Aileen Burford-Mason Ph.D. is an immunologist, cell biologist, former cancer researcher, and author of many research papers published in prestigious national and international scientific journals. For the past 15 years she has had a busy private nutritional practice in downtown Toronto. Known for her ability to take the complex field of nutritional research and make it accessible and practical for everyone, she currently teaches a popular course for doctors at the University of Toronto in the use of diet and supplements for disease prevention. For more information visit www.aileen burfordmason.ca.

Judy Stoffman has been a writer and editor on numerous publications, including the *Toronto Star*, *Globe and Mail*, and *Canadian Living* magazine, and has worked for the *CBC News*, *Ideas*, and *As It Happens* on CBC radio. Her essay about aging, "The Way of All Flesh," is included in two high school English textbooks used in Ontario.

Books of Merit

EAT
WELL
AGE
BETTER

EAT
WELL
AGE
BETTER

How to Use Diet and Supplements to
Guard the Lifelong Health of Your Eyes,
Your Heart, Your Brain, and Your Bones

Aileen Burford-Mason, Ph.D.
with Judy Stoffman

Thomas Allen Publishers
Toronto

Library and Archives Canada Cataloguing in Publication data available upon request

The information in this book is made available with the understanding that the
author and publisher are not providing medical advice or nutritional counseling services
to the reader. The information is not intended to replace medical treatment and should
be used in consultation with a competent health care or nutrition professional.

Editor: Janice Zawerbny
Jacket design: Karen Satok

Published by Thomas Allen Publishers,
a division of Thomas Allen & Son Limited,
390 Steelcase Road East,
Markham, Ontario L3R 1G2 Canada

www.thomasallen.ca

ONTARIO ARTS COUNCIL
CONSEIL DES ARTS DE L'ONTARIO

Canada Council
for the Arts

The publisher gratefully acknowledges the support of
The Ontario Arts Council for its publishing program.

We acknowledge the support of the Canada Council for the Arts, which
last year invested $20.1 million in writing and publishing throughout Canada.

We acknowledge the Government of Ontario through the
Ontario Media Development Corporation's Ontario Book Initiative.

We acknowledge the financial support of the Government of Canada
through the Canada Book Fund for our publishing activities.

12 13 14 15 16   5 4 3 2 1

Text printed on a 100% PCW recycled stock

Printed and bound in Canada

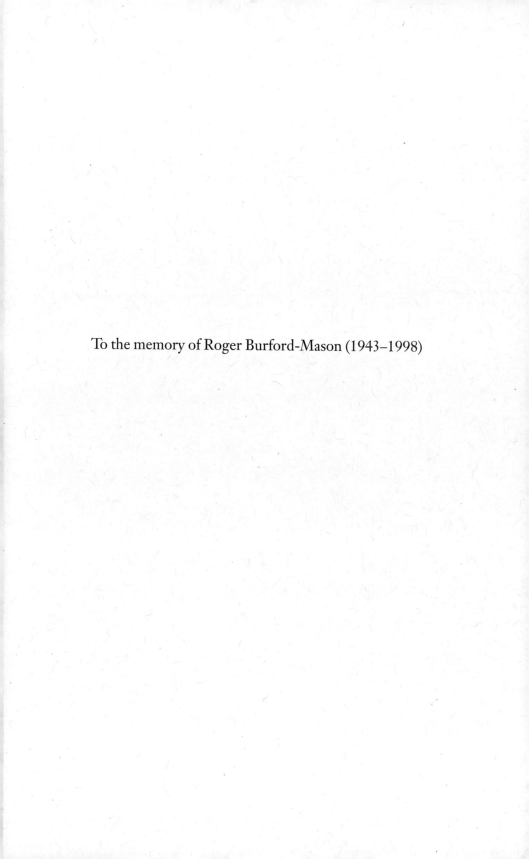

To the memory of Roger Burford-Mason (1943–1998)

I know of nothing so potent in maintaining good health in laboratory animals as perfectly constituted food; I know nothing so potent in producing ill-health as improperly constituted food. This, too, is the experience of stock breeders. Is man an exception to a rule so universally applicable to the higher animals?

— Sir Robert McCarrison, MD (1878–1960), pioneer in nutrition research

Contents

▼

Foreword

▼

This book you have in your hands is first and foremost a gift—a gift of knowledge and insight created for all those who want to age well. It is a gift for those who are willing to take responsibility for their own well-being, and use their discernment, their discipline and observational powers for the maintenance of their mental and physical health.

I speak of *Eat Well, Age Better* as a gift because it meets my definition of a great gift so well. A great gift is unique and does not duplicate something I already own; it is not just one more item to accumulate. It is something I need and can use right away. It becomes part of my daily life, and is not taken out only on special occasions, like Grandmother's teacups. The gift can be shared and can become the basis of conversations and explorations. Do keep these criteria in mind as you begin to read, and you will see how well they are met.

A set of central concepts permeates all pages of the book. First and foremost: be aware of the role of nutrition. Food and the environment profoundly affect us. Our global technological society badly needs to recognize what we as human beings need from our food to sustain us in the here and now. *Eat Well, Age Better* guides the reader's quest for optimal functioning of the complex and unique system entrusted to them: their very own body and mind.

Aileen Burford-Mason begins with a deep respect for the traditional time-tested knowledge of nutrition, then augments this with the findings of modern scientific research. Reflecting back on her clients' needs as well as on her own experiences, she offers us non-specialists a way to cope with the almost daily outpouring of new health information.

Yet this is only one feature of the book that I treasure. Maybe the aspect of the work that I most admire stems from the author's ability to integrate her sharply focused analytical approach with her holistic perception of wellness and health. She is not narrowly prescriptive, telling us simply to take this or that vitamin, but instead looks at the whole body, mindful of its individual needs and differences.

Aileen understands the distinction made by the philosopher Immanuel Kant between a mechanism, which is a functional unit whose parts exist for one another in the performance of a particular task, and an organism. The clock is the historical archetype of a mechanism, where pre-existing parts, designed to play a specific role, are assembled together into a unit whose dynamic action serves to keep track of the passing of time. An organism, on the other hand, is a functional and structural unit, in which the parts exist for and by means of each other. Thus, a plant's roots, leaves and flowers are not made separately and then assembled, but arise as a result of interactions within the living organism.

Eat Well, Age Better is a book that does not allow the reader to be complacent or lazy. There is the temptation to say "It's in my genes. My mother was also fat" or "My father also had high blood pressure. There is nothing I can do." But Aileen will have none of that.

Do accept her gift and use it, accept the privilege and obligation of being a functioning organism that requires maintenance and nourishment. None of us can afford to see ourselves as a clock, running slowly down, meanwhile looking for a good watchmaker, just in case.

Ursula M. Franklin
University Professor Emerita
University of Toronto
Companion of the Order of Canada
Member of the Royal Society of Canada

Introduction

▼

My fascination with vitamins and the immune system began almost 30 years ago when I was a young mother preparing for my Ph.D. at a small university in England. I was working full time and studying, and had a five-year-old son who was constantly getting sick. Very sick. If he so much as coughed once in the night, we knew that next day we would get a message from school to come and take him home. He always needed antibiotics to get better, so on our way home I would fill the undated prescription from his doctor I always kept on hand.

Then one day I was working in the library and read an article by endocrinologist and nutritional researcher David Horrobin. He wrote about immune cells and their nutritional needs; how they could fight infection only if they had the right nutrients to do the job. He talked about the role of essential fatty acids, the B vitamins, especially B6, vitamin C and zinc in fighting infection, and described how the need for these nutrients increased during infection.

The next time my son was ill I decided I would try giving him tiny doses of all these nutrients four times a day, just as if I was giving him antibiotics. It worked, and he got better quickly without medication. I then started giving him supplements routinely—a daily multivitamin, extra vitamin C and some cod liver oil. From then on he was rarely sick, and if he was I'd revert to my four-times-a-day routine. We no longer needed an undated antibiotic prescription at the ready, and I could see that his immune system could fight, given the right ammunition.

Since those days, taking vitamins has become less of a rarity. Vitamins are sold everywhere. Most people have a few bottles in the house, which does not mean that they know how to take them or why they are needed. A great deal of research has been done on nutritional supplements over the last few decades, and the scientific underpinning for their benefits is becoming more and more compelling. At the same time, the push-back from conventional medicine has increased.

The resistance from doctors is understandable. They still get little or no nutrition education during their medical training. In 1985 the U.S. Food and Nutrition Board, an advisory board on nutrition policy in North America, proposed that doctors receive a minimum of 25 hours of nutrition education over the course of their studies. However, 25 years later only 27 percent of American medical schools meet even those meagre require-ments, and the current average is 19.6 hours.[1] A recent survey of Canadian medical students found that 87.2 percent wanted more curriculum time devoted to nutrition, and over half felt handicapped by their lack of nutritional knowledge when it came to counselling patients.[2]

The buzz term in medicine right now is "evidence based," meaning that health practices should be based on sound research evidence. When it comes to supplements, however, the main-stream view is that there is not yet enough evidence to support their use. But how much evidence is enough? One test of whether something has been well researched is the number of scientific papers that have appeared about it in peer-reviewed journals. Let us compare the evidence base for a popular class of drugs—

the statin drugs, widely used to bring down cholesterol—with the more controversial but equally popular vitamin D.

If you search the medical literature under "statin therapy," you'll find 19,400 papers—that's a lot! And because of all those publications, these drugs are considered evidence based. Search the medical literature under "vitamin D therapy" and you'll come up with slightly more: 20,723 papers. These papers suggest that we need more vitamin D than we are getting to prevent a wide range of diseases, from diabetes to cancer, heart disease and dementia. Yet a recent joint U.S.-Canadian review of vitamin D came to the conclusion that there was still not enough evidence to suggest that vitamin D had a role to play in preventing any condition other than bone disease—rickets and osteoporosis—despite the fact that only about 7 percent of the existing papers on vitamin D are about bone health.

The argument against the use of vitamin D for preventing other chronic diseases is that its effectiveness is largely backed by observational studies, whereas the evidence that supports the use of drugs is based on randomized controlled trials (RCTs). RCTs compare a group of patients taking a drug with a similar group taking a placebo or dummy pill and are the gold standard in drug research, essential to proving that a drug actually works. But the RCT approach for vitamin D is difficult, for both ethical and practical reasons. In the first place, you cannot completely deprive your control group of vitamin D without making them sick. And since we make vitamin D from sunshine, how do you keep all the participants out of the sun for years at a time? Thus an RCT of vitamin D is always comparing variable and fluctuating levels of vitamin D in both the supplement group and the controls. This blurs the boundaries between the two groups, and the outcome of such studies frequently results in scientists arguing among themselves as to what, if anything, was proved.

In observational studies researchers simply observe whether certain habits or behaviours increase the risk of disease by comparing patients who have engaged in a certain activity with those who have not. A good example is smoking. In the 1950s British researcher Sir Richard Doll showed that smoking caused lung cancer. This came as a surprise because back then smoking was considered a healthy habit, and most doctors smoked. But Doll's studies were enough for governments throughout the Western world to recommend that people quit smoking and, as a disincentive, to tax cigarettes heavily. As a result, rates of lung cancer fell and Doll's observations were vindicated. No RCT was required. Imagine asking a group of non-smokers to smoke 20 cigarettes a day for 10 years to "prove" Doll's observations. It would simply be unacceptable.

We are in the same situation with vitamin D today. We know that, worldwide, vitamin D blood levels are dropping. We work indoors and use sun block when outside. Observational studies show us that in parallel with these lifestyle changes we are getting sicker. With an epidemic of vitamin D deficiency on our hands, it is time to accept that the observational data is strong and can tell us all we need to know. To do intervention trials now would be difficult and possibly unethical.

Why is it that nutrition experts frequently differ and fight among themselves? The media bombard us with contradictory reports: one day they showcase research that suggests vitamin E is helpful in preventing heart disease or Alzheimer's. But before long a different research group issues a contrary press release. Their research shows that vitamin E supplements make no difference or may even harm us. One week vitamin D is a panacea for all our ills. The next week we are warned that vitamin D supplements roughly equivalent to ten minutes of noonday summer sunshine are dangerous. The public is confused, and so are doctors.

Introduction

As you read this book, you will see how marvellously complex the body is, with all the essential nutrients being required by every tissue of the body, and every nutrient doing many different jobs. Often contradictory studies in nutrition are a result of ignoring this biological reality—that all nutrients are needed at all times. Vitamin D, for example, requires vitamins A and K, and the minerals magnesium, calcium, boron and zinc to be effective. If you test single nutrients in isolation from the other nutrients they interact with, you are likely to come up with conflicting data.

The famous parable of the blind men and the elephant, retold in humorous verse by the American poet John Godfrey Saxe (1816–1887), illustrates how this sort of deductive reasoning, where we move from something that is complex to examining its individual parts in isolation, can lead us down the wrong path. Six blind men of Hindustan want to understand what an elephant is and decide to go into the jungle to investigate. Being blind, each one describes the elephant based on the part of the elephant he happens to have hold of. One, who finds the leg, says it's plain to see an elephant is like a tree. Another has hold of the tail, and claims the elephant is just like a rope. The blind man who holds the ear thinks the elephant is like a fan, and the one who comes up against its flank pronounces that the creature is more like a wall. In the end, writes Saxe, each of them was partly right, but all of them were wrong.

And so it is for the advocates of single foods or nutritional supplements. One will swear by oat bran, the other by vitamin C, the third by omega-3 fats, without considering that they are all part of one complex system. In this book we will attempt to piece together the whole nutritional elephant.

Aileen Burford-Mason
January 2012

1

The Crisis in Nutrition

1

Adding Life to Your Years

▼

*What makes me so certain that the natural human lifespan
is far in excess of the actual one is this. Among all my autopsies
(and I have performed over 1000), I have never seen a person
who died of old age. In fact, I do not think that anyone has ever
died of old age yet. We invariably die because one vital part has
worn out too early in proportion to the rest of the body.*

— Dr. Hans Selye (1907–1982)

MORE PEOPLE are living long lives than ever before in history. Industrialized countries are experiencing a surge in centenarians. According to the 2006 census, Canada had 4,635 people aged 100 or older, up more than 50 percent from a decade earlier.

Enormous strides in life expectancy in all the developed countries in the past century are due largely to public health measures, such as vaccination, better sanitation and improved access to medical care. In that time, the average national gain in life expectancy at birth has been 66 percent for males and 71 percent for females, and in some countries, life expectancy for both men and women has more than doubled.[1] In the United States one in nine baby boomers will survive into his late nineties, and one in 26 will reach her hundredth birthday.

Before we congratulate ourselves on our amazing luck to be born in the twentieth century, consider the reality behind these figures. Extended life does not equal extended health. In 1993, researchers published the results of a study in which they compared the health of elderly persons in Manitoba in 1971 with the health of people in the same age cohort in 1983. Over that period, longevity increased by 29 percent, but the increase in the number of elderly in poor health was much greater. In their article "Living Longer but Doing Worse," they reported that 73 percent were either unable to perform the usual activities of daily living due to poor mental health or required hospitalization.[2] Similar worrying trends can be seen throughout the Western world.

In 1999, the World Health Organization (WHO) decided for the first time to determine how many years we could expect not just to live, but to live in good health. Out of 191 countries studied, Japan had the highest disability-free life expectancy with nearly 75 years of healthy life out of a total life expectancy at that time of 79. Canada came in 12th with a healthy life expectancy of 72 years, while the big shock was the United States. It was in 24th place, with an average life expectancy of just 70 healthy years.

"The position of the United States is one of the major surprises of the new rating system," commented Dr. Christopher Murray, director of Global Health Policy for the WHO. "Basically, you die earlier and spend more time disabled if you're an American rather than a member of other advanced countries." Since then, life expectancies have continued to climb, with Japan's current combined male/female life expectancy reaching 83, Canada's 81 and the United States 78. *Healthy* life expectancies, however, have improved very little. Weakened by illness, many older people find little pleasure in the extra years of life.

It does not have to be this way. As a biomedical researcher

and practicing nutritionist, I know that there is now overwhelming evidence that dietary changes and appropriate nutritional supplements can help us maximize our healthy years. What I teach health care professionals and my private clients I want to share with the readers of this book.

Why life expectancy and healthy life expectancies differ

The divergence between life expectancy and *healthy* life expectancy is due to chronic degenerative diseases, such as diabetes, heart disease and stroke, dementia, liver disease and arthritis, that increase in incidence with age. One of the hallmarks of degenerative diseases is that they are persistent. They cannot be prevented by vaccines, nor do they just disappear. They require medication for the rest of the sufferer's life—often multiple drugs—but the drugs do not cure, they only manage the symptoms. Many have serious side effects. At the root of these chronic diseases is lack of physical activity, chronic stress and inadequate nutrition.

The WHO blames in particular the widespread adoption of a western-style diet, high in fat, starch and sugar. "Worldwide, the adoption of this diet has been accompanied by a major increase in coronary heart disease, stroke, various cancers, diabetes and other chronic diseases," noted a WHO report in 1997 titled *Conquering Suffering, Enriching Humanity*.

There are, of course, factors that are out of our control: heredity, stress and the growing burden of chemical pollutants in the environment, which are now believed to play a part in the development of many degenerative diseases, cancer in particular. In spite of that dire news, it is in our power to control our nutrition and lifestyle.

The incidence of degenerative diseases is rising fast in all developed countries, putting enormous strain on health care resources. Approximately 9 million Canadians live with diabetes, 10 percent with type 1, and the remainder with type 2 or pre-diabetes. Type 1 is a failure of the pancreas to make insulin due to autoimmune destruction of its insulin-producing cells; it can be controlled with insulin injections. Type 2 is caused not by the body's inability to produce insulin, but by its inability to use it, and is therefore called insulin-resistant diabetes. Type 2 diabetes is considered a lifestyle disease, meaning that it is preventable.

Type 2 diabetics are at increased risk of contracting other chronic diseases, such as heart disease, stroke, kidney disease, blindness and Alzheimer's disease—exactly what you would expect if there was a common nutritional basis for all these conditions. Other epidemics we are facing in the near future include liver disease and age-related macular degeneration (ARMD), the leading cause of blindness in those over 50. ARMD affects an estimated 25 to 30 million people in the Western world, and the incidence is expected to triple over the next 25 years. We are also becoming less mobile, our movements restricted by excess weight, arthritis and osteoporosis. We worry about the possibility of dementia and Alzheimer's disease.

Many chronic diseases are striking at ever younger ages. Type 2 diabetes used to be called age-onset diabetes because it was confined to the elderly, but is now being diagnosed in young adults. The beginnings of heart disease can be identified in children. In one recent study one in six U.S. teenagers were shown to have arteriosclerosis, a thickening and hardening of the arteries, which is early but silent evidence of heart disease.[3]

Diabetes, heart disease and cancer rarely appear overnight. Their incubation period extends over months, years or even decades. During that time we may notice that something is amiss. We may find ourselves more susceptible to colds and flu and take longer to recover. We tire more easily. The optometrist spots signs of serious vision problems ahead. Mechanisms that once kept blood pressure and cholesterol under control and bones in good shape begin to falter.

If we have had a less-than-ideal diet most of our life, the signs of a cumulative shortfall of nutrients will become more obvious with age, as tissues and organs begin to show signs of wear and tear. Appetite may diminish, leading to still lower nutrient intakes.

Many prescription drugs deplete nutrients

People take more prescription medications[4] as age-related health issues arise. A large proportion of people over 50 that I see in my office are on blood pressure medications or cholesterol-lowering drugs. Menopausal women might be on hormone replacement therapy or drugs for osteoporosis. The problem is that many commonly prescribed drugs deplete nutrients or interfere with their absorption (see Table 1). This depletion often accounts for their side effects.[5] The side effects might then be treated with yet another medication that may deplete nutrients still further. Few doctors warn their patients about this or are even aware that the problem exists.

Several other changes in the aging body also call for increased nutrients. Low stomach acid is one. The secretion of stomach acid, which is essential for protein digestion, decreases as we age. In addition, many people in their forties, fifties and older are on medications that suppress stomach acid, because of indigestion or acid reflux. Without stomach acid we cannot break down proteins into their component amino acids. These amino acids are the building blocks for hormones, enzymes, and all the tissues and organs of our bodies.

Table 1
Common prescription drugs and the nutrients they may deplete

Drug type	Examples	Nutrients potentially depleted
Anti-anxiety	Valium, Xanax	Melatonin
Antibiotics	Penicillin, ciprofloxacin (cipro), tetracycline	All B-vitamin, vitamin K, calcium, iron, magnesium, zinc
Antidepressants	SSRIs: Paxil, Prozac, Zoloft Amitriptyline (Elavil)	Co-enzyme Q10, vitamin B2, melatonin
Anti-diabetic	Metformin	Vitamins B1, B12, folic acid
Anti-inflammatory	Aspirin NSAIDs (ibuprofen, etc) Steroids (Prednisone, Pulmacort, etc)	Vitamin C, folic acid, iron Folic acid, iron Vitamins A, B-6, B-12, folic acid, vitamins C, D, calcium, magnesium, potassium, chromium, selenium, zinc
Anti-ulcer and anti-reflux (GERD)	H2-receptor antagonists (Pepcid, Tagamet, Zantac, etc.)	Vitamin B12, calcium, chromium, iron, zinc, vitamin D, protein
	Proton pump inhibitors	Beta carotene, vitamin C, B12, folic acid, calcium, chromium, iron, zinc, protein
Asthma drugs	Beta-2-agonists (Ventolin, Alupent)	Magnesium, potassium
Blood pressure medications	ACE-inhibitors (captopril) Beta-blockers (inderal) Loop diuretics (Lasix)	Zinc Co-enzyme Q10 Calcium, magnesium, potassium, vitamins B1, B6, C, folic acid

	Potassium sparing diuretics (Aldactone)	Folic acid, calcium
	Thiazides (hydrochlorothiazide)	Magnesium, potassium, zinc, vitamin B1, folic acid
Cholesterol-lowering drugs	Statins (Crestor, Lipitor, Zocor)	Co-enzyme Q10
Hormones	Birth control pills; hormone replacement therapy (HRT)	Folic acid, vitamin B6, vitamin C, magnesium, zinc

Sources: http://naturaldatabase.therapeuticresearch.com (Accessed 22-10-2011); University of Maryland Medical Center.

Why acid-suppressing drugs can be harmful

Acid suppression not only makes for incomplete protein digestion and an inadequate supply of amino acids, but over time leads
to vitamin B12 deficiency. Before vitamin B12 can be absorbed
by the small intestine, it requires a carrier protein called intrinsic
factor (IF) produced by the stomach's acid-secreting cells. Suppressing acid will cause a decrease in IF and reduce absorption
of B12. Older people with insufficient stomach acid may eventually develop pernicious or megaloblastic anemia—a sign of
serious B12 deficiency. They need to supplement their diet with
vitamin B12. Vegetarians will have problems getting enough
B12 because B12 is found mainly in animal products.

Magnesium deficiency increases with age, and acid-suppressing drugs make this worse. In early 2011, the American Food
and Drug Administration (FDA) issued a warning to doctors
to be on the lookout for magnesium depletion as a side effect of
powerful acid-suppressing drugs called proton pump inhibitors

(PPIs); for example, the widely used drugs Nexium, Prevacid and Prilosec. According to an FDA bulletin, "Low serum magnesium levels can result in serious adverse events including muscle spasm (tetany), irregular heartbeat (arrhythmias), and convulsions (seizures)." Magnesium supplements will overcome the side effects in some people, but for others discontinuing the drug is the only solution. Unfortunately, not all doctors keep up to date on drug warnings and may continue to prescribe PPIs and offer other medications to treat the resulting arrhythmias or seizures without considering the issue of nutrient depletion.

What can we do to address this cascade of prescription medications, where one drug leads to the use of another? Try working with a nutritionally oriented physician who will assess whether the drugs you are taking are absolutely necessary, and if there really is no alternative, will suggest supplements to replace depleted nutrients. Pharmacists trained in the use of nutritional supplements are also a good resource. Ask at the drugstore next time you have a prescription filled.

Type 2 diabetes and metabolic syndrome (pre-diabetes) due to diets high in fat, starch and sugar are reaching epidemic proportions, and result in more frequent urination.[6] Frequent urination causes depletion of water-soluble nutrients such as B vitamins and vitamin C, as well as minerals, which are also water soluble. Although we need to drink fluids to stay hydrated, drinking too much water leads to valuable nutrients being flushed down the toilet.

Heavy sweating also leads to vitamin and mineral loss. If you are a runner or enjoy hot yoga (done in a very warm room to promote sweating), you will need to replace lost nutrients. Women who experience hot flashes and night sweats also lose vitamins and minerals. Of particular importance is magnesium loss.[7] In women with breast cancer, magnesium supplements have been shown to reduce the annoying menopausal hot flashes that follow treatment.[8] In men, night sweats are invariably a sign of magnesium deficiency.

We also need more vitamin D than we did in our youth because skin becomes less efficient at manufacturing vitamin D from sunshine. Moreover, middle-aged spread will affect vitamin D levels because vitamin D is trapped in fat cells. It is released only when you burn that fat through vigorous activity or weight loss.

If we ate poorly in our youth, can we correct for it in later life?

It is never too late. The body constantly repairs and renews itself, a process that continues even in old age, provided it receives ongoing nutritional support. All the nutrients are needed for cell manufacture, for brain maintenance, for the refurbishment of bones and cartilage, and must be consumed regularly in generous amounts. Our diets need to deliver sufficient nutrition to replace, on average, one hundred billion cells that die each day—heart cells, brain cells, skin and liver cells, red blood cells and cells of the immune system, and the cells that line the gastrointestinal tract that are damaged each time we eat. If those cells are not replaced, the tissues and organs they were once part of inevitably deteriorate. This cell turnover has been estimated as the equivalent of replacing a 70 kilogram adult body every 18 to 24 months,[9] a huge task that cannot be accomplished without adequate building materials.

Bones, tendons, ligaments, the cartilage in knees and hips and the discs between the vertebrae are also in a constant state of renewal. If we develop osteoporosis, degenerated discs, worn-down cartilage in our knees and hips so that replacement surgery is required, then something is amiss with the nutritional support of those tissues.

When I was a university student, an enormous metabolic map hung on the wall of the biochemistry lecture room. It showed the vast web of interconnected chemical reactions involved in the everyday functioning of our bodies—the digestion of food, the production of energy, the making of hormones and neurotransmitters, and the detoxification of tissues. These countless chemical reactions required all the essential fats and amino acids. And, as we have seen, they also required vitamins and minerals as catalysts to drive those chemical reactions, if they were to proceed at anything other than a snail's pace.

When my mind wandered from the day's lecture I would find my attention drawn to this map, whose complexity still makes my head spin. I wondered then how we ever knew if we were getting enough nutrients to guarantee that those metabolic pathways ran smoothly. The assumption was that our diets could provide everything we needed in the right amounts and at the right time. And what happened when our diets provided maybe 60 percent of the vitamin C or half the magnesium we needed? Was that 60 percent randomly allocated? Or were there specific metabolic needs that were satisfied first, and others that had to wait in line?

The notion that food alone can provide an optimal daily intake of vitamins and minerals has always been, at best, a hopeful guess, an assumption that is being steadily undermined by modern research. Individuals who carry certain common genes now known to increase the need for vitamins and minerals would always have been at a nutritional disadvantage. The extreme variation in iron needs, for example, makes it unlikely that diet alone could satisfy those with the highest requirements, no matter how carefully they ate.

Many Canadians do not even meet the standard recommendations for vitamin and mineral intake. The most recent data we have is from the Canadian Community Health Survey of 2004, conducted by Statistics Canada.[10] Magnesium is a serious deficiency and vitamin A is another. Note that government health agencies use a measure called the EAR (Estimated Average Requirement) when deciding how well nourished we are as a population. The EAR is the estimated amount of a nutrient that would meet the daily needs for *half* the population. It does not tell us anything about the needs of the other 50 percent, for whom the amounts are presumably insufficient. The older we are, the less likely we are to meet the EAR not only for vitamin A and magnesium, but also for zinc, vitamin C and the B vitamins. It is clear that as Canadians age, deficiencies increase across the board.

Why problems associated with nutritional deficiencies get worse as we age

There is evidence for a direct link between deteriorating health and deteriorating intake of vital nutrients with age. One evolving theory suggests that where modest deficiencies of vitamins and minerals persist over time, the body performs a sort of triage whereby nutrients first go to maintain the functions[11] most essential to survival: keeping the heart beating, maintaining body temperature, clotting the blood. Even minor deficiencies will mean that the maintenance of a strong immune system, pain-free joints, the building and rebuilding of bones, and the maintenance of smooth skin or clear vision will get short shrift.

This is how degenerative diseases creep in, unnoticed at first. Nutritionally oriented physicians and natural health practitioners focus on ensuring an abundance of nutrients so that over the long term all parts of our metabolic map are equally well supported. The daily task of tissue renewal and repair may be challenging, but not impossible. It's never too late to improve our diets, eat more mindfully and, if necessary, take supplements. It is indeed possible to have a healthier body at 70 than we had at 50.

Some people resist degenerative diseases better than others, and therefore can be said to age more slowly. We probably all know someone in her sixties who plays tennis several times a week, takes no medications and doesn't smoke. Her blood pressure, triglycerides and cholesterol are all normal and her bones are like those of a 30-year-old. This person might have an overweight friend the same age, whose doctor has pronounced her pre-diabetic. She takes medications to control her blood sugar, blood pressure, cholesterol and osteopenia, and she wheezes when she walks upstairs. Both these women are the same chronological age, yet their biological ages are different.

Many Internet sites (for example, www.growyouthful.com or preventdisease.com) exist to calculate your biological age based on questionnaires that ask, among other things, about your blood pressure, your level of physical activity, your body mass index (BMI), how long your parents and grandparents lived and whether you take blood pressure or cholesterol medications. (The need for such medications is a sign that your body processes are not under control.) When you hit "calculate," you hope that your biological age will be younger than the age on your birth certificate.

A way to tell how well we are aging

A more precise indicator of biological age is telomere length. Telomeres are tiny caps at the ends of chromosomes. They stabilize chromosomes and protect our DNA. Visible under a high-powered microscope, telomeres are sometimes compared to the tags at the end of shoelaces that prevent them from unravelling.

Each time a cell divides, telomeres shorten. Just as a shoelace unravels if the end tag is destroyed, making it useless, so it is with chromosomes.

Eventually, when telomeres become too short, the chromosomes fray and cells stop dividing, compromising the body's ability to repair tissues. Cells with worn-out telomeres are also more vulnerable to cancer because errors are more easily integrated into DNA when chromosomes are unprotected. The discovery of how chromosomes are protected by telomeres won the Nobel Prize in Medicine in 2009 for Elizabeth Blackburn, Carol Greider and Jack Szostak. Telomere length can be measured in the laboratory and is now widely accepted as a marker of biological age. The longer your telomeres the younger your cells, and consequently, the more resistant you are to disease.[12]

Elizabeth Blackburn is working with a new company called Telomere Health in California that is developing the technology to measure telomere length in the doctor's office. In a recent interview with the journal *New Scientist*, she said that at the moment the company offers the tests only as a part of research studies, but tests for the public will eventually go on sale at a cost of about $200. She explained that measurements will come from blood samples, cheek swabs or saliva, and will measure the telomere length in white blood cells, because cells from the immune system are the ideal report card for a host of conditions.

An enzyme called telomerase can restore telomere length and allow cells to keep on dividing. However, most cells contain only a limited supply of it. The rapidly dividing cells of a fetus contain high levels of the enzyme, and so do cancer cells. The ability of cancer cells to manufacture telomerase helps make them immortal. The race is now on among pharmaceutical companies to find telomerase-like drugs that will slow down or reverse aging, but the concern is that any drugs that could elongate telomeres would also make us more cancer prone. While we may not at present have drugs that can safely elongate telomeres, we know that poor diet and lifestyle can shorten them prematurely.

Throughout this book I will show you the steps you can take to protect telomeres and prolong the life of your cells. For example, telomeres are longer in people with high blood levels of vitamin D and in those who exercise regularly. Consuming high amounts of omega-3 fats found in fatty fish protects telomeres, as does a daily multivitamin. Conversely, smoking, obesity, excess alcohol consumption, environmental toxins, lack of sleep and chronic stress all tend to shorten telomeres.

Studying the old and healthy

Centenarians have been extensively studied in an effort to understand healthy aging. Concentrations of people who are active and mentally alert at 100 and beyond have been found in Canada (Nova Scotia study), the United States (the New England study, based in Boston University and Loma Linda, California) and Japan (the Okinawa study).

Longevity is in part genetic; most of the centenarians studied in the research above have at least one parent or sibling who lived into his or her late nineties or beyond. However, studies of identical and fraternal twins show that genes don't tell the whole story and have only a modest effect on longevity.[13] Lifestyle and nutrition also play a large part. In Okinawa, where Japan's largest concentration of old people live, 900 centenarians and others in their seventies, eighties and nineties have been studied. Here the elderly are active and have excellent diets. They grow their own vegetables, walk to market, practice martial arts, dance for fun in the evening and don't overeat. In fact, they have a saying at table—*haro hachi bu,*—which means "eat to no more than 80 percent full." The women have very little osteoporosis, perhaps due to their high early intake of soy, which contains estrogen-like compounds, and their regular physical activity.

Such studies demonstrate that old age and degenerative illness do not have to go hand in hand. Even if we lack those desirable longevity genes, we can adjust our diet and lifestyle to our advantage. Dr. Raymond Rodriguez, director of the Center of Excellence in Nutritional Genomics at the University of California, Davis, who studies the interaction between nutrition and genes, insists that were it not for poor nutrition most of us could stay healthy well into our eighties. "We're not slaves to our genes," he has said, "and we're not victims of genetic determination. We ate ourselves into a disease state and we can eat ourselves out of that disease state."[14]

2

A Short History of Eating

▼

Nature delights in the most plain and simple diet. Every animal but man keeps to one dish. Herbs are the food of this species, fish of that, and flesh of a third. Man falls upon everything that comes in his way; not the smallest fruit or excrescence of the earth, scarce a berry or a mushroom can escape him.

— Joseph Addison (1672–1719),
English essayist, poet and politician

*F*OR ALL BUT a tiny portion of the 200,000 years that our species has been in existence, we have lived as hunter-gatherers. Our earliest human ancestors would have eaten whatever was available in their region, and they tried everything. Communities that evolved around rivers, lakes and oceans ate fish and the surrounding vegetation. People of the plains ate large game and few fruits and vegetables; in the Far North they survived chiefly on fish and sea mammals. Hunter-gatherers ate whenever they could, and were no doubt often hungry since the energy density of the food they consumed was low.[1]

They were constantly on the move, chasing after buffalo or wildebeest, catching fish, gathering wild greens, berries and nuts for their survival. Sheer hunger would have compelled them to expend a lot of energy foraging for edible vegetation and tracking game. When their hunger was satisfied, they would rest to conserve energy. Today, the majority of people are engaged in sedentary work and food is available everywhere. Yet even in our current age of plenty we are born with the same drive to eat and eat and eat. That drive once assured our survival and is deeply embedded in the most primitive parts of our brain,[2] which explains the difficulties we have with our modern diet and lifestyle.

Our healthy ancestors

The skeletal remains of ancient hunter-gatherers have been studied for more than 50 years and provide a gold mine of information. Researchers found that, depending on geographical location, hunter-gatherers could be surprisingly tall. Moreover, they found that those who lived in equatorial regions had bones with few signs of osteoporosis, but those who lived farther north had weaker bones, presumably due to less sun exposure and therefore less vitamin D. We can't tell much about cardiac health from such remains, since soft-tissue evidence has vanished, but research has shown few degenerative changes and deformities.

Without modern medical know-how, our hunter-gatherer forbears were susceptible to infectious diseases and most lived short and brutal lives, dying early from infections, trauma and in childbirth. Infant mortality was high, and average life expectancy at birth varied from 25 to 45 years. If they survived to adulthood, life expectancy increased, and many lived into their seventies. In the past 25 years, researchers have shown increasing interest in the diet and health of living hunter-gatherer tribes, who survive on food in its natural state. Eighty-four such tribes have been identified and studied in South America's Amazon region, in Australia and south Asia. They appear to have life expectancies similar to ancient hunter-gatherers.

In his 1989 book *Health and the Rise of Civilization*, anthropologist Mark Nathan Cohen showed that humans evolved to eat the widest range of foods of any creature, and meat was important to them. He found that the strongest, largest and healthiest ancient peoples lived in parts of Africa where an abundance of big game exists to this day.[3]

The Inuit of the Far North had little vegetation, and stayed healthy on a diet consisting almost exclusively of meat and fish. They showed great ingenuity in figuring out how to obtain essential vitamin C without vegetables or fruits. The animals they hunted provided vitamin C in their raw, fresh meat. Because cooking would have destroyed the vitamin C, the Inuit learned to avoid scurvy by eating fresh seal and other uncooked meats.

How agriculture changed the human diet

Evidence has been found of farming communities established about 10,000 years ago, but agriculture may have started earlier in some places. Remains have surfaced in Sri Lanka of a 30,000-year-old woman whose stomach and intestinal contents contained grain, evidence of farming activity. Agriculture was an inevitable development. Observant people noticed that where seeds fell, they would eventually sprout and grow, and thus realized they could intentionally cover them with soil and obtain a crop. Change must have been driven by starvation, since hunter-gatherers were extremely vulnerable to famine. If a steady supply of food were available, wandering tribes would have likely been content to settle in one place.

In Asia, rice-type grains have been found with prehistoric skeletal remains. Like wheat and barley, rice could easily be stored after the harvest. Thus hunter-gatherers who became farmers exchanged a broad range of foods for less variety and a diet that was largely cereal based. Archaeological remains indicate that in regions from India to Europe and the lower Mississippi Valley this new cereal-based diet resulted in people generally being shorter and living shorter lives. But population density increased as more efficient food storage ensured that more infants survived into adulthood and famine became less frequent.

Pima Indians: decline of a vibrant community

The change from hunting and gathering to farming was gradual, with many communities combining both. Such was the case of the Pima Indians, who had migrated from Mexico and settled in an area of two great rivers in Arizona. The Pima have been much studied because they experienced in a century changes in diet that other peoples went through over thousands of years.

Along the Gila and Salt rivers in Arizona, the Pima found that the soil was rich but nothing grew. The reason? The river flooded, washing out the plants in the rainy season, while in the dry season the rivers dried up entirely. The Pima brought their sophisticated irrigation methods from Mexico, and soon tamed the river. They grew squash and corn and, after their encounter with missionaries, wheat. They supplemented the products of their agriculture with fish; they ate eggs from wild birds and hunted jackrabbits. In the nineteenth century, they were a lean, tall, athletic people whose young men would run up mountains for sport. Fleet of foot, they were used as message carriers during the American Civil War.

Competition for water began with the settlement of immigrant farmers along the river. The most drastic changes came in the early decades of the twentieth century, when the river was dammed to provide water to the new city of Phoenix. Little by little the Pima's crops failed and they began to starve. They sent heartbreaking letters to the U.S. government pleading to get their water back, to no avail. Instead of water, the government sent them supplies of white flour, sugar and lard. The Pima developed recipes using these ingredients, notably bannock and fried bread, and they were no longer hungry. Gradually the Pima started to get sick. Generation by generation they gained weight and are now one of the heaviest people on earth except for the Samoans, with the highest rate of diabetes in North America.[4] A large number are in wheelchairs, since so many Pima—even some in their thirties—have had amputations due to their diabetes.

The National Institutes of Health (NIH) has established a research branch in Phoenix, Arizona, where researchers have put some of these diabetic descendants of the original Pima back on their traditional diet. Those who stay on the traditional diet find that their blood sugar falls, and so does their cholesterol.[5]

The rise of the modern food industry

Over the twentieth century, the U.S. population more than tripled from 76 million in 1900 to 281 million in 2000. During the same period, Canada's population increased almost six-fold from 5.3 million in 1900 to 31 million. These increases in population drove the development of food technology in the twentieth century. Public health measures such as improved sanitation, vaccinations and the assurance of clean drinking water meant that more children survived and thus more people needed to be fed. The modernization of our food supply began with the invention of commercial canning in the nineteenth century. By applying heat and sealing the food, it was preserved, but a good deal of sugar and salt had to be added to make the canned food palatable. Canning changed the nutritional quality of food, and because early cans used lead, introduced toxic substances into the food supply.

Agriculture became intent on maximizing food production, growing more crops in less time and on less land than before to supply an expanding market. Chemical fertilizers, herbicides and pesticides allowed high-yield crops to grow on less fertile soils. New cultivars tolerant of these chemicals were developed. This intensification of cultivation was remarkably successful. Food production increased dramatically, and the new agribusiness was considered a social and scientific triumph.

Recently, questions have been raised about how much nutrition these new crops deliver. Studies comparing vitamin and mineral content of crops from the 1950s to the end of the twentieth century do show changes in the nutrient content of commonly consumed fruits and vegetables. In 2004, researchers at the University of Texas compared 13 major nutrients in fruits and vegetables from 1950 to 1999 and showed declines in 6 of them, ranging from a drop of 15 percent in iron and 16 percent in calcium to a 20 percent drop in vitamin C and a 38 percent drop in riboflavin (vitamin B2).[6]

There are many possible reasons for these declines in nutritional content over the years. One may be that new high-yielding varieties are often lower in minerals than older varieties. Or nutritional declines may be due to loss of soil nutrients because of continuous planting of the same land without crop rotation, an explanation that is hotly contested by government agencies and agricultural scientists. Whatever the reasons, it is likely that a tomato eaten today does not provide the same nutritional benefits as one eaten by our parents and grandparents.

Breakfast-in-a-box

In the late nineteenth century, the North American food industry evolved to meet the needs of an industrialized society in which people had less time for food preparation. One of the men who shaped the new eating patterns was John Harvey Kellogg (1852–1943), a doctor at the Battle Creek Sanatorium, in Michigan. When the overfed women and men of America's Gilded Age had digestive problems, they came to partake of Dr. Kellogg's austere regime at Battle Creek. One of their chief problems was constipation, which at the start of the twentieth century was considered the "disease of diseases." The theory at the time was that if stagnation occurred in the bowel, microbes would ferment food, producing toxins that were absorbed into the blood and circulated to different organs of the body, causing disease at distant sites.[7]

Dr. Kellogg, a Seventh-day Adventist, encouraged lifestyle changes to combat the problem, including daily exercise in the open air. His patients were given one pint of yogurt every day, half of which was eaten and half given as an enema. Dr. Kellogg invited his brother William to be business manager of the clinic and together they set up a laboratory to develop high-fibre foods, since it was known that fibre was low in North American diets, and that was a major cause of constipation. In the lab, they came up with a technique to take soaked corn kernels, crush them flat and toast them. The result was the first cornflakes and they were quite palatable. The brothers Kellogg also developed All-Bran, still popular today. Patients were given these cereals for breakfast.

William Kellogg wanted to keep their flaking process secret and patent it, but John Kellogg was delighted to show it to anyone who was interested. A patient who was very interested indeed was C. W. Post, who immediately saw its commercial

potential. He founded the Postum Cereal Co., later known as
Post Cereals, in 1895 and made his fortune. William eventually
left his brother and started his own highly successful company,
Kellogg's.

The immense popularity of these cereals was due not so
much to their health effects, but to their convenience. At the
time, breakfast was a cooked meal, consisting of sausages or
lamb chops with eggs, or for people of modest means, porridge
or grits. These foods took a lot of preparation, whereas cornflakes took seconds to pour out and serve with milk and sugar.
Today very few people eat a traditional breakfast. Breakfast-in-
a-box has become one of the most detrimental nutritional lega-
cies that American culture has spread throughout the world.

When you look at John Kellogg's other ideas and obsessions,
you have to question many of his ideas about health. He advised
various harsh methods to curb masturbation in children. He
frowned on sexual intercourse because he believed that each
individual was born with a limited degree of vital energy and
intercourse depleted it. He and his wife raised some 40 foster
children, and adopted seven of them, but never consummated
their own marriage. He strongly believed in eugenics, the drive
to create perfect people. Interbreeding with immigrants and
blacks, he believed, would weaken the American Caucasian
population. He died in 1943, around the time this idea came
to its horrific pinnacle with the Holocaust in Europe.

John Kellogg's nutritional ideas have been remarkably persistent. To this day, most people who suffer from constipation
believe that bran, bran and more bran is the healthiest way to
achieve regularity. It isn't. In the long run, phytates—chemicals
contained in bran—bind minerals, and people who eat too much
bran will not derive full nourishment from their food because
the bran reduces absorption of essential nutrients. Kellogg also
unwittingly kick-started a trend towards packaged and processed

convenience foods whose effects, as we shall see, are still being played out today.

The self-experimenters: Luigi Cornaro (1464–1566)

Knowledge about the relationship between health and food originally came from curious individuals who experimented on themselves and recorded their observations. Among the earliest was Luigi Cornaro, a contemporary of the artist Titian, who lived in Venice during the Renaissance, the period of cultural ferment that brought forth many new areas of inquiry.

A common assumption at the time was that the more you ate the healthier you'd be. The young Cornaro indulged himself in every type of food, but although he ate and drank heartily, he was constantly ill. By the age of 40, he wrote, he'd "fallen into different kinds of disorders such as pains in my stomach and often stitches, and a species of gout and attended by what was still worse, an almost continuous low fever, a stomach generally out of order and a perpetual thirst."

He decided to investigate what would happen if he ate less. He restricted the amount but not the variety in his diet. A typical day would begin with a cup of milk with a little bread. His lunch was soup with an egg, and his dinner, a modest portion of meat with vegetables and a glass of the light wine of the region. His health started to improve. As the years went on, he continued to restrict his food, consuming no more than 12 ounces of solid food and 14 fluid ounces of wine a day. In *Discourses on the Sober Life*, published when Cornaro was 84, he paints a delightful picture of his old age, noting that his current state of health was excellent and his psychological and mental health was also excellent:

My spirits not oppressed by much food, but barely kept up are always brisk especially after eating, so I am obliged then to sing a song and then to write. Nor do I ever find myself the worse for writing immediately after meals, nor is my understanding ever clearer, nor am I apt to be drowsy, the food I take being in too small quantity to send any fumes up to my brain.

After publishing several more books, Luigi Cornaro died at the age of 101.

William Stark, physician (1741–1770)

The dietary experiments of the British physician William Stark contrast sharply with Cornaro's in that they ended tragically. Stark wanted to determine the minimum amount of food one could live on. The idea was sparked by a comment made by his friend the American diplomat Benjamin Franklin, who told Stark he had once survived for two weeks on bread and water when he was a printer. Stark set out a number of experiments, in which he would consume a severely restricted range of foods. He began by consuming only bread and water and a little sugar, starting with 20 ounces of bread and working up to 38 ounces— more than a loaf and a half of bread. He ate that daily for 31 days.

Later, he added olive oil to the bread and water. Still later, he stopped olive oil and added boiled beef. For another period he lived exclusively on flour, suet or lard, water and salt. He devised a total of 24 diets, none of which included fruits or vegetables. Each combination of foods was eaten for a few weeks at a time. Each day he recorded his weight as well as his excretions, his moods and his sense of physical and mental well-being.

Although there were periods when he felt perfectly well, as his experiments continued his health declined. In his diary he wrote that after a few months his gums became swollen, and that he "now perceived small ulcers on the inside of my cheeks and particularly near the back tooth and the gums of the upper jaw of the same side were swelled and red and bled when pressed with the finger. The right nostril was also internally red and purple and very painful."

Stark died at 29, just eight months after he started his restricted way of eating, apparently from an acute intestinal infection. At the end of his life, he was eating only honey puddings and Cheshire cheese. The description of his gums we would now recognize as signs of scurvy, caused by vitamin C deficiency. Eighteen years after his death, an account of his self-experiments was published as a book by James Carmichael Smythe.

The contrasting experiments of Cornaro and Stark led to an unavoidable conclusion: A wide variety of foods in modest amounts is more conducive to health and longevity than an ample intake of a very limited diet. What we eat or don't eat can make the difference between a long life and early death.

William Banting (1797–1878)

Although widespread obesity is a late-twentieth-century phenomenon, affluent societies have always produced overweight individuals. Ancient Egyptian artefacts show the occasional fat person among the mainly slim ones. The Greek physician Hippocrates (ca. 460 BC–377 BC), father of Western medicine, observed that sudden death was more prevalent in obese men.

William Banting was a Victorian-era cabinetmaker in London and a distant relative of Frederick Banting (1891–1941), the co-discoverer of insulin. Unlike the rest of his family, Banting was grossly obese and hated it. He was so fat, he was unable to tie his shoelaces and could walk upstairs only if he did so slowly and backwards. For 20 years he tried to lose weight. He fasted, went to spas, tried punishing exercise regimes, to no avail. On the advice of Dr. William Harvey, an ear, nose and throat specialist, he cut sugar, bread and all cereal products out of his diet. The diet worked and he lost the excess weight. He wrote and self-published a monograph describing his weight-reducing regime titled *A Letter on Corpulence*. In it he emphasizes that he didn't restrict the amount of food he ate; he ate anything he liked except sugar, bread and cereal.

Banting's was the first low-carbohydrate diet and became popular throughout Europe through his widely translated monograph, which sold 63,000 copies in England in its first three editions. Banting died in 1878, at the age of 81. The term "to bant" came to be used as a jocular synonym for low-carbohydrate dieting and is still used that way in Sweden.

Morgan Spurlock's contemporary food experiment

Once North Americans became habituated to William Kellogg's breakfast-in-a-box, they were ready for other quick and convenient meals bought at the store. By the late twentieth century the availability of highly processed fast food was commonplace in North America, and had become a major export to other industrialized nations. Food still looked like food; it even tasted like food. And it was cheap. But the mass-produced burgers, chicken nuggets, french fries, soft drinks and milkshakes purchased at ever-expanding chains of popular restaurants were high in fat and sugar and low in fibre, vitamins and minerals, reducing the chances of eating a balanced meal.

Morgan Spurlock is a contemporary self-experimenter, a twenty-first-century version of Luigi Cornaro and William Stark. In 2003, at the age of 32, Spurlock decided to put himself on a fast-food diet, after watching a television news item about two women who sued the McDonald's chain for making them overweight (they lost). Eating all meals at McDonald's for six weeks, Spurlock set himself two rules: If the server asked him, "Do you want that supersized?" he had to say yes, but he would take the supersized portion only if asked. His other rule was to try everything on the menu.

At the start of his experiment, Spurlock had himself weighed, measured and tested by an internist, a cardiologist, a nutritionist and an exercise adviser, and he was found to be healthy and fit. Three weeks into the experiment, his blood sugar, triglycerides and cholesterol levels had risen, and his liver functions were abnormal. He felt sluggish and disinclined to exercise. His doctor diagnosed him as pre-diabetic and was also concerned about Spurlock's fatty liver. There were changes in his blood tests comparable to those of a heavy drinker. But Spurlock wasn't drinking alcohol. Instead, his diet was high in sugar, starchy carbohydrates and saturated fats and lacking in fruits and vegetables.

In the movie he made to document his experience, *Supersize Me*, his doctor tells him, "If you were drinking alcohol I would say to you, stop it immediately or you are going to kill yourself. I would never have believed that junk food alone could do such harm." Although there is now growing evidence that a high-starch, high-sugar diet will damage the liver just as effectively as excess alcohol, Spurlock's doctors were still shocked that his health could have deteriorated so fast. It took Spurlock over six months to take off the weight he gained and for his blood tests to return to his pre–*Super Size Me* days.

Such self-experimentation would certainly not pass muster today as rigorous scientific research. Yet these self-experimenters powerfully illustrate of the old adage "You are what you eat." The link between overeating, obesity and low dietary intakes of fruits and vegetables to chronic diseases like diabetes, heart disease, dementia and cancer is self-evident. Mounting scientific evidence is validating the nutritional lessons of Cornaro, Stark,

Banting and Spurlock: the best diet to delay the onset of these diseases, which become more widespread as we age, is one that is modest in calories, low in saturated fats and high in fruits and vegetables.

3

Hidden Hunger: The Discovery of Micronutrients

▼

Man is a food dependent creature. If you do not feed him he will die. Feed him improperly and parts of him will die.

— Emanuel Cheraskin (1916–2001), American physician

L ONG BEFORE VITAMINS were isolated and named, people knew that there were some hidden substances in food needed for good health. Many ancient cultures, including the Chinese, Egyptians and Romans, realized that eating raw liver could cure night blindness, a condition in which vision is normal in bright light but weak or even absent in the dark. They did not, of course, know that it was the vitamin A in liver that made it an effective treatment, only that raw liver had a curative effect.

Cod liver oil was perhaps the earliest nutritional supplement to be widely used. The first mention of it occurs in a scientific thesis, written in Latin and published in 1645, which describes the use of cod liver oil to cure rickets.[1] Rickets is a debilitating disease of infants and children, which causes their bones to soften and break. A woman with rickets would have a pelvis so twisted that childbirth would be extremely difficult, and her children likely stillborn. Rickets was widespread in crowded, smoggy areas, where people worked indoors or underground and rarely got any sun.

Cod liver oil, rich in the sunshine vitamin, was made by extracting the livers of codfish, leaving them in piles to putrefy, and collecting the oil that ran out. By the end of the eighteenth century it was widely used in medicine, but had been popular among the peasants of Europe long before that. Dr. Robert Darley wrote in 1782 about his success using cod liver oil to treat his patients, and noted that "the poor clamoured for it," even though it tasted and smelled loathsome.[2] Case histories from that period showed that it was used not only to prevent rickets but to help "the rheumatism" (what we would now call arthritis) and osteomalacia, the adult version of rickets.

In the eighteenth century, the British navy pioneered the use of lemons and limes as important nutritional supplements. Before that time, many luckless sailors died of scurvy before their ship reached its destination. The disease was then attributed to a lack of hygiene, but the Scottish naval surgeon James Lind (1716–1794) believed that it was caused by the absence of fresh food, especially fruit. To test his hypothesis, Lind conducted one of the first clinical trials. He gave some sailors a lime every day and observed what happened to those who did not get the limes compared to those who did. The sailors who were not given limes developed scurvy, whereas those who ate limes stayed well. From then on, all British sailors were issued a lime a day, which is one of the explanations of how the English came to be nicknamed Limeys.

Two centuries before Lind, the French explorer Jacques Cartier (1491–1557) also recognized the importance of vitamin C, though he would not have called it that. When Cartier's ship was marooned in the St. Lawrence ice on his second voyage in 1535, his crew was near death from scurvy. Aboard his ship was the son of the great Chief Donnacona of the St. Lawrence Iroquoians, who, sickened from scurvy, crawled away but later returned cured.

"How is it that you are well again?" Cartier asked him.

"My people cure this disease with a tea brewed from the bark and needles of the white cedar," replied the sailor. The tree was *arborvitae*, whose needles are rich in vitamin C. Even today, members of the Canadian First Nations will chew cedar buds to relieve a sore throat, and make a strong tea from cedar boughs, which they drink over the winter months.

Discovering the vital amines

At the end of the nineteenth century, there was an explosion in the study of microbial infections, at that time considered to be the cause of every disease. Beriberi, a fatal condition of the nerves and heart, was one of these. Observing that beriberi occurred in populations who ate white or polished rice, and not in those who ate brown rice, led some scientists to propose that beriberi was not caused by infection, but that the outer husk of rice contained something special that prevented the disease— what they called an accessory food factor.

The Polish biochemist Casimir Funk (1884–1967) isolated the "anti-beriberi" substance, which he named thiamine, and went on to systematically study other food factors that, when eliminated from the diet of animals, caused the animals to become ill and eventually die. He called these essential food factors "vital amines" because thiamine contained a chemical group called amines ($-NH_2$). But when this didn't hold true for some of the later discoveries, the term was changed to vitamins and the name eventually applied to all accessory food factors.

Vitamin B1 was the first vitamin isolated in 1911, followed by vitamin A, in 1913. The 1920s and 1930s was a time of rapid progress in isolating and identifying other vitamins. By the 1940s, the idea that we were made ill not only by trauma and infection, but also by what might be missing from our food, was well established.

How many vitamins are there?

Thirteen vitamins were identified, classified into water soluble and fat soluble. Vitamins A, D, E and K are fat soluble and can be stored in body fat and organs. The B vitamins and vitamin C are water soluble and not well stored by the body. They are easily eliminated in urine. Vitamin B is a complex of eight different vitamins: Although chemically they are quite different from each other, they often occur together in food and complement each other biochemically; where you need one of them, you usually require the others.

Most of the vitamins are identified by letters and numbers, and the letters correspond to the order in which they were discovered. But they also have chemical names (see Chapter 16). Vitamins do not provide energy or the raw materials to make cells or tissues, but are catalysts—substances that in tiny amounts speed up reaction time in the production of energy, the generation of hormones, and in countless other metabolic processes needed to run the body. Without these enzymes, chemical reactions in the body would take place slowly, if at all, and metabolism would slow to a standstill.

Later researchers recognized that another class of nutrients—minerals—worked alongside vitamins as essential cofactors in metabolic reactions. Minerals are classified either as macrominerals or trace minerals depending on the relative amounts we need of each. Macrominerals include calcium, magnesium, potassium, phosphorus, sodium, chloride and sulphur. Trace minerals include iron, iodine, copper, zinc, fluoride, nickel, chromium, boron and selenium, as well as the less familiar molybdenum and vanadium. Although vitamins are frequently destroyed during metabolism, minerals are not. But they, too, are water soluble and lost in urine, blood, sweat and feces.

The new science of phytochemicals

In the latter part of the twentieth century, scientists identified a new class of chemicals in foods they called phytochemicals, which are not essential—that is, we do not die if we are deprived of them. Nevertheless, they are needed for good health. *Phytos* is Greek for "plant," and these chemicals were found mainly in fruits and vegetables as well as in whole grains, herbs and spices. They too were known in ancient times. They were not called phytochemicals, of course, but herbalists recognized their curative properties. In fact, phytochemicals are the basis of herbal medicine.

Phytochemicals give plant foods vibrant colour and unique aromas and flavours. They evolved to help plants survive in hostile environments, protecting them from UV damage or predatory insects. Some are natural antimicrobials. Garlic, for instance, is as strong an antibiotic in the laboratory as penicillin. It also has antiviral, antifungal and even antihistamine properties.

The colour pigments of fruits and vegetables are antioxidants. When the earth was young, there was less oxygen in the air than there is today, and the planet could not support life forms that depended on oxygen for their survival. Plants take in carbon dioxide and release oxygen, and over time this process made the atmosphere more hospitable to oxygen-dependent life forms. At the same time, plants needed to protect themselves from the damaging effects of some forms of oxygen generated in the process—oxygen free radicals—and thus evolved antioxidants. Antioxidants are chemicals that neutralize this damage. A diet rich in phytochemicals also helps us to detoxify, especially from fat-soluble toxins such as herbicides, pesticides, PCBs and other man-made chemicals that persist in the environment and are now thought to put us at increased risk of a host of diseases.

The evidence is compelling that eating a variety of plant-based foods, including herbs and spices, legumes and whole grains, has a huge payoff, promoting disease resistance and increased life expectancy. Current research shows that a high intake of vegetables and fruits has the potential to protect us against diabetes, cancer, cardiovascular disease and dementia. The phytochemicals that protect plants and enable them to survive can be used to maintain our health.

New directions in nutritional research

In the second half of the twentieth century, evidence emerged for individual differences in nutritional needs: we all need the same range of essential nutrients, but vary widely in the amount that we require.

This interesting idea was first put forward by one of the great vitamin researchers, Roger Williams (1893–1988). He synthesized and named folic acid and was the discoverer of pantothenic acid, one of the B vitamins. He talked about biochemical individuality more than half a century ago, and suggested that wide variations in individual nutritional needs might explain many baffling health problems. Williams's book *Biochemical Individuality*, first published in 1956 and republished in 1998, still makes wonderful reading today.[3] In it, Williams describes simple experiments from the 1940s that support his theory.

For example, he wrote about an experiment in which subjects were deprived for months of thiamine. Some of them developed clinical signs of beriberi but others did not, even though they were all on the same experimental diet. Williams also noted that the American author Richard Dana, in his 1840 account of a two-year sea voyage, *Two Years Before the Mast*, described a sailor near death in the last stages of scurvy. The rest of the crew, who received the same vitamin C–deficient rations, appeared free of the disease. Williams argued that if everyone had the same needs for vitamins, all volunteers deprived of thiamine and all the sailors on vitamin C–deficient diets would have become ill at roughly the same time.

Today, modern science is taking Williams's ideas a step further. It has been demonstrated at the most sophisticated level of molecular biology that our requirements for any one of the essential nutrients is highly individual. The need for iron, for example, can vary as much as 40-fold from one individual to another.[4] This may explain why some women seem always to teeter on the verge of anemia and require iron supplements, even when postmenopausal.

The really big breakthroughs of the twenty-first century are in two new and fertile fields of biological science, nutrigenomics and nutrigenetics, spinoffs from the Human Genome Project. These sciences explore the interaction between diet and genes. Individuals with slight alterations (polymorphisms) in their genes called SNPs (pronounced "snips") have been found to have increased needs for certain nutrients, compared to individuals who lack those particular SNPs. Although these sciences are in their infancy, it is already clear that Roger Williams got it right. When it comes to vitamin and mineral needs, one size does not fit all.

Keep this in mind the next time you read about a government agency's pronouncement on how much vitamin D a person needs. Despite the fact that every tissue in the body is now known to use vitamin D, current supplement recommendations in North America are the same for a small child and an obese 69-year-old. Whether you live in sunny Florida year-round or in the frozen North, the amount recommended for you does not vary. Nor does the RDA (Recommended Dietary Allowance) take into account a number of common genetic variations that have been shown to alter vitamin D needs.

Bruce Ames of the Department of Biochemistry and Molecular Biology at the University of California, Berkeley is a scientist following new directions in nutritional research. Ames's groundbreaking research, for which he has received countless awards, was for many years focused on identifying cancer-causing agents (mutagens) in food and in the environment. More recently, he has turned his attention to vitamins and minerals. While life-threatening deficiency diseases such as scurvy, beriberi and rickets are now rare, his research shows that cellular and metabolic damage can occur at intakes of vitamins and minerals that fall between the RDAs and the rock-bottom intakes that cause the classic deficiency diseases. This damage accelerates the onset of the diseases of aging. Moreover, he maintains, the deterioration of cells and tissues is easily and cheaply prevented by taking supplements.[5]

2

Red Flags

4

Fatigue

▼

The best six doctors anywhere
And no one can deny it
Are sunshine, water, rest, and air
Exercise and diet.
These six will gladly you attend
If only you are willing
Your mind they'll ease
Your will they'll mend
And charge you not a shilling.

— Nursery rhyme quoted by Wayne Fields,
    What the River Knows (1990)

L ISTEN TO YOUR BODY. If you are not getting the nutrients to maintain yourself in good health, your body will
let you know. You will notice signs, seemingly minor at
first, that something is amiss. Fatigue is one such red flag and a
common complaint as we get older.

If you feel tired all the time, you will first want to see your
doctor because fatigue may signal a medical condition that needs
treatment; you may be anemic or have thyroid problems. Once

you doctor has ruled out a medical condition, he or she might attribute your fatigue to your age or work schedule. Perhaps your doctor will say, "We are all tired—I'm tired, too. It's the pace of modern life."

Many people arrive at my office after having been given this unsatisfactory explanation. I take their complaint very seriously. The first thing I want to do is evaluate how fatigued they are. I ask them to estimate on a scale of 1 to 10 what their energy level is. We talk about the difference between sustained energy and driving energy. Some people can rise to the occasion and push themselves hard to meet a deadline, but feel exhausted when there is no emergency. I need to know how well they are sleeping, because anyone who does not get enough restorative sleep is unlikely to feel energetic the next day. Short sleeping, whether due to overwork or to burning the candle at both ends, could be the source of the problem. A less obvious and frequently overlooked cause of fatigue, however, is vitamin and mineral deficiencies.

Lessons from history

In the heyday of vitamin research in the 1930s and 1940s, healthy volunteers agreed to be put on diets deficient in one or another vitamin so that the researchers could see how soon the volunteers exhibited signs of illness. The researchers kept records of when human guinea pigs deprived of vitamin C developed scurvy, how long before those deprived of vitamin B3 (niacin) showed the three signs of pellagra—dementia, diarrhea and dermatitis—and so on for other vitamins. Regardless of what the missing vitamin was, the first symptom the subjects reported was the same: fatigue.

Some of these studies were described in a 1942 book entitled *The Vitamins in Medicine* written by two British researchers, Franklin Bicknell and Frederick Prescott. In their book, Bicknell and Prescott wrote that the volunteers who agreed to go on diets short of one or another of the vitamins "generally complain of tiredness before any other recognizable sign of deficiency occurs. This 'tiredness' is one of the commonest complaints in the doctor's surgery and it is not unreasonable to associate it in some cases with vitamin deficiency in the patient."[1] All this research has been somehow forgotten by modern medicine.

Today, vitamin and mineral intakes of a significant number of Canadians are less than adequate. It would not be surprising, therefore, if vitamin deficiencies were at the root of cases of otherwise unexplained fatigue. The Canadian Community Health Survey of 2004 showed that between 10 percent and 35 percent of Canadians over the age of 19 did not meet the Estimated Average Requirement (EAR) for vitamin C, a number of B vitamins, and zinc, and that 40 to 65 percent of Canadians, depending on age and sex, failed to meet the EAR for vitamin A and magnesium.

Measuring deficiency

As we have already mentioned, the EAR—defined as the amount that will satisfy the requirements of *half* the population—is a rather odd measurement. While it may be a useful standard for public health planning purposes, the EAR has little bearing on individual health requirements and is not helpful to you or your doctor. The Recommended Dietary Allowance (RDA) or Recommended Daily Intake (RDI) is somewhat more useful. About 20 percent higher than the EAR, the RDA is the amount of a nutrient expected to maintain good health in the average healthy person at each life stage.

The problem here is that there is no "average person"; the actual amount of each nutrient needed to maintain good health differs from one individual to the next. The RDA assumes you are healthy and does not apply if you are sick with the flu or recovering from surgery, if you take nutrient-depleting medications, or if you have a condition such as diabetes or heart disease, all of which influence daily needs. Nor does it take into account your height, weight, or age. The most recent RDA for vitamin D is the same for people from age 1 to 70.

Since we know that many Canadians are not meeting the EAR, it seems an even higher proportion would not meet the RDA. Concern about deficiencies appears to be increasing. A poll conducted by Ipsos Reid in 2010 showed that two-thirds of Canadians say they "sometimes" or "frequently" take supplementary vitamins.[2] Taking a good daily multivitamin and mineral supplement (how to choose one is described later in this book) is the first step in dealing with fatigue.

Fatigue and magnesium

Mineral deficiencies can also cause fatigue. Magnesium is needed for sustained energy, and insufficient magnesium will certainly reduce your energy levels.

Before food can be used as energy, it must be converted inside cells into adenosine triphosphate (ATP). ATP is the currency of energy transfer between cells, needed for the countless metabolic reactions that run the moment-by-moment functioning of our bodies. No cell in the body can work without it, whether it is a brain cell that needs to make neurotransmitters such as dopamine or serotonin or the memory chemical acetylcholine; pancreatic cells that need to make insulin; muscle cells that contract and relax as we move.

ATP has to be bound or "complexed" to magnesium to be activated biochemically. I like to think of ATP as a jack-in-the-box, ready to burst out and provide energy as needed. I picture magnesium as the catch on the lid. Without the catch, the jack will not jump out of the box. This requirement for magnesium to be complexed to ATP is fundamental for sustained energy production in the body.

Getting enough magnesium

A multivitamin will usually contain no more than 50 to 75 mg. We can get a certain amount from food (see Table 1), but foods richest in magnesium are not plentiful in the average diet. Sources include spinach and other leafy greens, since chlorophyll, which gives plants their green colour, is a magnesium-containing molecule. Nuts, seeds, seafood and whole grains are also good sources of magnesium. Water sourced directly from mountain streams or artesian wells traditionally contributed to our magnesium intake, but city water is not a good magnesium source, since minerals are usually removed from it to soften water for laundry use and industrial purposes.

Some bottled mineral waters are high in magnesium—check the label.

Table 1
Food sources of magnesium

1 cup pumpkin seeds	700 mg
1 cup mixed nuts	300 mg
3 oz halibut	70 mg
1 cup cooked oatmeal	56 mg
1 can tuna	50 mg
1 cup spinach	44 mg
1 shredded wheat	40 mg
3 oz shrimp	31 mg
4 oz steak	22 mg
1 slice whole wheat bread	18 mg

Magnesium is tricky to supplement since it is easy to take too much. Later in this book I will describe a method you can use to judge how much you personally need. As a basic, I recommend an extra 100 mg in addition to the multivitamin. There is another issue: refining and processing foods reduces their mineral and vitamin content. As the use of processed foods has risen in Western countries, magnesium intake has diminished.[3] The other culprit in reducing tissue stores of magnesium is prescription drugs. Many of the top-selling medications are known to have this magnesium-depleting effect. The FDA has alerted doctors that proton pump inhibitors (PPIs)—drugs commonly used to control acid reflux and similar digestive problems—can increase the symptoms of magnesium insufficiency such as muscle cramps, heart arrhythmias and even heart attacks. Because of the need for magnesium to activate ATP, the chemical energy of cells, it's not surprising that people taking these drugs feel fatigued.

The role of sugar and starch in fatigue

Many people reach for something sweet when tired. Sugar gives us a quick burst of energy. A little later, however, it leads to an energy crash so that we feel even more fatigued than before we ate it. Most people know this about sugar, but are not always aware that starchy foods—bread, potatoes, rice and pasta—are just sugars in disguise. These complex carbohydrates are glucose molecules linked together, and when they are digested will also push up blood sugar, although the upward swing is delayed 20 or 30 minutes. Although starchy carbs don't taste sweet, ultimately they will have the same effect on blood sugar as sweets.

Foods that cause a rapid rise in blood sugar are dangerous because high levels of sugar in the blood damage tissues and cause alterations in proteins. Called cross-linking, this interferes with how the proteins function. When blood sugar rises rapidly, the pancreas goes on high alert and releases insulin. Insulin moves sugar from the blood and stores it in liver, muscle and fat cells. The immediate danger is reduced, but the brain and tissues no longer have enough glucose available to them. The spike is thus followed by an energy drop. To avoid this, we have to learn to eat carbohydrates that will break down slowly, providing a steady supply of energy to the brain and muscles without provoking this exaggerated insulin response. That means a high daily intake of vegetables and fruit.

In 1980, a team of scientist at the University of Toronto led by Dr. David Jenkins set out to identify which carbohydrate foods would be slow to raise blood sugar, and therefore be best for diabetics. Their research led them to develop the concept of the glycemic index (GI) with which we are now quite familiar.[4] The position of the foods on the index is a measure of their ability to raise blood sugar when compared to glucose or white bread. Carbohydrates such as muffins and cookies that are digested quickly into glucose have a high GI, while carbohydrates that break down slowly and enter the bloodstream at a leisurely pace have a low GI. GI has become a useful measure not only for diabetics but for all of us.

Why we cannot think clearly when we are fatigued

Eating in a way that leads to spikes in blood sugar and insulin, followed by a drop in blood sugar, naturally affects the brain. The brain is a nutrient hog. It uses up glucose, oxygen and all the nutrients at about 10 times the rate of other tissues. Therefore, the brain is the first to feel the drop in blood sugar. When the brain senses that blood sugar is low, it demands that you eat something. Everybody knows the feeling, that midafternoon low when you feel as if someone had removed your brain and replaced it with a bunch of soggy cotton batting. If your lunch was high in carbohydrates, it will have sustained you for a while, but then, by midafternoon, your blood sugar has dropped and you find yourself thinking about the cookies in the coffee room. Or about a walk to the convenience store for a candy bar.

What is the ideal frequency for eating to maintain energy?

Depends on the individual. Many people do well eating regular small amounts. If you go longer than five hours without food, the brain reads that as starvation and your blood sugar will start to rise by itself by a process called gluconeogenesis. This process makes glucose from amino acids, the building blocks of protein, and from stored fats. Lunch to dinner is often more than five hours, particularly if one is going out to eat. To stabilize blood sugar, you need a high-quality afternoon snack. A candy bar won't do. The ideal thing would be a piece of cheese and an apple or pear, or a small container of unsweetened yogurt and a piece of fruit. Almonds and walnuts have a neutral effect on blood sugar and provide the added benefit of reducing cholesterol, according to some studies.

Unless you work at home, such healthful snacks are not always at hand. In an emergency—for instance, when you are out and know it will be a long wait until the next meal—you can look for the nearest coffee shop. In any town or city, you'll now find cafés on just about every corner. Order a caffè latte, unsweetened. The milk in it will contain just enough protein and milk sugar (lactose) to keep you satisfied. It will tide you over and keep your blood sugar from dropping too low.

I see both men and women with fatigue, though men are perhaps less likely to recognize it and seek help. Some time ago, a couple came to see me because the wife had had cancer and she wanted to prevent a recurrence. Eventually she came alone, without her husband. Then, after a while, I saw his name on the appointment list. He filled out the usual forms about his health history, and reported that there was nothing much wrong with his health. He slept fine and was not on major drugs. He said he just wanted help to develop a basic supplement regime and check that his diet was appropriate. He started a multivitamin, learned how to optimize his magnesium and vitamin D intake and started taking fish oil for the omega-3 fats. Six months later he came back and told me: "I could never have believed how well I would feel taking these supplements." I asked him what was different. He said, "I have more energy, feel less irritable and I just feel so much better."

When he came to me I believed his needs were generally being met from his diet. He had no obvious health issues. But when you look at the Community Health Survey results, it stands to reason he could have been missing one or more of the nutrients he needed for optimal well-being. The benefits of his new regime have been sustained and he comes to see me now just once a year. Each time, he mentions that he has never felt so well in his life.

High energy levels are attainable at every age. Taking a daily multivitamin makes good sense, since a deficiency of any essential nutrient can cause fatigue. The potential benefits are high and the risk is close to nil. The right diet, one that is high in fruits and vegetables and low in sugar and starch, is also important whatever your age. If you eat balanced meals and snacks throughout the day, and learn how to use magnesium, you can maintain steady blood sugar levels without insulin spikes. You will be able to say goodbye to that tired feeling.

Percentage of Canadian women and men 19 years and older who do not meet Estimated Average Requirements (EAR) for selected vitamins and minerals.

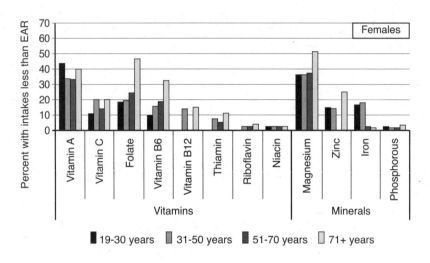

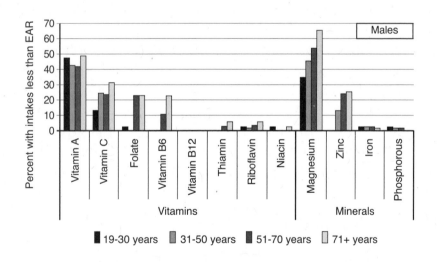

Source: Do Canadian Adults Meet Their Nutrient Requirements Through Food Intake Alone? Health Canada www.hc-sc.gc.ca/fn-an/surveill/nutrition/commun/art-nutr-adult-eng.php

5

Hair, Skin and Nails

▼

*I want to grow old without facelifts. I want
to have the courage to be loyal to the face I have made.*

— Marilyn Monroe (1926–1962), movie star

DOCTORS ROUTINELY ASSESS the general health of a
new patient by noting on their chart, "Looks younger
than her age" or "Looks older than his age." They base
that conclusion almost entirely on hair colour and smoothness
of skin. Theirs may be a snap judgment, but recent research suggests that it has some validity as a measure of health status. Prematurely wrinkled skin seems to indicate that a person is aging
abnormally fast. In one study, volunteers were asked to guess the
age of 1826 pairs of twins aged 70 years or older. The volunteers
were not told that the subjects were all twins. Those whom the
volunteers guessed to be younger than their twin were found to
have longer telomeres, better memory and better mental-
processing capacity than their older-looking sibling,[1] who, of
course, was the same age. When the subjects were followed for a
number of years, the researchers found that those picked as older
looking generally predeceased their younger-looking twin.

Collagen, the skin's chief protein

The health of skin relies on our ability to continuously produce several protein molecules, the most important of which is collagen. Protein makes up roughly 50 percent of the dry weight of the human body, and of that, collagen accounts for a quarter, making it the most abundant molecule in the body, after water.

Collagen is not only the chief protein of skin, but also gives resilience to bones, and strength and flexibility to tendons and ligaments. It is the cement that holds the blood vessels and other tissues together. Under a high-powered microscope, it appears fibrous, coiled like a spring or a three-stranded rope. Collagen is a dynamic tissue, constantly being worn down or damaged, so that it must be replaced on a regular basis. Throughout our lifespan, cells synthesize and degrade collagen. The balance between synthesis and degradation is critical not only for the renewal of skin, but also for muscle and heart health.[2] For example, collagen forms scar tissue and if the body cannot make it rapidly enough, wounds will heal poorly.

Collagen and sugar—a fatal attraction

A high-sugar, high-starch diet is damaging to collagen. Such a diet will elevate the circulating blood glucose. Glucose binds to collagen and triggers a series of chemical reactions that result in the production of molecules called advanced glycation end products (AGEs). AGEs make collagen molecules stick together, or cross-link. This then causes rearrangement and dehydration of collagen, an irreversible process that results in skin losing elasticity and forming deep lines and wrinkles. Some cross-linking is essential to the stability of collagen, but excessive cross-linking gives skin an aged appearance. The accumulation of AGEs, which are yellow in colour, also causes skin to discolour.

Noticeably wrinkled skin is an indication of poorer health status because wrinkles signal an excessive cross-linking of collagen. Not all the damage is visible. The same cross-linking will simultaneously cause stiffening of veins and arteries, which need to be flexible to control blood pressure and maintain circulation. Cross-linked collagen increases the risk of heart disease; diabetics with poorly controlled blood sugar levels are at increased risk of heart disease and circulation problems, particularly in the lower legs.[3] Remember, too, that collagen is not only the major protein of skin and blood vessel walls, it's also required for the integrity of the discs between spinal vertebrae and the cartilage in knees and hips. Moreover, healthy eyes depend on collagen, as do healthy teeth and gums. In short, strong collagen is an essential component of a healthy, young-looking body.

Nutrients needed for collagen health and replacement

When I talk about collagen in my office, I use a Slinky toy. I explain that while DNA is a double helix, collagen is similar but a triple helix—three spirals wound around each other. Like a Slinky, collagen has to be stretchy and elastic. And the triple-helix structure makes it very strong. Foods rich in protein are needed to provide the two amino acids—lysine and proline—that are the raw materials for collagen synthesis. Vitamin C is then needed to transform these two building blocks into the collagen molecule. Scurvy, the dreaded disease of old-time seafarers, is simply the inability to replace worn-out collagen.

The first sign of scurvy is fatigue, followed by generalized weakness, particularly in the legs. Skin becomes thin, and reddish-purple blotches appear around hair follicles. The hairs themselves are twisted like a corkscrew and break off easily. In the later stages of scurvy, extensive purple bruises called ecchymoses appear. Ecchymoses are often seen in frail elderly individuals, but often go unrecognized by attending physicians as a symptom of ultimately fatal scurvy.[4]

Magnesium is another important nutrient involved in collagen replacement, since it is required for protein synthesis. Stress rapidly depletes vitamin C and magnesium, which is why some people become wrinkled like a walnut after a period of extreme stress. Though clients do not seek me out for advice on how to lessen wrinkles, I ask them if they have noticed any sudden increase in facial lines. If they answer yes, I make sure they are taking enough vitamin C. The lines that I worry about on the face are not laughter or frown lines but the lines that travel diagonally across the cheeks. I often see that in people with high personal needs of vitamin C.

Magnesium is anti-inflammatory, meaning it will damp down inflammation. Many people, particularly women, complain of red spidery veins on their cheeks and nose, caused by a condition known as rosacea. Before the availability of drugs, an old-fashioned remedy for rosacea was to put milk of magnesia (magnesium hydroxide) on the face every night before bed to counteract the inflammation.

Mineral hot springs is a traditional European treatment for many diseases. The three strands of the collagen molecule have to be connected to each other for strength, and it is sulphur bonds that connect them. Many of Europe's thermal springs are rich in sulphur, source of the rotten-egg smell. Traditionally, visitors drank the water as well as bathed in it. Dietary sources of sulphur are equally effective. The anti-inflammatory Mediterranean diet is rich in onions and garlic, a significant source of sulphur. Egg yolks, too, contain sulphur.

Why dry skin is common among older people

If you look at a flake of skin under the microscope, you'll see a sheet of dead cells. Skin cells replace themselves every 21 to 28 days on average, but replacement time slows down with age. Cells can die off faster if they don't have the right nutritional support. The result is dry, flaky skin. The fine balance between cells dying and cells being replaced needs to be maintained if skin is to remain healthy. If your skin is drier in winter, the cause could be vitamin D deficiency since we cannot make vitamin D from October to March in most of Canada, and the period of vitamin D deprivation lengthens the farther north you go. The skin needs vitamin D for two important functions: to stimulate the production of new collagen and to encourage new cell growth.

I sometimes see people who have gone on a low-fat diet develop dull, dry and itchy skin. Increasing the good fats in the diet is important, since these fats play a vital role in strengthening cell membranes. Consume fatty fish such as salmon, trout and sardines that contain plenty of omega-3, or take fish oil supplements. Omega-3 is an essential constituent of cell membranes and also has an anti-inflammatory effect. People find that when they start taking omega-3 fats, their hair is shinier and their skin more supple. Olive oil, a component of the Mediterranean diet, likewise keeps skin youthful.

Preventing ugly age spots

Many women spend a lot of money having brown age spots (also known as liver spots) removed in the doctor's office without considering how they originate. These spots are an accumulation of a fatty brown pigment called lipofuscin. Lipofuscin is not only deposited in skin, but also in internal tissues—the heart muscle, kidneys, brain, adrenal glands. Stress, aging, even exercise can increase their numbers. I have seen age spots develop not only in the elderly but in young people who have been through an extended and serious health crisis. Made up of fats and proteins that have been damaged by free radicals, these spots are a sign that the body needs more antioxidants.

You will recall that the vitamins A, C and E, and the minerals selenium, manganese and zinc are antioxidants. They work in synergy with the phytochemicals present in colourful fruits and vegetables. Plants produce phytochemicals for their own protection from oxidation, which is what gives them their antioxidant properties. Green tea is known to have powerful antioxidant properties, and inhibits the formation of age-induced collagen cross-linking (see above), as do vitamins C and E.[5] Two to three cups of green tea a day may not only help prevent age spots and wrinkles, but may also protect against cardiovascular and other diseases caused by damaged collagen.

The big message from studies of the protective effects of antioxidants is that focusing on single nutrients, like vitamin C or E alone, is not the solution. It is the synergy amongst all the antioxidant vitamins, minerals and phytochemicals that offers the greatest benefit.

Getting age spots to disappear

It's a slow process, but it does happen. The first thing I expect when I work on a supplement regime is that my client will stop getting *new* age spots. Both diet and supplements I recommend will focus on antioxidants and include regular modest portions of protein throughout the day, a high intake of colourful vegetables and fruit, as well as low sugar intake and modest amounts of starch. Over time, age spots can fade on this regime, but they often leave a small ghost or footprint that will darken again when antioxidant levels in the blood decline, when sun exposure is excessive or following a prolonged illness.

Absorption of medications through the skin has been studied

since the 1950s, and many medications are given now as transdermal patches. Few people realize that we can also absorb the antioxidant ACE vitamins, and minerals such as magnesium and zinc, through the skin. To improve the appearance of skin, I sometimes recommend topical application of antioxidant vitamins. Vitamin C is easily oxidized and is best obtained in single-use capsules. To penetrate the skin, the concentration of vitamin C needs to be at 10 percent. Such capsules are readily available at health food stores and some pharmacies and can help to keep wrinkles from coming too fast or brown spots from getting browner.

My focus, however, is to look at skin with the aim of discovering what it reveals about the nutrition of an individual. Creams are useful for enhancement of your appearance, but you really need to feed the skin from the inside. The same nutrients that support your skin health are also needed by your brain, your bones and your vascular system. Simply applying antioxidants to your skin is not going raise blood levels sufficiently to nourish other organs.

What nails tell us

Nails, like skin, are an important indicator of the nutritional status of an individual. Doctors examine them for clues to underlying diseases; ridged nails, for example, can signal certain types of arthritis.

White spots, or leukonychia, are a striking feature sometimes seen in nails. They are due to trauma or a bang to the nail bed while the nail was forming. Leukonychia is known to be related to zinc deficiency.[6] In a supermarket recently, I saw a young woman at the checkout whose fingernails were marred by white spots on the nails of both hands. I wanted to ask her if she got a lot of colds and flu, or had a problem with dandruff, because all three can be a sign of zinc deficiency. She might just have a poor diet, and not meet the daily recommended intake of zinc, or she could have higher than average needs for zinc.

Stress depletes zinc,[7] and white spots may form when there is trauma to the nail bed at the same time as one is undergoing stress caused by an illness, or pressure at work to finish an urgent project, or the breakup of a relationship. It takes six months for the nail to grow from nail bed to tip. A white mark halfway up suggests that the trauma and stress occurred three months ago, especially if there are white marks at the same level on other nails. If you then ask, "Did something stressful happen to you three months ago?," the person with the white-spotted nail may well be astonished by the question and ask how you knew. It's a neat party trick. Because the girl in the supermarket had white spots all over her nails on both hands, they were likely due to on-going inadequate zinc intake.

How much zinc do you need? Zinc has a narrow therapeutic range, meaning that there is not a lot of wiggle room between not having enough and having too much. For most women, 10 to 15 mg a day is sufficient, an amount contained in a good multivitamin. Men have higher needs than women, especially after age 50, and a good multivitamin for men of that age should contain 20 to 25 mg of zinc. If you still have white spots on your nails after six months of taking a multivitamin, you may need to add more zinc. Consult a knowledgeable health care practitioner about the amount. You could also eat more oysters, the richest food source of zinc.

Beau's lines are horizontal ridges on the nail. They indicate a complete, if temporary, arrest of nail growth, usually after a serious illness. I see them in chemotherapy patients when they stop and start chemo, but nail growth can stop due to any sort of severe prolonged stress. Vertical ridges are common as we age, often due to poor circulation to the nail bed.

Splinter hemorrhages are fine lines under the nail, near the tip, caused by vitamin C deficiency. Splinter hemorrhages may be accompanied by other signs of vitamin C deficiency in the skin such as red or purple spots called petechiae, caused by minute hemorrhages. If I see those two together, I can be sure that an individual needs more vitamin C.

People who have experienced soft or peeling nails will often comment on the fact that by the end of summer their nails are harder and stronger. That they notice improvement in summer is a sign that the problem is caused by a shortage of vitamin D. Vitamin D is needed for calcium to be absorbed into bones, nails and teeth, and lack of D leads to soft, peeling as well as brittle nails. Brittle nails are also seen in people who have sharply reduced their protein intake.

Spoon-shaped nails that curve slightly upwards, frequently at the tip, can indicate iron deficiency. If anemia is the cause, the nail will look quite pale, especially around the nail bed. Insufficient B vitamins can also cause spoon-shaped nails, but it's more often iron that is lacking in the diet. After you start taking the needed supplements, the nail must grow out before it can resume its normal shape, a process that takes at least six months.

What can we do about hair loss?

Hair loss can be a sign of a serious underlying illness in both men and women, especially thyroid disease. If your hair is falling out, be sure to report it to your doctor. Once illness is ruled out, there are some other causes to consider. Hair shedding may occur two to four months after childbirth, or as a result of any type of stress. People who go on crash diets for a time and people with eating disorders have thin, poor-quality hair. Many common medications causes hair loss as a side effect, including the contraceptive pill, acne medication, heart medications called beta blockers, some types of blood pressure medications, antidepressants, and blood thinners such as heparin and warfarin (Coumadin).

Male pattern baldness is hormonal and genetic. It comes through the mother's genes and affects some men starting as early as their twenties. Preventing it through nutrition is difficult. Hair regrowth needs all of the nutrients, but particularly vitamin D. In the summer months, hair grows faster, which shows the beneficial effect of the sunshine vitamin. Apart from vitamin D, other deficiencies can cause diffuse hair loss, including shortfalls of iron and zinc and the omega-3 fatty acids.[8]

Dandruff is another problem related to nutritional health. People with white flecks on their shoulders are likely to be short of zinc, particularly if they also have white flecks on their nails; selenium is another mineral likely to be in short supply. Some people develop dandruff as a result of a fungal infection of the scalp, a condition which can be helped by taking selenium. If you have a shampoo that seems to control your dandruff well, check the ingredient label. If the product contains zinc or selenium, that will be a clue that these nutrients are missing from your current diet.

Dandruff is not all that different from dry skin. A dry, flaky scalp might indicate a shortage of omega-3 fatty acids. The first thing to do is swap the bad fat in your diet—trans fats from processed foods and saturated fat from meats—for the monounsaturated fats in olive oil and avocado. A scalp treatment of mashed avocado applied before you shampoo your hair can help. Flaxseed oil, fish and fish oils, salmon, trout and sardines are sources of good fats for hair health.

Slowing down the greying of hair

Vitamins B12, B6 and folic acid are all at the root, so to speak, of healthy hair. The B vitamins work together, which is why we need to supplement with a B complex to retain our natural hair colour longer. The B vitamins and magnesium are needed to make melanin—the colour pigment of hair and skin—from the amino acid tyrosine. (You will read more about tyrosine in Chapter 10.)

Early loss of hair colour can be genetic. I always ask people with grey hair, "When did you start to go grey?" If they answer, "In my twenties," I know there is probably a strong family history of premature greying, along with a family history of heart disease. The link? The same B vitamins that are needed for the production of hair colour are required to reduce levels of a toxic amino acid called homocysteine in the blood. Homocysteine is produced by normal metabolism, but it should disappear quickly from the circulation by being further metabolized into non-toxic amino acids. If it hangs around, it will damage blood vessel walls, cause abnormalities of blood coagulation and therefore increase the risk of heart disease.[9] Since homocysteine is a recognized indicator that you are short of B vitamins, it is a good additional test to ask for at your annual checkup. The lower your level of homocysteine, the better.

A breed of laboratory mice—the Agouti mouse—has demonstrated how diet can trump genetics with respect to hair colour. Agouti mice generally have pale yellowy-grey coats and are prone to obesity and diabetes. Scientists at Duke University in Durham, North Carolina, managed to change the hair colour of baby Agoutis by feeding their mothers extra B vitamins during pregnancy. The new generation of Agouti mice not only had lustrous brown coats, they grew into lean, disease resistant adults.

And when they had offspring of their own, the next generation kept their brown hair even though they were not fed extra B vitamins before birth.[10]

A cancer patient came to me after undergoing chemotherapy of a type that did not cause hair loss, but caused her brown hair to turn white. Her hair was black at the ends but growing in totally white at the roots. We worked on increasing her nutrient intake, and after she started taking a full range of B vitamins, the new roots started growing in black. The result was a bizarre striped effect for a time, but eventually she regained her full head of black hair.

Antibiotics deplete B vitamins. Bacteria in the gut—the good kind—actually produce B vitamins and vitamin K. Antibiotics are on a mission to kill disease-causing bacteria, but they cannot distinguish them from the good bacteria that our intestine needs. The result is B-vitamin depletion. This unwanted side effect is well known, and when antibiotics were first marketed, they were always given together with B vitamins. I don't know when that practice stopped or why doctors decided that depletion of B vitamins by antibiotics was unimportant. Yet today we have more antibiotic exposure than ever before.

Skin, as well as hair, can lose its pigmentation. Vitiligo, a condition that causes large white patches to appear on the skin, has also been associated with high levels of blood homocysteine. In a two-year Swedish study, researchers showed that folic acid, vitamin B12 and sun exposure helped repigmentation of the skin in 64 of 100 patients they treated.[11]

Since everyone eventually goes grey, does that mean every old person is vitamin B deficient?

We don't know. We do know that the B vitamins and magnesium work together and both are depleted by stress. Advanced age might itself be a stressor. Many medications commonly used by older people deplete magnesium and B vitamins, as we have seen.

It's not possible to say exactly how much B vitamins are needed by a particular individual, but I normally advise older people to read the label before buying and choose a multivitamin with the highest level they can find. Some of the common drugstore vitamins have Bs in such trivial amounts that they are not useful for a majority of people. If someone is particularly stressed, I may add in some extra Bs on top of their multivitamin.

6

Vision and Hearing

▼

When Mozart was composing at the end of the 18th century, the city of Vienna was so quiet that fire alarms could be given verbally, by a shouting watchman mounted on top of St. Stefan's Cathedral. In 20th-century society, the noise level is such that it keeps knocking our bodies out of tune and out of their natural rhythms. This ever-increasing assault of sound upon our ears, minds, and bodies adds to the stress load of civilized beings trying to live in a highly complex environment.

— Steven Halpern, New Age composer/musician

BECAUSE OUR EYES AND EARS connect us to our environment and to each other, any diminution in their function is distressing. But not inevitable. Complaints about vision and hearing loss are common among some of the older people I see in my office. Both sometimes occur in the same individual, perhaps because the same lifestyle and dietary habits can affect both sensory functions.[1] A high-sugar and -starch diet is a shared risk factor,[2,3] along with a low intake of vegetables and fruit.[4,5] Since both hearing loss and vision impairment are hard to reverse once established, we need to focus on prevention.

The most common age-related eye problems are cataracts, macular degeneration and glaucoma. Research indicates that in each of these conditions, nutritional deficiencies play a central role.

Causes of cataracts

The lens of a healthy eye is transparent and allows light to travel through it. A cataract occurs when the lens becomes cloudy, dense and inflexible. Apart from water, the lens is mostly protein, and damage to this protein causes the cataract. Compare it to the protein of an egg white, which is clear when fresh but starts to become opaque when heated. The change in opacity of the lens is due to the same cross-linking process discussed in the last chapter. Cross-linking rearranges the protein molecules so that they no longer let light pass through.

The protein damaged is largely collagen. As we have already discovered, collagen is a dynamic molecule, constantly being broken down and replaced. Healthy collagen requires high levels of antioxidants to protect it against free radical damage. It also needs all the essential nutrients, such as vitamin C and magnesium, for its replacement and stabilization.

Elevated blood sugar will cause the lens to deteriorate and reduce blood flow to the eye. Because of this, we see a higher incidence of cataracts in people with diabetes; diabetic cataracts are a well-known complication of the disease. Smoking, excess alcohol consumption and UV light exposure are other risk factors. Controlling blood sugar, keeping alcohol intake modest, not smoking and wearing sunglasses in bright sunshine are all effective preventive measures.

Cataracts grow slowly, and you may be unaware of them at the early stages. But almost everyone over the age of 65 has some sign that they are developing the condition. Cataracts can be successfully operated on once "ripe," and for most people, surgery to implant an artificial lens restores their sight. But not everyone tolerates the implants well.

Although they are most frequently seen in older eyes, cataracts can occur at any age. One client who came to see me had had cataract surgery in her early thirties. Even children can have cataracts, in which case the cause is genetic.

Are people with early-onset cataracts aging poorly? Research suggests they are. I have already described a laboratory test that can reveal how fast we are aging by noting the length of telomeres in our chromosomes. A recent study looked at telomere length in cataract patients and found that people with more dense and widespread opacities in their lens had shorter telomeres than people of the same age without cataracts, suggesting that indeed aging is accelerated in people with age-related eye disease.[6]

Preventing cataracts

The first thing to do is avoid frequent spikes in blood sugar by eating a low-sugar, low-glycemic diet. The glycemic index (GI) of a food indicates how fast and how much it will raise blood sugar. A related but slightly different term is glycemic load (GL), which takes into account the portion size of a carbohydrate food you eat as well as its glycemic index. Some foods have a high GI but a low GL. Watermelon is an example. You need to eat an awful lot of watermelon—more than 4 cups—to ingest the equivalent of 50 g of sugar.

The second thing to do is include a wide assortment of colourful fruits and vegetables in your diet. Eat a rainbow. The colour pigments of fruits and vegetables are powerful antioxidants that prevent free radical damage of delicate tissues. Eyes and ears will both benefit from a diet high in antioxidants.

What are antioxidants?

Vitamins A, C, E, zinc, selenium and manganese are the chief vitamin and mineral antioxidants. Provided it has the right raw materials from food, the body manufactures other protective antioxidants, for example, glutathione, coenzyme Q10, super-oxide dismutase (SOD) and melatonin. We need antioxidants to prevent tissue damage caused by free radicals, a by-product of oxygen consumption. Free radicals cause damage to the cells and tissues they were produced in. This is known as oxidative stress.

If you remember your high school science class, you'll recall that the nucleus of an atom is surrounded by electrons orbiting around it, like planets revolving around the sun. These electrons occur in pairs, with one electron in the pair spinning one way and its partner in the opposite direction. If an oxygen molecule loses an electron, it becomes very reactive, and will try to stabilize itself by stealing an electron from a neighbouring molecule. This electron "theft" in turn forms a new free radical, and what follows is a chain reaction resulting in escalating damage to tissues. One current theory suggests that excess free radical damage is at the root of many serious chronic diseases associated with aging.[7]

The body makes free radicals in the process of normal metabolism, but their manufacture is increased by stress, exercise, and exposure to ultraviolet radiation and pollution. The harm caused by smoking is thought to be largely due to the free radical damage it causes. The accumulation of man-made chemicals collectively called POPs (persistent organic pollutants) in our environment and in our bodies is a major contributor to free radical damage. Infection and inflammation also dramatically increase free radical generation.

An excess of free radicals results in unhealthy aging. Free

radicals will damage not only eyes and ears, but also cause premature aging of skin, impair the immune system and damage the brain and heart. We can counteract such damage with a high intake of antioxidants, which neutralize free radicals. Some antioxidants are of particularly lively scientific interest, for example, resveratrol. Found in red wine, resveratrol became the subject of numerous human and animal studies after it was noticed that people were healthier in the wine-drinking countries around the Mediterranean. Red grape juice is also a good source of resveratrol. Other foods that have been shown to be high in this antioxidant include beet juice, peanuts, cranberries and blueberries. These tasty foods are easily incorporated into our diets.

Measuring antioxidants

The antioxidant capacity of a food can be measured and is called an ORAC score. ORAC stands for "oxygen radical absorbance capacity." The U.S. Department of Agriculture (USDA) recommends consuming 5000 ORAC units each day to protect tissues. Mother was right when she told you to eat your vegetables, but even eating five a day may provide only 1000 to 2000 ORAC units.[8] Certainly not enough to offset the daily onslaught of free radicals caused by stress and an increasingly toxic environment.

Dark chocolate, rich in antioxidants, is a treat you can include in your diet. Milk chocolate contains too much sugar and provides too low a concentration of flavanols, specific antioxidants found in cocoa. Cocoa powder that has not been processed with alkali (non–Dutch processed) has the highest ORAC score yet recorded per 100 mg of food. The protective potential of chocolate is just beginning to be studied. Evidence is emerging that chocolate benefits vascular health by lowering blood pressure and cholesterol.

Synthetic antioxidant supplements

Many people take antioxidant vitamins and minerals, sometimes as an antioxidant supplement or as part of a multivitamin. We usually take vitamin C and E separately, since they are too bulky to add to multivitamins in anything but tiny amounts. Of all the antioxidant supplements, vitamin E is the most controversial. Clinical trials investigating its use to treat and prevent a host of diseases have been contradictory, and a few have even suggested that it might be harmful.[9]

There are two forms of vitamin E—natural and synthetic. While some synthetic vitamins are identical to their natural counterparts (vitamin C, for example), this is not true of vitamin E. In nature, vitamin E occurs as eight chemically related compounds—the tocopherols (alpha, beta, delta and gamma) and the tocotrienols (alpha, beta, delta and gamma). All of these are present in foods like spinach, nuts and seeds, wheat germ and wheat germ oil, and all have antioxidant activity.

In North America and elsewhere only one part of vitamin E, alpha tocopherol, has a recommended daily intake.[10] This is because until recently researchers have claimed that only alpha tocopherol has health benefits. This idea is now hotly disputed and a growing body of research shows that the different forms of vitamin E complement each other.[11] The benefits of vitamin E in protecting against dementia, for example, seem to be related to the combination of different forms, rather than to alpha tocopherol alone.[12]

Food source alpha tocopherol, written as d-alpha tocopherol on supplement bottles, or cheap synthetic vitamin E, dl-alpha tocopherol, are the usual forms of vitamin E used in clinical trials.[13] This is unfortunate because large doses of alpha tocopherol are known to reduce blood levels of other beneficial forms of vitamin E that would normally be present in healthy diets and could conceivably do harm.[14] Synthetic beta carotene presents a similar problem. In one clinical trial, a synthetic form of beta carotene given to smokers at risk of lung cancer—they had been exposed to asbestos—increased rather than decreased the risk of cancer. Beta carotene is one of hundreds of orange-yellow pigments called carotenoids, which include the vitamin-like compound lutein, essential for eye health. The synthetic beta carotene has been shown to block the absorption of lutein[15] and is likely to also block absorption of other cancer-preventing carotenoids present in diet.

When we take supplements, they should mimic closely what is present in food. That is why I recommend only full-spectrum vitamin E supplements, containing all eight forms, to maximize antioxidant protection. Since it is easy to obtain beta carotene in the diet by including carotenoid-rich foods like carrots, tomatoes and cantaloupe, it is unnecessary in my opinion to take beta carotene as a separate supplement.

Macular degeneration—a growing epidemic

The leading cause of vision loss in Canada among those 65 and older, macular degeneration is occurring now at ever younger ages. The comedian Mary Walsh, for instance, was diagnosed with macular degeneration when she was in her mid forties. She is now blind in her left eye. The macula is a fatty yellow cushion on the retina surrounding the optic nerve and protecting it from damage. The optic nerve relays visual images to the brain. Blue light is the most energetic and damaging part of the light spectrum; the yellow pigments in the macula absorb the blue light, deflecting harm from the optic nerve. In the process of absorbing the blue light the macula itself is damaged, and therefore needs constant repair and maintenance. That repair requires a daily supply of several carotenoids, the pigments found naturally in yellow-orange vegetables and fruits.

A source of lutein and zeaxanthin that was a daily part of most people's diet in the past is eggs. Egg yolks, which have been demonized in recent years, are an excellent source of lutein and zeaxanthin. Carotenoids are fat soluble and since the yolk is fatty, the body readily absorbs the lutein and zeaxanthin in eggs, making these nutrients highly bioavailable. Lutein and zeaxanthin are also available as supplements.

In praise of egg yolks

Recent research has shown that the more eggs people consume, the less likely they are to have macular degeneration. In one study, a group of people with severe macular degeneration were each given an egg every day. After 12 weeks the researchers could detect significant increases in the thickness of the subjects' maculae.[16]

One egg a day does no harm at all. Many people are in the habit of discarding the yolk—the most nourishing part of the egg—and eating only the whites, worried that the fatty yolk will affect blood cholesterol. In fact, there has never been any evidence that avoiding eggs has any effect on cholesterol levels. Studies have shown no increase in cholesterol levels in people over 65 who ate an egg every day.[17]

Choosing which eggs to buy has become complicated. No difference exists nutritionally between brown and white eggs; they just come from different breeds of chickens. However, there *is* a difference between regular eggs and omega-3 eggs, which come from chickens fed flaxseed. The balance of fats they contain is healthier, with more of the anti-inflammatory omega-3 fatty acids than the eggs of conventionally fed chickens. For the most healthful eggs, you generally have to choose between omega-3-enriched eggs and organic eggs, which come from chickens raised without hormones or animal by-products added to their feed. Omega-3 eggs that are also organic are hard to find, but if they are available, I recommend them.

Supplements that prevent macular degeneration

There are two types of macular degeneration: wet and dry. In the wet form, abnormal fragile new blood vessels begin to grow under the macula, which tend to hemorrhage or leak, eventually resulting in scarring and loss of central vision. The wet form is less common but more serious than the dry form, in which the macula itself becomes thin and less able to do its job defending the optic nerve. Both forms eventually lead to loss of vision.

If you have a family history of either type of macular degeneration, you would be wise to take the so-called AREDS supplement to protect your eyes. The Age-Related Eye Disease Study (AREDS) is a long-term clinical trial sponsored by the National Eye Institute in the United States.[18] It studies the use of antioxidants and other supplements in the prevention and treatment of macular degeneration and cataracts. The actual supplement that arose from this study has changed as the study progressed. Today this over-the-counter product generally includes lutein, zeaxanthin, beta carotene, vitamins C and E, copper and zinc. The study found that together these nutrients reduced the risk of developing macular degeneration by about 25 percent.

If you are at risk for macular degeneration, you will want to take all possible steps to protect against this devastating disease by consuming both eggs and supplements. An egg is the original convenience food. With just 75 calories, the egg contains everything required to create a new life—it's a nutritional treasure chest. Because of its fat content, the lutein it contains is readily absorbed and used by the body. AREDS supplements should be taken with a meal containing some fat, though this is not noted on the pill bottle.

If you take an AREDS supplement should you stop taking a multivitamin?

Multivitamins for people over 50 usually contain lutein, but often only a fraction of what is in the AREDS supplement. The AREDS formula has not been shown to prevent cataracts, even though it contains antioxidants. In contrast, a multivitamin preparation containing similar antioxidants to the AREDS formula, plus a full spectrum of other essential vitamins and minerals, appeared to provide protection against cataracts, too.[19] Thus there is an advantage to taking a multivitamin, and the National Eye Institute in the United States suggests additional benefit can come from taking both. A concern I have about taking both together, however, is the possibility that you might get more zinc than needed, which can cause nausea in some people. The question of how much zinc is too much will be addressed later in the book.

Higher blood levels of vitamin D may also help to prevent macular degeneration. Researchers found that postmenopausal women who got the most vitamin D had a 59 percent decreased risk of developing age-related macular degeneration compared to women with the lowest vitamin D intake.[20]

One controversial study investigated the role of vitamin C in eye health. Published in the February 2010 issue of the *American Journal of Clinical Nutrition*, the study found that a high dose of vitamin C (1000 mg daily taken as a supplement) increased the risk of developing cataracts. Those taking hormone replacement therapy or corticosteroids in addition to vitamin C were at even greater risk of developing cataracts. It's difficult to work out why this one study has shown an increased cataract risk while AREDS and many other studies found vitamin C to have a protective effect on the eyes. More research is needed to settle the issue.

What is glaucoma?

Glaucoma is caused by the rise in pressure within the eye; this, too, can cause damage to the optic nerve. Glaucoma has no obvious symptoms at first, but if left untreated, vision becomes blurred around the edge, and the field of vision is gradually restricted. The condition can eventually lead to complete blindness. Have the pressure checked during visits to the optometrist to make sure yours is in the normal range. This is particularly important if you know your blood pressure is elevated.

Nutrients involved in controlling blood pressure, especially magnesium, also help control glaucoma. Deficiency of magnesium can be readily identified. If you plunge your hands into ice-cold water and feel a spasm, you are probably short of magnesium. One study found magnesium effective in reducing intraocular pressure in people who exhibited cold-water hand spasms.[21] This is exactly what one would expect, since we know that high blood pressure responds well to magnesium supplements.

An antioxidant not previously mentioned that is also useful in the treatment of glaucoma is lipoic acid. Lipoic acid, which is available as a supplement, is normally made by the body but not always in high enough amounts. Tiny amounts are present in green vegetables like spinach, broccoli and peas, and in organ meats. Needed to convert carbohydrates into energy, lipoic acid can also help to control blood sugar. One of its major strengths lies in its ability to help recycle other antioxidants such as vitamins C and E, selenium, glutathione and coenzyme Q10. This may be one of the ways it helps protect against cataract and glaucoma.[22]

I once had a woman in her sixties come to my office, concerned about the rising pressure in her eyes. Her doctor recorded pressures of 26 mm Hg (millimetres of mercury measured by an instrument called a tonometer) in one eye and 24 mm Hg in the other. Normal pressure is below 21. She was reluctant to start prescription medication and her doctor agreed to let her try another approach. I recommended lipoic acid supplements and within a few weeks the pressure was coming down. Six months later it was down to 16 in one eye and 14 in the other—well within the normal range. Lipoic acid is considered by anti-aging doctors to be one of the key supplements to add as a protective antioxidant for all tissues, not only eyes.

Another problem of aging eyes: poor night vision

Many people over age 60 are reluctant to drive after dark, preferring to be passengers. This is no mere personal quirk, but more likely a sign of declining night vision. Poor night vision can be caused by developing cataracts or other eye diseases, but is also a milder form of night blindness, a condition documented in the 1930s among fishermen in Newfoundland and Labrador. The fishermen worked in bright light reflected off the water in the daytime, and saw well enough during the day. After nightfall they had great difficulty seeing or were totally blind. They did not, of course, wear sunglasses at work and, in addition, were found to be deficient in vitamin A. They could also have been deficient in zinc, a partner to vitamin A in preventing loss of vision at night.

Vitamin A is a fat-soluble vitamin that is essential for healthy vision but also for normal growth and development, immunity and reproduction. It is obtained either preformed in animal foods such as liver, eggs, milk and butter, or from plants that have yellow/red pigments called carotenoids, which can be converted into vitamin A in the body. Although beta carotene is plentiful in carrots and other orange vegetables, raw carrots are not the best source. Cooking carrots in a small amount of water with a knob of butter makes the beta carotene bioavailable, so that it can be more efficiently absorbed and converted in the body to vitamin A. Cooking softens the cells to release the carotenoids, and the butter helps their absorption.

Fat increases the bioavailability of all phytochemicals, often dramatically. A can of vegetable juice drink is a healthy snack, but absorption of the phytonutrients in it may be increased as much as eightfold if you have it with a small piece of cheese. In one experiment, two groups of subjects were each given the same salad with tomatoes and carrots. No oil-based dressing was put on the salads, but one group of subjects ate their salad topped with avocado, which is, of course, fatty. The addition of 150 g of avocado increased absorption of beta carotene and two other important carotenoids, lutein and lycopene, by as much as 15-fold, compared to the group not given avocado.[23]

Causes of age-related hearing loss

Noise is known to be a major cause of hearing loss, whether it's a sudden loud whistle or explosion, or the continuous clamour of a noisy workplace. A serious concern is the amount of noise ears are exposed to at a young age through personal listening devices turned up way too high. These devices operate in proximity to the sensitive hair cells of the ear that are easily damaged. Rock musicians typically suffer premature hearing loss.

Exposed to excessive noise, the small sensory hair cells in the inner ear may die. These cells convert sound energy into electrical signals that travel through the auditory nerve to the brain. Death of the hair cells (apoptosis) may be caused by circulatory problems and diseases such as diabetes. Once damaged, those cells are not easily replaced. Magnesium has been shown to protect ears from noise-induced hearing loss and in some cases even reverse it.

In one interesting experiment, 300 U.S. military recruits were given a fairly small dose (173 mg a day) of magnesium, while another group of recruits was given a placebo. The objective was to see if magnesium would protect them from hearing loss brought on by repeated exposure to gunfire over a two-month training period. Recruits who had daily magnesium were less likely to experience hearing loss than those who were given a placebo, and if they did, it was less severe.[24]

Other causes of gradual hearing loss

Hyperviscosity of the blood can affect hearing as well as vision. Blood may thicken as we age, causing it to travel more slowly through blood vessels, which puts us at increased risk of blood clots and stroke. If sluggish blood is a problem in large vessels, it is even more of a problem in the fine capillaries that feed the eyes and ears. Blood too thick and too viscous will have a much slower passage through these capillaries, reducing the flow of oxygen, glucose and other nutrients to eyes and ears. Over time, cells in those structures starve and die.

Diets high in saturated fats increase blood viscosity, while diets high in fruits, vegetables and omega-3 fats found in fish and fish oils will keep blood thin naturally. Eating two or more servings of fish a week has been shown to reduce the risk of age-related hearing loss by 42 percent compared to those eating less than one serving a week.[25] Vitamin E, high in nuts and seeds and vegetable oils made from them, is a well-known blood thinner. Other natural blood thinners that have been studied and found to be effective are ginger and garlic. Eating large amounts of fatty fish such as salmon and trout is risky unless you know the source. Instead, take fish oil supplements, from which mercury, PCBs, dioxins and other contaminants have been removed.

Tinnitus, or ringing in the ears, can drive people crazy. It sounds like a background buzzing or hissing. Those who have a severe case describe it as a roar in the ears. Often a side effect of drugs including antibiotics and the long-term use of aspirin, tinnitus could also be the first sign of hearing loss due to noise exposure. However, in common with other hearing disorders, low circulating levels of antioxidants seem to be one cause of the problem.[26] One antioxidant in particular—melatonin, released during sleep—has been suggested in the treatment of tinnitus.[27]

By the time serious deterioration is detected, vision or hearing loss is probably irreversible. All we can aim for is to support eye and ear health so that the damage does not progress any further. Age-related deafness and vision loss are serious degenerative diseases with roots in poor nutrition. Remember too that both can be caused or at least exacerbated by smoking, since smoking restricts blood flow and generates large amounts of free radicals. Smoke rises so that the eyes are irritated externally by cigarette smoke, but internally as well.

Bottom line: It's best to be proactive and keep your hearing and vision in good shape through supplementing with key nutrients. How to use omega-3 fatty acid supplements and optimize your intake of antioxidant vitamins, minerals and phytochemicals will be discussed later in this book.

7

Osteopenia and Osteoporosis

▼

*All parts of the body which have a function, if used in
moderation and exercised in labours to which each are
accustomed, thereby become healthy and well-developed:
but if unused and left idle, they become liable to disease,
defective in growth, and age quickly.*

— Hippocrates (460–377 BC)

O STEOPOROSIS is a degenerative condition in which normal bone becomes spongelike, weak and brittle. This condition is increasing at an alarming rate as the population ages, not only in Canada but around the world. According to Osteoporosis Canada, the disease affects one in four women and one in eight men aged 50 and over. In Canada, the cost of treating osteoporosis and its consequences adds up to $2 billion a year.

Fractures of the wrist, spine and hips are the most feared outcome of osteoporosis. These fractures in turn can lead to other serious complications, including blood clots, chronic persistent pain, depression and loss of independence. You might have osteoporosis and, if you are lucky, never break a bone. But the likelihood of a break is high, and the personal consequences of that can be devastating. Many elderly people who fracture a hip will never recover and eventually die of it.[1]

If we are to remain active and avoid frailty in old age, we need to keep our bones strong. Most of us look forward to retirement as a time for travelling, dancing, golfing and chasing after grandkids. No one wants to be that shaky, fragile person afraid of leaving home for fear that a slip on the sidewalk will lead to life in a wheelchair. Which is why both men and women should learn how to protect themselves against osteoporosis, sometimes called the silent thief.

Osteopenia: early warning sign

Bone health is presumed to be optimal in young adulthood. Osteopenia is a milder form of bone thinning, a loss of bone density when compared to the bone of a young adult. Some doctors consider osteopenia to be the earliest stage of osteoporosis, although not everyone who has osteopenia will go on to develop osteoporosis. Osteopenia should nevertheless set off some alarm bells, since it does increase the risk of full-blown osteoporosis.

Adolescence and early adulthood are our peak bone-building years, and poor diet and lifestyle during those years, including smoking and lack of physical activity, can increase the risk of osteopenia in later life. Even before we are born, fracture risk may be programmed into our bones, depending on our mother's diet and whether she smoked during pregnancy.[2] The good news is that if you are diagnosed with osteopenia, you can arrest the condition and restore normal bone strength regardless of what happened to your bones in your youth or before you were born.

Bones are 50 percent protein, largely in the form of springy, supple collagen. Collagen forms the matrix upon which the hardening minerals—the remaining 50 percent of bone—are laid. Calcium and phosphorus are the two main minerals in bone; approximately 98 percent of the 1 to 2 kg of calcium, and 85 percent of the 1 kg of phosphorus in a human adult are found in the bones. Calcium and phosphorus occur together as calcium phosphate, also called hydroxyapatite (HA), which gives bones their strength, while the protein matrix provides their resilience. Hydroxyapatite is needed to glue together the collagen fibres, stabilizing the matrix and acting as tiny internal shock absorbers.

Bones are constantly being reshaped or remodelled by two types of specialized cells: osteoblasts, which build bone, and osteoclasts, which break it down. Bone remodelling is needed to repair micro damage. First, old or damaged bone is digested by osteoclasts, leaving holes or pockets. Then osteoblasts lay down new, stronger bone to fill in the gaps. Osteoblasts first manufacture collagen and other proteins, then add minerals to the new bone matrix. Once osteoblasts become entrapped in their own collagen matrix they mature into osteocytes, the main cell type of bone.

Bones feed the whole body

Osteocytes have many functions. One important role is the homeostatic maintenance of the balance of minerals in the blood.[3] Osteocytes are responsible for the constant exchange of essential minerals such as calcium from bone to blood and back again. Depending on diet and the needs of other organs and tissues in the body, osteocytes can remove minerals from bone in a matter of moments.[4] Other macrominerals that play an important role in bone health and in regulating cellular and organ functions in the rest of the body include magnesium, potassium, sodium and chloride.

Think of bone as a savings account of minerals—we make deposits and we make withdrawals. The daily withdrawal of minerals from bone is essential for the smooth running of our metabolism. But we also have to make regular deposits or, sooner or later, the account will be overdrawn.

Causes of osteoporosis

In a person with osteoporosis, the body fails to make enough new bone to replace the old bone and the two processes—destruction and replacement—fall out of balance. This change will eventually lead to bones that are not strong enough to resist a small bang or minor fall. The process happens slowly and progressively with no outward symptoms until suddenly there is a fracture; thus the catchphrase "the silent thief." Hips and wrists are the two most common areas of breakage, but spine and even ribs can be susceptible. Eighty percent of hip fractures are due to osteoporosis.

Loss of bone density and increased risk of fractures are a known adverse effect of many commonly prescribed medications, including prednisone and other steroids, which are used to treat inflammatory and autoimmune conditions such as rheumatoid arthritis. Anti-cancer treatments such as aromatase inhibitors for breast cancer (for example, Arimidex) and anti-androgen therapy for prostate cancer also deplete bones. Other drugs with this side effect include SSRI antidepressants such as Prozac, anticonvulsants, blood pressure medications called loop diuretics, blood thinning medications like heparin and warfarin, and the antacid drugs, proton pump inhibitors (PPIs).[5]

Muriel, one of my clients, came to me when she was well past menopause. She had been taking prednisone for more than 40 years to treat her rheumatoid arthritis. Prednisone is a steroid drug that weakens bones. Suddenly and without any bone-building drugs, her bone density started to improve, as we worked to optimize her vitamin D levels. At first it looked as though she needed 4000 IU to achieve good blood levels, but now with the consent of her doctor, she takes 7000. Her blood level is in the upper end of the normal range and her bones are fine. That's an extremely difficult feat to accomplish after such a long time on steroids. She recently acquired a new rheumatologist and asked him what he thought of her bone health. "It's surprisingly good," the doctor reassured her.

Diseases that cause inflammation of the gastrointestinal tract such as Crohn's disease and ulcerative colitis will affect bone density because inflammation will interfere with calcium absorption. Celiac disease, an intolerance to the wheat proteins gluten and gliadin, also puts people at high risk of osteoporosis. If you have any of these predisposing conditions or are on bone-depleting medications, your bone density and vitamin D level should be closely monitored.

Measuring bone density

Testing bone density is done with low-dose radiation, using a technique called dual-energy X-ray absorptiometry, shortened to DEXA or sometimes DXA. Measurements are taken at the spine and hip. The opaqueness of the bone at these two sites is an indirect measure of how well it is mineralized. If the image obtained from the scan shows light areas against a generally dark background, these are the areas of reduced mineralization and therefore reduced bone density.

When you receive the results of a bone scan it will consist of two numbers: a T score and a Z score. The T score indicates how much the density of your bones differs from young healthy bones. At age 30, people are believed to have built up all the bone density they will have; the T score is the deviation from the bone density of 30-year-olds. If your T score is between +1 and -1 your bones are considered normal. A T score between -1 and -2.5 is considered osteopenic and a T score lower than -2.5 means you have osteoporosis. However, because the norm varies by race and sex, what is normal for you will be different if you are a woman of African heritage than if you are, say, a Caucasian male.

The Z score measures the state of your bones compared to the bone density of others who are your own age, sex and race. A 45-year-old Asian woman, for example, will be compared to other 45-year-old Asian women. The Z score is considered the more significant measure for men of all ages and women under 50.

What bone density testing does not tell you

Although DEXA testing is considered the most accurate way of assessing bone health, the results do not tell the whole story. A DEXA scan measures how dense but not how strong your bones are. Dense bones can still be brittle, especially if the bone matrix is weak and poorly maintained. A friend of mine knocked her wrist against the kitchen cupboard one day—just a minor glancing blow—and shattered her wrist. Her bone density, last time it was measured, had been fine. At the moment, we cannot measure the strength of bone, only its density. The resilience of bone—whether or not the bone will bounce or shatter if you fall on it—is also difficult to ascertain. Resilience is related to the architecture of the bone and the health of the bone matrix.

If you receive a diagnosis of osteopenia or osteoporosis, you will be offered medications to increase bone mass. Before you embark on drug treatment, however, consider whether this is the first time you have been tested. If so, you need to know if your bones are stable, or if they are continuing to lose density.

New laboratory tests such as the N-telopeptide test (known as NTx) are being developed that can answer that question. These tests pick up breakdown products of the bone matrix in blood or urine and reveal if there is active bone loss. If the NTx test comes back normal, your bones are probably stable and treatment may not be necessary because your risk of fracture is not high, even if you are considered osteopenic.

For accurate assessment of osteopenia or osteoporosis, make sure that repeat bone scans are preformed on the same machine, as there can be wide variations in the density readings from one machine to another.

Adverse effects of osteoporosis drugs

The most commonly recommended drugs for osteopenia and osteoporosis belong to a class of drugs called bisphosphonates. These drugs work by killing off osteoclasts, the cells that remove old bone, or by restricting their functioning. Osteoblasts may then lay down new bone on top of old inferior bone so that bone density may appear to improve, but the underlying structure of the bones can still be unsound—a problem that has only recently surfaced. A small but significant proportion of those on bisphosphonates for osteoporosis are at risk of serious side effects, including osteonecrosis (bone death) of the jaw and, ironically, an increased risk of hip fractures.[6] The consensus among doctors now is to have patients stay on these medications for no longer than five years, and to avoid their use in individuals at low risk of fracture.

Although the benefits of bisphosphonates often outweigh the risk of the fractures that might occur without them, prevention is always the better approach. To maintain strong bones, you also need to think about how diet and lifestyle affect bone health.

Getting enough exercise

As we have seen, bones are dynamic tissues, constantly breaking down and being rebuilt. They need weight-bearing high-impact exercise to nudge osteoblasts into doing their work. When we walk, run, climb stairs or lift, we stimulate bone building; the less active we are, the more likely we are to develop osteoporosis.[7] Good exercises for bone strength include lifting weights, running, jumping, dancing and skipping. Low-impact sports like swimming and cycling, while they have other health benefits, do not help to build bone.

It is interesting to note that a "threshold" effect appears to exist: both too little and too much exercise have the same detrimental result. Chronic overexercise in young women, sufficient to cause disruption to their normal menstrual cycles (amenorrhea) will cause bone loss.[8] And both male and female athletes are at high risk of osteoporosis, especially if they restrict their calorie intake to keep their weight low for competitive reasons.

Some people lose calcium at an accelerated rate because of their diet. Normal digestion results in acid production, a regular and entirely natural process. Stomach acid is produced to activate digestive enzymes needed to break down food. But the acid must ultimately be neutralized, and a diet rich in fruits and vegetables will do that. If the diet is low in fruits and vegetables and high in acid-producing proteins, animal fats like cheese, and refined grains—in other words, a typical western diet—it will trigger osteoclasts to pull calcium out of the bone to neutralize the acidic conditions that result. The fewer fruits and vegetables in the diet, the more likely we are to call on bone stores of calcium to deal with what is called metabolic acidosis.[9] The DASH diet (Dietary Approaches to Stop Hypertension), which is high in fruits, vegetables and whole grains and low in starches and sugars, has been shown to reduce bone turnover in osteoporosis.[10]

Vegetarian diets and bones

If vegetables and fruit protect against acidosis, does this mean that a vegetarian diet is best for preventing bone loss? Studies carried out over the last few decades found no difference in bone loss between meat eaters and lacto-ovo-vegetarians, whose diet consists of dairy products, eggs and vegetables. A few studies found bone mass to be significantly lower in vegans, who eat no animal products at all. In these cases, the higher rate of bone loss is likely due to underconsumption of protein. Remember that 50 percent of bone is protein and that bone resorption involves destruction of the collagen matrix, which is so critical for bone support.[11]

Until recently, the daily recommended intake of protein was set at .8 g per kilogram body weight for all adults, regardless of age. Current advice for everyone over the age of 70 is to increase this amount to 1.5 g per kilogram body weight, or almost double previous recommendations. The recommended increase is due to mounting evidence that a higher protein intake in the 70-plus age group improves not just bone health, but also muscle mass and strength, immune health and wound healing. A 70 kg man needs 105 g of protein daily.[12] Protein-rich foods contain only a fraction of their weight as protein. An egg weighing 75 g is only 6 g protein. A 4 oz (115 g) steak or a chicken breast will have 20 to 25 g protein. If you increase your protein intake, make sure that fruits and vegetables are still the foundation of your daily diet to prevent metabolic acidosis.

Calcium and bones

Calcium is, as we have seen, the most plentiful mineral in bone, and many older women have been advised to take calcium supplements for bone health. But current thinking is that the amount of supplemental calcium recommended in the past—

anywhere from 1000 to 1200 mg a day—may be unnecessary and even harmful. A recent study from Sweden showed that while intakes under 700 mg did increase the risk of osteoporosis, calcium intakes above that amount did not offer any additional benefit.[13] Current guidelines, however, recommend 1000 mg of calcium daily for women up to 50, and men up to 70 years. After that, 1200 mg are recommended for both.

Table 1
Some good sources of calcium

1 can of sardines	350 mg
¾ cup non-fat yogurt	330 mg
1 cup 1% milk	300 mg
1 cup soy, rice or almond milk (fortified)	300 mg
½ cup ricotta cheese	250 mg
4 oz tofu (made with calcium)	225 mg
1 oz cheddar cheese	200 mg
4 oz canned salmon	200 mg
1 cup frozen cooked kale	170 mg
½ cup cooked spinach	125 mg
½ cup cooked collard greens	120 mg
½ cup cottage cheese	70 mg
½ cup broccoli (chopped, cooked)	50 mg
1 oz almonds (about 24)	75 mg

Ricotta is a rich calcium source because it is not as high in fat as hard cheeses. Cottage cheese is not as good a source because some calcium is lost in making it. Milk is fine. I generally suggest that people buy 1 or 2 percent milk. You do not need to worry about fat in yogurt or milk, when compared to cheeses. In cheddar cheese, the saturated fat content is 40 percent, whereas in yogurt, fat content is, at most, 10 percent. One or 2% milk is a wise choice because it contains conjugated linoleic acid (CLA), a beneficial fat found only in dairy products. CLA may be helpful in controlling weight and could also have some cancer-prevention properties. The amount of CLA has been found to be higher in milk and beef from cows who have been pasture-fed rather than corn-fed—a good reason to seek out organically produced milk in your local supermarket.

New controversies about vitamin D

We need vitamin D to absorb calcium. Without adequate circulating blood levels we will not absorb sufficient calcium to make bones strong. Excess intake of calcium, with or without vitamin D, has recently been shown to increase the risk of heart disease in women.[14] The effect has been observed only in women taking calcium as supplements, rather than ingesting it as food.

The Institute of Medicine (IOM), which is the health arm of the National Academy of Sciences in the United States, recently published new recommendations on vitamin D and calcium.[15] The committee the IOM convened to review research into vitamin D, calcium and health was a joint Canada-U.S. panel, and their recommendations apply to both countries. The committee increased the daily recommended supplemental dose of vitamin D from 200 to 600 international units (IU), and declared a safe upper limit of 4000 IU daily, double the previous upper limit.

Since its publication in 2010, the report has generated a great deal of controversy, especially over the amount of vitamin D that is appropriate. We can easily have our vitamin D checked with a blood test that measures 25-hydroxy D, the storage form of vitamin D circulating in blood. The Institute of Medicine's report insists that quite low blood levels of 25-hydroxy D—50 nmol/L (nanomoles per litre)—will keep bones strong. The idea that such a low blood level of vitamin D is enough has led to strenuous arguments from scientists around the world, many of whom have spent a lifetime studying vitamin D and its relation to health. Health practitioners who regularly check patients' vitamin D report that they frequently see osteoporosis in patients with 50 nmol/L, the supposedly adequate blood level.

I work closely with doctors to monitor the blood levels of my clients and in my experience, people with blood levels of 50 nmol/L never succeed in increasing their bone density. However, on getting blood levels up into the high end of the normal range (normal range is 75 to 250 nmol/L), I do see improvements. One perimenopausal client, Yvette (not her real name), had experienced a 17 percent decrease in her bone density over the past few years as shown by DEXA testing (see pages 87–88). Since she did not want to go on medication, her doctor agreed to let her try a supplement regime first. Over a two-year period, I worked with her to raise her vitamin D level, which had been very low to begin with. When her blood level reached 150 nmol/L, her bone density began to improve. She had had osteopenia at one site and osteoporosis in another. Now, two years later, her bone density is normal.

An internationally recognized expert, Dr. Walter Willett at Harvard School of Public Health, is one of the many scientists who has challenged the IOM's recommendation, basing his criticisms on established clinical evidence. He considers the IOM off base in their recommendations for both calcium and vitamin D—"too low on vitamin D and too generous on calcium."[16] The IOM continues to suggest calcium intakes up to 1200 mg for women 51 and older, despite new research indicating that this may be too much. The IOM does, however, agree that most of us can get the calcium we need from diet (see Appendix B), without resorting to supplements.

Do we all need vitamin D supplements?

Vitamin D3 (cholecalciferol) is essential for calcium metabolism, and the consequences of vitamin D deficiency for bone health have long been recognized. Severe deficiency causes the bone diseases rickets and osteomalacia, the adult form of rickets.[17] Deficiency of vitamin D is much more common than previously thought. Anyone can suffer from it, but it is especially common in elderly patients in developed countries. It also affects those with darker skin and those who spend too much time indoors or cover up completely when they go outside, making it a serious problem among Muslim women who wear traditional dress.

We make vitamin D when our skin is exposed to ultraviolet radiation, either from sunshine or artificial UV light. Anyone living in northerly countries is at risk of vitamin D deficiency during the winter months.[18] The angle of the sun is too oblique at higher latitudes to permit vitamin D synthesis. But concern about vitamin D deficiency is not confined to northern climates. Even in sun-drenched countries, changing lifestyles mean more time is spent indoors, in front of computers in offices or in air-conditioned apartments. Children spend more time watching TV or playing computer games and less time kicking a ball around the yard. Dark-skinned individuals need much higher exposure to sunlight—five to 10 times as much—than light-skinned people to produce the same amount of the vitamin D from similar sun exposure.

In Canada, our bodies are not able to make vitamin D during the long winter months, and that is why we have a higher incidence of osteoporosis than countries south of us. We use up our stores over the winter and our blood level bottoms out by about March. We then start from a low point to build it up during the summer, but over those few short months, it can never get as high as the vitamin D level of people exposed to sun year-round. And if you use a sunblock higher than 8, your skin will not make vitamin D at all during the brief Canadian summer.

People habitually exposed to sunshine, for instance those who live in Florida or Mexico, will naturally have blood levels near the top end of the normal range—around 175 nmol/L. Compared to those of us living at higher latitudes, they have lower risks of all the diseases now linked to insufficient vitamin D: heart disease, many cancers including breast, prostate and colon, autoimmune diseases and, of course, osteoporosis.[19] It appears that nature provided our ancestors with high blood levels of vitamin D, and since lower blood levels have a negative impact on many aspects of our health, I am comfortable mimicking, through the use of supplements, the sun conditions under which our ancestors evolved.

How much vitamin D should I take?

My advice is to have your blood tested before you decide. Without testing you will not know whether you are deficient or sub-optimal for vitamin D.

After you have your blood tested, the amount you need to maintain healthy blood levels of 25-hydroxy D will vary depending on your initial blood levels and your BMI. The heavier you are, the lower your blood levels will likely be. Your vitamin D needs are also governed by your genes. Some people have genetic variations that predispose them to have lower natural 25-hydroxy D levels, and also to require higher amounts of supplements to move their blood level into the therapeutic range.[20] I cannot say for certain if my vitamin D–deficient clients have these gene variants (called SNPs) but if they have low blood levels, that is all I need to know.

We have only recently begun to understand some of the signs

and symptoms of inadequate vitamin D—bone pain, muscle weakness, and an awkward, swaying gait or inability to walk in a straight line. When people report those symptoms to me, and there is no other medical reason for them, I can generally predict that their blood test will come back with low levels of 25-hydroxy D. A lawyer I'll call Lily, whom I saw recently, had been taking 2000 IU of vitamin D for a year before she came to me, but she still had many of the above symptoms, including foot and knee pain and poor grip strength—a sign of muscle weakness. She laughed when I asked her if she could walk in a straight line, and agreed that she could not.

Her blood test revealed a 25-hydroxy D levels of 51 nmol/L; she must have been at rock bottom before she began taking 2000 IUs a year earlier. When you start taking vitamin D, your blood level climbs slowly over a three-month period, and then reaches a plateau. At that point it is necessary to retest. I advised Lily to double her intake of vitamin D to 4000 IU. When she was retested after three months, she had still not reached 75 nmol/L—the beginning of the normal range quoted by most laboratories. Some of her symptoms have resolved, but not all. We'll watch and see what happens as she increases her dosage again and re-checks her blood levels.

There can be as much as a 10- to 20-fold difference in the vitamin D one person needs to achieve a desirable blood level compared to what another person needs to achieve the same level. If you were low to begin with, you will need to persuade your doctor to check your level every six months or so to track your progress. Some people take 2000 mg and get good results, others need 4000 or 6000 or 10,000 IU, while certain rare individuals might need 15,000 IUs. Once the desired blood level is achieved, you'll need only an annual blood test to stay on track. It is best to test for vitamin D in late fall or winter so that the results are not distorted by summer sun exposure.

What else do I need, in addition to vitamin D and calcium, to strengthen bones?

Phosphorus, potassium and particularly magnesium are other important minerals needed for bone health. Phosphorus can readily be obtained from a diet containing milk, fish and eggs, while a high intake of fruits and vegetables will provide ample potassium. Bones are stronger when magnesium and calcium are present together than when magnesium is low. In fact, magnesium by itself has been used in clinical trials to improve bone strength and has been shown to suppress bone turnover in postmenopausal women.[21] The recommended daily intake (RDI) for magnesium ranges from 350 to 420 mg, depending on gender, with men having higher needs. Since most people are not getting the RDI, an additional supplement of 200 to 300 mg of magnesium can be helpful, but some people need an even higher amount. In a later chapter we will discuss magnesium in more detail and how to personalize your magnesium intake.

Bones are half protein, and a substantial portion of that is collagen. As we have seen, collagen needs vitamin C for its formation. For bone health, I recommend at least 500 mg twice a day for most people. A good multivitamin will contain a little extra magnesium and vitamin C, and more recent formulas also contain vitamin K. Vitamin K's primary job is to help blood clot, but it is also central to bone health. We can get vitamin K from leafy greens, but most of our vitamin K is produced in the gut by good bacteria. K and D work together to strengthen bones. Research is now in progress to help us understand vitamin K's role in preventing osteoporosis. Other minerals like strontium and boron are also being explored as bone strengtheners. As yet there is no strong evidence that they can improve bone density on their own.

The link between thinning bones and aging

A number of explanations have been proposed. It's possible that older people have lower levels of the nutrients needed for strong bones, either because of lower intakes or poorer absorption. Estrogen protects bones and sustains the survival of osteoblasts. When estrogen levels drop as women go through menopause, more osteoblasts—the bone-forming cells—die off. Falling estrogen levels, however, don't seem to effect the survival of the bone-resorbing cells, the osteoclasts. This accounts for the fact that osteoporosis is more common in postmenopausal women, after estrogen production declines. Women who had early menopause are more likely to experience bone loss since they have spent a longer period without estrogen protection.

We have all known seniors who shrank visibly in their old age—another effect of osteoporosis. When bone is lost from the vertebrae, the spine shortens and the body changes shape. But shrinkage may also be due to the deterioration of the discs—the shock absorbers that separate the vertebrae and provide a cushion between them. These discs consist mostly of water and give the spine flexibility. As we walk about during the day, discs lose water and we shrink, while at night when we are resting they gradually rehydrate. Unsurprisingly, we are usually taller first thing in the morning. As we age, the ability of our discs to reabsorb water may diminish. Spinal compression, whatever its cause, will result in backache and restriction of movement, even if it does not lead directly to compression fractures.

I remember a woman who became my client in her seventies. She was a great golfer and after she lost her husband, she decided to buy a condominium overlooking a golf course because she planned to spend her remaining years playing golf. One morning after getting out of bed she suddenly felt incredible pain in her back. Tests determined that she had multiple stress fractures in her vertebrae. After that, she was mostly confined to a wheel-chair and had to wear a brace to support her back. The silent thief had struck and her golfing days were over.

Another problem both men and women are prone to develop with age is kyphosis, a curvature of the spine that causes a humped back. Kyphosis may be due to genetics, osteoporosis or even poor posture, or a combination of all three. Over time the liga-ments of the spine become stretched, allowing the upper body to curve forward. Often called a dowager's hump because it's seen in so many elderly women, the condition is becoming increas-ingly common in men.

Until recently, osteoporosis was considered solely a condi-tion affecting postmenopausal women, but men, too, need to be concerned about the health of their bones. Although they expe-rience half the rate of osteoporosis that afflicts women, the inci-dence (one in eight men over 50) is still considerable. Men haven't been considered to be at risk of osteoporosis until recently, and their bone density is rarely tested. Research into male bone health is just starting in earnest.

Optimizing vitamin D intake and a comprehensive regimen of exercise, a regular consumption of protein, a diet rich in fruit and vegetables, and a synergistic combination of bone-enhancing vitamins and minerals should provide the optimum regimen for preventing and treating osteoporosis.

The decrease in bone mass that happens as we age appears to go hand in hand with loss of muscle mass. This reduces strength and balance and contributes to falls. The relationship between muscle strength and bone health is thought to be linked through a complex interplay of dietary protein, calcium and vitamin D, all of which support the health of both bone and muscle.[22]

8

Sleep Problems

▼

How do people go to sleep? I'm afraid I've lost the knack.
I might try busting myself smartly over the temple with the
night-light. I might repeat to myself, slowly and soothingly,
a list of quotations beautiful from minds profound;
if I can remember any of the damn things.

— Dorothy Parker (1893–1967), writer, critic, wit

I SEE TWO TYPES of sleepless people coming into my office. For some it's a new problem. For others, it's a lifelong issue, and that is often more difficult to treat. Recently a young woman I will call Janet came to see me. Janet, who is 31, hasn't slept properly since she was a baby. She was also depressed and anxious, and had been for some time.

Her mother told me that when Janet was a small child the family couldn't go away with her on holiday due to her wakefulness. If she was sharing a room with her parents, she would ask them not to breathe because she could hear them, and that would keep her awake.

Janet had done the rounds of conventional and alternative practitioners. She had gone to sleep clinics and tried most of the sleep medications on the market, without success. She had explored relaxation therapy, herbal remedies and acupuncture. Nothing helped.

When she came to my office I explained that the nutritional approach to insomnia is based on understanding the complex chemistry of sleep. We know some of the biochemical pathways the body uses to put itself to sleep and the vitamins, minerals and other nutrients required by those pathways, beginning with an amino acid called tryptophan. Tryptophan is an essential amino acid that is the basic building block of serotonin in the brain. In turn, serotonin is converted into melatonin and it is melatonin that gives us deep refreshing sleep.

Depressed people are usually low on serotonin and don't have enough available for this conversion. However, there is another problem: the conversion of serotonin to melatonin in the brain is triggered by darkness—total darkness. Think of our early ancestors. They slept when darkness fell and woke at the first sign of dawn. Today, light leaking through our bedroom curtains from city streetlights mimics early dawn and triggers wakefulness throughout the night.

Melatonin has a major role to play in controlling our day-to-day circadian rhythms, the internal clock that influences when we sleep and for how long. Interference with melatonin production will intensify insomnia and lead to difficulty sleeping the next night.[1] With Janet, my first step was to make sure she had total blackout in her bedroom, or wore an eye mask overnight. For some people who have difficulty sleeping, this simple change is all they need to make a dramatic improvement in their sleep, but it was not sufficient for Janet.

Getting tryptophan to the brain

Tryptophan is one of 20 amino acids, nine of which are essential. This means it cannot be made by the body and must be supplied from food. All protein foods contain tryptophan; eggs, meat, chickpeas, peanuts, pumpkin seeds and milk are all good sources. Before it can induce sleep, however, tryptophan must cross the blood-brain barrier, a barricade of tightly packed cells that protects the brain from noxious chemicals and infections.

The challenge for tryptophan is to get past this roadblock. Since it is the least plentiful of the 20 amino acids in protein foods, it may be elbowed out of the way by competition from other, more abundant amino acids. The only time it has an easy ride across the blood-brain barrier occurs when you eat something sweet. This will push up your blood sugar, which will cause a rise in insulin.

As discussed earlier, insulin is a hormone needed to control blood sugar, storing the excess in liver, muscles and other cells for later use. But in the big picture insulin does much more, orchestrating the storage of all the nutrients we get from food, including vitamins, minerals and amino acids. When insulin rises, it binds a large proportion of amino acids in the bloodstream that would otherwise compete with tryptophan for transport over the blood-brain barrier. Insulin transports the competing amino acids to muscles and other organs, but it does not bind tryptophan. Thus, after we eat something sweet, brain tryptophan levels rise, triggering the chain of chemical events that brings on sleep.[2]

Many adults will recall being put to bed as children with a glass of milk and a cookie. I grew up in Ireland where I was given warm milk with a little honey. Milk contains tryptophan, and its entry into the brain is facilitated by the honey or the cookie, either of which will push up insulin levels. Parents may not know why, but they have learned that you can put a child to sleep with this simple trick.

In Janet's case, the ploy had not worked when she was young and it was unlikely to be sufficient to solve her sleep problems now. However, I did encourage her to maintain good blood levels of tryptophan by eating protein regularly throughout the day, and to include a small sweet treat and a glass of milk as a bedtime snack.

Not by milk alone

If milk and cookies fail to help with sleep, I begin to think about other essential nutrients involved in the manufacture of serotonin. Several B vitamins, including B6, B12 and folic acid, are needed. The mineral zinc is also involved in processing serotonin. Modern diets are short of zinc, but for most people a multivitamin will make up for any shortfalls. I suggested a well-formulated multivitamin for Janet, one that contained zinc and higher levels of B vitamins than are usually found in the average generic multivitamin. (Guidance on how to choose a well-designed multivitamin can be found at the back of this book.)

Perhaps the most overlooked nutrient involved in the biochemistry of sleep is magnesium.[3] It is needed for many of the metabolic steps involved in the manufacture and use of neurotransmitters, including serotonin. Leafy green vegetables are good food sources of magnesium because they contain chlorophyll. Chlorophyll, the molecule that gives these vegetables their green colour, contains magnesium. Nuts and seeds are also excellent sources of magnesium. These foods are not plentiful in the average North American diet, creating the need for supplements.

We know from surveys that most people in North America don't meet the recommended daily allowance of magnesium, which is 350 mg to 450 mg depending on activity level and gender (men need more). The average daily intake, which was 400 mg at the beginning of the twentieth century, has tumbled to between 250 mg and 300 mg by the beginning of the twenty-first century—approximately one-quarter to one-third less than it used to be 100 years ago.[4]

The age of anxiety

Many insomniacs report being kept awake by fear and worry hovering over the bed like a swarm of bees. Anxiety and sleep disturbance go hand in hand, and magnesium deficiency is often at the root of both problems.

My sister has a golfing friend, a woman of 82. When my sister inquired recently after her health, the friend replied: "At my age I shouldn't complain. I have few health concerns and a comfortable life. But recently I've started to feel very anxious, and for no real reason." My sister, who has heard a great deal from me about supplements, offered her friend her own bottle of magnesium gel—a topical form of magnesium that is easy to apply and quickly absorbed through the skin.

Two weeks later, she ran into her friend and asked how she was feeling. "I am almost scared to tell you," she replied. "First of all, I have no more anxiety. I put the magnesium gel on my arms and legs in the morning and before I go to bed and that seems to take care of [the anxiety]. I have more energy, too. I played a round of golf yesterday for the first time in a long while."

This outcome did not surprise me. One of the basic jobs for which magnesium is needed is the control of adenosine triphosphate (ATP), a molecule that directs the storage and release of energy. ATP is required for all metabolic reactions in the body, including the activity of muscle cells. Serious shortages of magnesium will compromise the action of ATP, which in turn will lead to fatigue and low energy.

Another major benefit seen by this 82-year-old was the effect of extra magnesium on her sleep. "I wasn't sleeping well," she reported, "and now I am." She had not mentioned sleep previously. The only problem she had described was her anxiety.

But back to Janet. I was not surprised to learn that she had been chronically constipated all her life—a sure sign that she had a higher than average need for magnesium. She was tense, complaining of shoulder tension that was only temporarily relieved by massage or hot baths. She also suffered from excruciating cramps in her calves, frequently at night.

Sleep problems, constipation, muscle cramps and tension are often seen together, signalling their common origin: an imbalance of calcium and magnesium in the body.

Your medications may be keeping you awake

One of the reasons that people can develop sleep problems as they age is that they start to use more prescription medications, many of which deplete magnesium. Among the worst culprits are blood pressure medications, especially diuretics. These drugs increase the flow of urine, which speeds the loss of many water-soluble vitamins and minerals, including magnesium.

A 2006 study of 2551 individuals by the Heart and Stroke Foundation of Ontario found that while 21 percent of the general adult population has high blood pressure, that figure rises to 52 percent among 60- to 79-year-olds. Blood pressure medications are therefore more commonly used as we age, and doctors are generally unaware of their effect on magnesium.[5] One of my patients, whom I will call Calvin, is a busy stockbroker nearing retirement. At 63, he is on several medications to control his high blood pressure. Calvin couldn't get to sleep however hard he tried, and when he asked his doctor about the problem, the doctor wanted to add another drug to the long list he was already taking. Calvin came to me wanting to know if he could use something other than a sleeping pill.

He was already taking magnesium in tablet form, but I suggested adding a topical magnesium gel, which he could apply to his arms or legs just before he went to bed. Magnesium is depleted very quickly, and a magnesium tablet taken earlier in the day might already have been used up.

If he were short of the magnesium needed for the brain chemistry that brings on sleep, that little extra might give him the boost needed at the end of a busy day. In fact, the gel can trigger sleep or relief of muscle tension in as little as five minutes.

The following week his wife was in my office for her own appointment and she marvelled at the quick results. "He applies this gel to his arms when he gets into bed, and almost before the bottle is out of his hands, his head has hit the pillow and he is asleep," she reported.

Watch those statins

Statins are another class of prescription drugs that can interfere with sleep. Prescribed for people with elevated cholesterol, these drugs are frequently taken by the same individuals using blood pressure medications. High blood pressure and elevated cholesterol tend to go together and both are major risk factors for heart disease.

Researchers at the University of Pisa compared adverse drug reactions in patients taking a variety of medications. The groups were drawn from a database of people in eight regions of Italy who reported adverse reactions going back to 1988. Of the various side effects reported, only insomnia was reported more frequently by those taking statin drugs than by those who were not.[6]

What is ironic is that both high blood pressure and high cholesterol have been linked to magnesium deficiency. Magnesium deficiency lowers blood potassium levels even when a person's diet contains ample potassium, and lack of potassium is known to drive up blood pressure. Simply by increasing magnesium, potassium levels can normalize, and this in turn will bring down blood pressure.[7]

Magnesium is known to play a complex role in the control and regulation of cholesterol production. The effects of statin drugs on cholesterol are similar to those of magnesium: both lower LDL cholesterol (the bad stuff). Magnesium, however, can also raise HDL cholesterol (the good stuff).[8]

Few doctors warn patients when they prescribe blood pressure or cholesterol-lowering medication of the possibility of sleep disturbance. Some may not even know of the medications' link to sleep, so that if a patient on these drugs complains of sleeplessness, he or she might be sent off to a sleep clinic where the insomnia is dealt with as an entirely unrelated problem.

How much magnesium do you need?

Some people have higher magnesium needs than others; how much you need is an individual matter. I have often seen sleeplessness and constipation running in families, which may be evidence of a genetically determined high magnesium need. Several genes are known to affect the absorption and retention of magnesium by the body, and alterations (polymorphisms) in those genes can cause magnesium wasting.[9] Individuals who have these gene alterations may take magnesium supplements to overcome their constipation and other signs of magnesium deficiency, but they do not retain it. For them, keeping magnesium levels topped up is like keeping a leaky bucket full of water; turn your back and it's empty. They have to be extra careful to take their supplements each day.

Some people may get by on below-average intakes, but it is safe to assume that, even without genetic problems, almost everyone is deficient. In one study carried out in American women between the ages of 15 and 50 years, 39 percent had magnesium intakes less than 70 percent of the recommended daily allowance.[10]

Magnesium requirements are tricky to figure out. If your doctor is concerned that you are iron or vitamin D deficient, you will be sent for a blood test to check the levels of these nutrients in your blood. A blood test for magnesium does exist, but most experts do not consider it reliable because the amount of magnesium in blood is only a tiny portion of total body magnesium— about 1 percent. This minuscule amount is kept fairly constant, tightly regulated by the body's homeostatic mechanisms, similar to the mechanism that assures, for instance, that our temperature remains steady. The remainder is stored in muscle and bone. These stores can be rapidly tapped and transferred to the blood, should magnesium levels happen to drop.

This tight control of blood levels of magnesium is not surprising when you consider that magnesium is needed to relax cardiac muscles after the heart has contracted, a vital process on which life itself depends. Blood tests, therefore, do not tell the whole story. In fact, they usually come back normal, even when there are clear indications that magnesium needs are not being met.[11]

Finding your optimal magnesium intake

In my practice, I try to train people to observe their own bodies and figure out if they have any symptoms that could possibly point to insufficient magnesium: sleeplessness, anxiety, leg cramps and foot cramps, particularly at night when magnesium need is highest.

Shortness of breath is another indicator. You may have enough calcium to contract your lungs when you exhale, but without magnesium, they will not easily relax again. Huffing and puffing as you walk upstairs or wheezing and asthma may be the result. Indeed, magnesium is given to asthmatics in distress when they come to hospital emergency departments.[12]

I also ask about frequency of urination. The bladder is a muscular sack that can store about 300 to 400 mL (1½ cups) of urine in most normal adults. As it reaches its capacity, the stretching of the bladder wall builds tension, which sends a message to the brain: "I am full, empty me." When we urinate we consciously contract the bladder to release its contents, and empty it completely. At this point the smooth muscle of the bladder wall should relax so that the now-empty bladder can return to storage mode. If you are short of magnesium your bladder may not relax fully, and its capacity is effectively reduced. A much smaller volume of urine will indicate to the brain that the bladder is now full, and the urge to pee is felt sooner than necessary.

As we age we often find ourselves waking more frequently in the night to urinate. While in men this may be due to prostate problems, it can also be due to insufficient magnesium. Adjusting the intake of magnesium can significantly reduce the number of nighttime bathroom visits for both sexes.

How much is too much magnesium?

When Janet first came to see me, I started her immediately on a small dose of magnesium before bed, and then asked her to increase her magnesium intake very slowly, every three days, until her bowels could take no more. This is called "titrating to bowel tolerance."

In Janet's case, just getting rid of her lifelong constipation made her feel much better. But the bonus was the reduction in muscle tension that had been a constant in her life. For the first time, her shoulders felt relaxed and free of nagging pain at the end of the day. We all experience tense shoulders at times, but Janet had become accustomed to the muscles of her entire body feeling tight and strained.

5-hydroxytryptophan—a natural sleeping pill

In addition, I also suggested a supplement for Janet called 5-hydroxytryptophan or 5-HTP. Given that milk and a cookie before bed had not been enough to help her sleep, she obviously needed more serotonin precursors than were being supplied by her diet. Some doctors prescribe tryptophan itself as a sleeping aid. It works for some patients but not for others, because tryptophan is not only used as the building block for serotonin but may be carried off for other metabolic processes. These include the manufacture of niacin (vitamin B3), should there be a deficiency.

An intermediate metabolite between tryptophan and serotonin, 5-HTP is found in minute amounts in certain foods such as cheese and the white meat of poultry. Supplements of 5-HTP sold in health food stores are usually obtained from the seeds of *griffonia simplicifolia*, a shrub native to West and Central Africa with a long history of use in African folk medicine.

Since 5-HTP cannot be sidetracked for other metabolic uses and easily crosses the blood-brain barrier, approximately 70 percent of the dose taken gets into the brain, compared with only 1 percent of tryptophan. It is usually available in doses of 50 to 200 mg per capsule. I advised Janet to start with 50 mg and increase the dose gradually (every three to four days) to find the appropriate level for her. That and the magnesium supplements I recommended previously caused her to sleep through the night for the first time in her life. On a recent follow-up visit, she reported still sleeping well two years later and was thrilled about this.

Why not just take melatonin?

You may be wondering why I did not simply recommend that Janet take one of the many melatonin supplements that are on the market. Would it not be simpler than pushing the body through all the steps of melatonin production? Travellers who cross several time zones take melatonin to cope with jet lag and reset their daily sleep-wake cycles disrupted by travel. There is also some evidence that our ability to make melatonin drops off after age 55 and that older people with insomnia may benefit from taking it as a supplement.[13]

But there is no set dose that works for everyone, and varying doses have been used in clinical trials from very low (0.3 mg) to high (6 mg or more). Finding your effective dose may be difficult, as taking more than you need may have the opposite effect to what you intended—disrupting your normal sleep-wake cycle and producing irritability and anxiety the next day. I believe it is far better for you to provide your body with the raw material and cofactors needed to manufacture your own natural melatonin. However, if you want to try melatonin, which has been shown to be effective, especially in older individuals, work with a knowledgeable practitioner to find the dose that suits you best.

Sleeping well is crucial as you age

We used to think of sleep as just downtime for the brain, but it is so much more than that. It's an active process. The different phases of sleep are important for different aspects of health. During deep sleep, the first phase, we are replenishing muscles and restoring our physical bodies. If you have ever tried to wake someone in deep sleep, you'll know that it's extremely difficult. After that comes REM (rapid eye movement) sleep, a time of intense brain activity. We might also be tossing and turning. Throughout this period of sleep, the brain is consolidating memories and setting up the production of hormones to regulate appetite and metabolism for the next day.

Researchers in sleep labs have woken their subjects during the different stages of sleep and found that if people who have been taught something new the previous day are awakened during REM sleep, they cannot remember what they learned. But if they are awakened during deep sleep, they can remember.

A growing problem

One theory about the cause of sleep difficulties as we age is the decline in growth hormone production. The less we make, the more difficulty sleeping. Growth hormone, manufactured during sleep, is made in large amounts during pregnancy and in early childhood; we have all seen the enormous capacity of children and teenagers for sleep as they grow and develop.

After we finish growing, we still need growth hormone for tissue repair, particularly when we are recovering from an illness. The decline of growth hormone production in our senior years is not all bad; scientists think that high levels of such hormones tend to support the development of certain cancers. That's the trade-off. Giving growth hormone to older people will improve their skin, increase their libido and the ability to sustain exercise, but studies of growth hormone for these uses were discontinued when it became apparent that it made subjects more cancer-prone. Some doctors still prescribe growth hormone if they believe that the benefits outweigh the risks. It does help people sleep.

How much sleep do we need?

Although we may get less sleep as we age, the need for sleep does not decline once we have reached maturity. Twin studies have revealed genetically determined differences in the amount of sleep people need. One teenager might need 10 hours, another 14. Newborns need the most sleep of all. As adults, we need seven to nine hours and that does not change over time. Older people may get away with more broken sleep, but the total amount they require remains unchanged. However, nutritional deficiencies increase with age, and that can bring on sleep problems, leading to the common misconception that older people do not need much sleep.

Sleep apnea—a momentary cessation of breathing—will increase with age and weight, waking you in the night. Restless leg syndrome will increase with age, but the latter is not difficult to correct with the right balance of calcium and magnesium. Restless leg may cause jerking of the legs during sleep. Towards the end of the day your legs may feel antsy or uncomfortable unless you are moving around. Going to a movie or play with someone who has restless leg syndrome is no fun because he or she will not be able to sit still, and wriggle as if the seat is uncomfortable.

Is there a link between poor sleep and mental deterioration?

Possibly. Doctors have long noticed that demented people sleep less and less. At the moment, however, we have no studies that show a causal relationship between not sleeping and dementia or Alzheimer's disease. It may be that the link is indirect. We do know that there are other symptoms that precede dementia, such as insulin resistance or metabolic syndrome. Metabolic syndrome reduces the body's ability to store nutrients, including the nutrients required for sleep.

Are you getting enough sleep?

While many people have difficulty sleeping as they age, other people I see in my practice short sleep on purpose. They have decided they have to get to the gym at 5 a.m. or perhaps they tend to work very late into the night before getting up at the normal time. Short sleeping can have negative effects on health. There are, of course, individual variations in the need for sleep and some people may need fewer than eight hours, but if someone falls asleep during the day, or nods off on the sofa after coming home from work, the body is signalling that five or six hours are not enough.

Short sleepers will miss out on the part of sleep called REM sleep, when the brain is reorganizing data. It happens at the end of every 90 minutes of sleep, and becomes longer within successive cycles, being longest in the last 90-minute period. We deprive ourselves of that final extended REM sleep if we set the alarm too early.

Check yourself: Are you getting enough sleep? Not sleeping, whether deliberately or because you can't, is stressful. All stress depletes magnesium, and this includes not only emotional stress, but also medical stressors such as surgery or illness, and the physical stress of pregnancy, exercise or heavy manual work.[14] If you have been busy during the day and your brain is overactive, if you are in the middle of a divorce, if your creditors are calling, or if you are stressed for some other reason, you may not be able to relax enough to fall asleep.

Anxieties that wake us up or keep us awake can usually be treated with another useful supplement called GABA, or gamma-amino butyric acid. GABA is an amino acid that also acts as an inhibitory neurotransmitter. Anxieties that wake us up or keep us from falling asleep can usually be helped by taking it before bedtime in the form of a powder or pill. Used with magnesium, GABA can be surprisingly helpful, stopping the whirring of a busy brain.

Night sweats

Overactive sweat glands may be another thing disturbing your sleep. A distressed middle-aged man once came to me because he was sweating so much he had to take two extra shirts with him to the office daily in order to change out of his damp clothing. Roy (not his real name) had tried coal tar and other topical ointments with no effect and his doctor was now advising him to undergo surgery to strip out his sweat glands. Before taking such an invasive approach, he decided to try natural remedies, if there were any.

Perspiration is known to deplete magnesium.[15] As magnesium drops, contracting sweat glands are unable to relax and the sweating gets even worse. After we balanced Roy's calcium and magnesium, his sweating problem was solved. No further need to change shirts during the day, and he slept better, too. He was careful to take his supplements from then on. I heard from him years later after he was in a skiing accident and had to be hospitalized in France. Sitting in a wheelchair, he was bothered by a twitching leg. He asked for magnesium but was told that he needed the anti-anxiety medication Ativan (lorazepam) to relax his leg muscles. Being a forceful character, he insisted until he got some magnesium. The twitching stopped.

You may be woken by dawn light, which switches off the production of melatonin. Light should wake you up—that is the natural response of the brain. Dawn woke our hunter-gatherer ancestors long before the arrival of alarm clocks. If light seeps into the room, you may be asleep, but your melatonin production will decrease. Failure to make an optimal amount of melatonin triggers disruptions in the sleep-wake cycle, further exacerbating sleep problems.

Many sleepless people turn in desperation to prescription sleep medications. While researchers try to develop medications that do not interfere with the normal cycle of sleep, some of these meds do affect REM sleep, which can, in turn, affect memory and learning. Prescription sleep medications work, though they can make people feel groggy the next day and can create dependency.

In short, there seems to be no really good substitute for natural means to get sleep. If you take a drug as a substitute for treating a deficiency, you are not doing yourself any favours. If you are low on magnesium, ultimately you will experience other problems related to magnesium deficiency. Go the nutritional route first and if you fail to find a solution, then you can turn to sleep medication.

9

Constipation

▼

*Not only does it [constipation] indispose the mind to exertion
and the body to exercise but it casts a gloom over the spirits,
and is productive of that general discomfort which ruffles the
temper and embitters the ordinary enjoyment of life.*

— Dr. John Burne, from *A Treatise on the causes and
consequences of habitual constipation* (1840)

T HOUGH PEOPLE ARE RELUCTANT to discuss the condition, constipation can cause extreme distress. Given
that a surprising number of people consider it a reason
to stay home from work, it also has an impact on the economy
due to lost workdays.[1] Constipation affects 10 to 20 percent of
the general population, but a much higher proportion—more
than 40 percent—of those 65 and older. The incidence among
women is two to three times as high as among men. In the
United States, it is one of the most common gastrointestinal
complaints. More than 4 million Americans have frequent
constipation, accounting for 2.5 million physician visits a year.
Around $725 million is spent on laxative products in the United
States annually.

Constipation is not a recent health problem, and we can't simply blame it on the rapid growth of the fast-food industry in the last two decades. It is a direct result of gradual changes in the food we eat, from the natural unrefined diets of hunter-gatherer societies and rural populations, to the refined and sugary foods common in the West today. One of the chief reasons that the well-to-do flocked to see Dr. Kellogg at his clinic in the early 1900s (see Chapter 2) was to rid themselves of the discomfort of constipation. Constipation may be a product of affluence, found chiefly in the wealthy nations of the West, but it is increasingly showing up in developing countries as well, following the introduction there of processed foods.

There is no universal agreement on what exactly constitutes constipation, but both infrequency and hardness are involved. The National Institute of Diabetes, Digestive and Kidney Diseases in the United States defines it as fewer than three bowel movements a week. The people who complain to me of constipation say that they may have a movement every two or three days, and then they have a great deal of difficulty passing it. But I have also seen people who have movements only every second day and do not consider themselves constipated. In my view, one or two comfortable movements a day are optimal, and possible to achieve naturally.

While sleep problems may be caused by factors other than lack of magnesium, constipation almost always points to insufficient magnesium. Or more precisely, an imbalance of dietary magnesium to calcium. As we have previously seen, magnesium and calcium work together to control muscle function. Calcium needs to rise within cells for muscles to contract, and a proper balance of magnesium is needed for those same muscles to relax again. This biochemical rule applies to all the muscles of the body—skeletal muscles, heart muscle and the smooth muscle that controls the contraction and relaxation of the lungs and bladder. It also applies to the rhythmic contraction and relaxation of the gut (peristalsis) that moves food through the digestive tract.

The reason constipation usually signals insufficient magnesium is simple. By the time food reaches the colon or large intestine, it is liquid waste and the main job of the colon is to compact this food waste by reabsorbing some of the liquid, together with electrolytes (minerals and salts) that the body can then reuse. If gastrointestinal muscle is sluggish, food waste remains too long in the colon, allowing too much water to be withdrawn back into the tissues. The result: hard, infrequent stools.

However, magnesium deficiency is not the only cause of constipation. If your bowel function changes suddenly, you should see your doctor to rule out a bowel obstruction or other serious medical reasons such as colon cancer for your condition. If no obvious physical cause is found, you will likely be given a laxative prescription or told to eat more bran. Bran consumption, as we will see later, may work temporarily, but if insufficient magnesium is the cause of constipation, ultimately bran will further deplete your magnesium and increase other physical symptoms of magnesium deficiency, such as leg cramps and muscle tension.

The case of the constant gardener

A woman in her late fifties I will call Kay came to see me one day. When I walked into the waiting room to invite her into my office, I noted from the way she struggled to her feet that she was in a great deal of pain. She took off her coat carefully and lowered herself slowly into the chair in my consulting room. She explained she had worked for a long time in her garden the previous day, and although she felt okay afterwards, her back soon began to hurt. The pain got progressively worse, she told me, and finally her back had gone into spasm.

Kay had not, in fact, come to my office because of back pain, but because she wanted to learn more about healthy eating and to ask about taking supplements. I knew she had elevated blood pressure because earlier she had filled out a questionnaire that asked about her health issues and any medication she was taking. I saw that she was on several blood pressure medications and it occurred to me that she may be deficient in magnesium.

The first question I asked was whether she was constipated and she said yes, constipation had been an ongoing problem in recent years. She tried to deal with it by drinking lots of water and taking fibre supplements. I asked if she was out of breath sometimes, and again she said yes, when she was going upstairs. I asked about leg cramps, foot cramps, charley horse (muscular pain, cramping, stiffness), especially at night. She agreed that, absolutely, she was having a problem with foot cramps. She wasn't experiencing them every night, but when she got them, they were severe.

To her doctor, all those conditions—constipation, foot cramps, high blood pressure—would be separate problems, each one addressed with a separate medication. To an orthomolecular practitioner like myself, each health issue is a clue to a common underlying nutritional problem. "Ortho" comes from the Greek for correct, and the term "orthomolecular" refers to the correct molecular environment in the body for proper functioning. The Nobel Prize–winning chemist and molecular biologist Linus Pauling (1901–1994) coined the term in an article in the journal *Science* in 1968.[2]

It was Pauling's genius to see the importance of the exciting work being done on individual nutrients in the first half of the twentieth century and the health problems that could result if these nutrients were not present in sufficient amounts in the body. He insisted that the scientific approach to health meant that nutrition must not be considered an optional add-on, but should be the first thing we look at in our efforts to solve any medical problem.

The crucial mineral

Let me explain why I read Kay's back spasms, pain and constipation as signs that her body was crying out for more magnesium. Magnesium is an energetic multitasker, required as a cofactor for more than 300 enzymes that regulate our metabolism. In my opinion, it is the most important mineral in the body. As we have seen, it is needed for the production of energy and for regulating blood sugar and cholesterol. We need it to make proteins, including DNA itself. Magnesium has sedative properties and is needed for sleep, as we saw in the previous chapter. It serves as a muscle relaxant, a characteristic of magnesium we've known about for decades. Insufficient magnesium in tissues causes hyperexcitability of nerves and this contributes to muscles tensing up. And since we need magnesium to relax muscles again after they have contracted, a deficiency in tissues can cause painful spasms in many parts of the body, especially the legs and hands (remember the ice water test?).

Kay was eating well, but you can be eating carefully and still not have ingested enough magnesium—magnesium deficiency is not necessarily a problem caused by a careless diet. As we saw in Chapter 1, the 2004 Canadian Community Health Survey showed widespread deficiencies of many nutrients, and magnesium was a particular concern, with up to 65 percent of Canadians failing to meet the estimated average daily requirement for this crucial mineral. The likelihood of magnesium deficiency in any single individual is therefore high. Office workers, for example, cashiers, and others who perform repetitive tasks, may experience sustained muscle tension. If their hands go into spasm or their shoulders feel tight and tense when they try to relax at the end of the day, magnesium deficiency is very likely to be at the root of the problem.

The treatment of chronic constipation is at the moment highly unsatisfactory and surveys show that most patients feel disappointed by traditional treatment options.[3] Even when they work, laxatives have unacceptable side effects such as bloating, abdominal pain, diarrhea and gas. Because constipation is such a common condition, many drug companies are currently looking for new and better medications. I hear from sufferers who have tried one drug after another without success, causing them to give up on the prescription drugs and go on to try over-the-counter medications, either from the drugstore or health food shop.

If you have been troubled by constipation and have found no satisfactory solution to the problem, try increasing your magnesium intake before you explore further drug treatment. Remember always to check with your doctor to make sure there are no medical reasons for your constipation, and then discuss the possibility of gradually increasing your magnesium intake with the help of a knowledgeable health care practitioner, using the method described in Part 3 of this book. If your constipation is caused by magnesium deficiency, you will have a constellation of symptoms, and correcting the constipation should help with all of them; you may find you enjoy higher energy levels, better sleep and blood pressure control. Indeed, taking magnesium is not simply a band-aid solution to your constipation, but an enhancement of total body health.

How do laxatives work?

Most over-the-counter laxatives are irritants that cause the bowel to increase its contractions. Stool softeners work to generate more mucus in the colon, which will allow easier passage. Except to those who suffer with it, constipation is usually considered a mere nuisance, something you have to put up with. In the long run it will do you no harm, or so it was once thought. But that is not turning out to be true. Researchers at the Mayo Clinic followed patients over the age of 65 with and without constipation for 10 years. Over that period, those who suffered from constipation had a 20 percent higher mortality rate than those who were not generally constipated.[4]

The Japanese have a better diet and longer lifespan than North Americans. Yet constipation is also a problem in Japan. According to another study, chronic constipation is associated in that country with early death from any cause, and an increased risk factor of cardiovascular disease.[5] And this side of the ocean, older women bothered by constipation have recently been shown to be at higher risk of heart disease than those with more regular bowel habits.[6] In short, constipation should not be ignored. People who are constipated are uncomfortable and hate the feeling, and in addition to its possible effect on longevity, this debilitating condition seriously affects quality of life.

Kay had been given the standard advice to drink lots of water and supplement her diet with lots of bran, and that is how she was dealing with her problem. Fibre stops too much resorption of liquids from the colon, maintaining bulk and moisture in stools. But all fibre is not created equal as far as bowel function is concerned. Both cereal fibres like wheat bran and fibres in legumes contain chemicals called phytates that bind magnesium. When magnesium binds to fibre, it is eliminated rather than absorbed, and thus bran, bran and more bran as a solution to constipation will exacerbate magnesium deficiency. The fibre in vegetables is different. Unlike cereal fibre, which can interfere with both magnesium and calcium absorption, fibre in vegetables helps magnesium absorption, while not affecting calcium, and so allows magnesium to be absorbed from diet and supplements.[7] Of course, vegetables themselves, especially green vegetables, are often a good source of magnesium.

The other thing Kay was doing was drinking a huge amount of water. Excessive water intake tends to override the capacity of the colon to withdraw water from the liquid food waste back into the tissues. In effect, you swamp the colon. That softens the stool somewhat, but is not the right solution, either, since more water will not replace missing magnesium.

Why the calcium-to-magnesium balance changed

Back in our evolutionary past, we lived in a magnesium-rich environment. As hunter-gatherers, we slaked our thirst by drinking from lakes or mountain streams whose waters contained magnesium. Our magnesium intake varied depending on the hardness of the water in a particular region. In most urban areas today, however, water is softened for industrial purposes by removing magnesium as well as other minerals such as calcium and iron.[8]

Our natural, unrefined plant-based diet as hunter-gatherers was also chock full of magnesium. But calcium was scarce, since dairy farming had not yet developed. Most of the calcium we consumed came from plants and water, both of which also contained magnesium. In such a diet, the balance of calcium to magnesium was almost equal. The table below compares the calcium-to-magnesium balance in a diet of natural, unprocessed foods—a modern version of a hunter-gatherer diet—to the balance of minerals found in a contemporary diet high in refined foods and dairy products. As you can see, a dramatic shift has taken place so that the typical Western diet now, on average, yields a calcium-to-magnesium balance of about five to one.

Table 1
Comparison of calcium-to-magnesium ratios in two different diets

Diet 1. Modern version of a hunter-gatherer diet—high in lean protein, essential fats and unrefined carbohydrates	Calcium-to-magnesium ratio in 100 g of food	Diet 2. Typical Western-style diet—high in refined foods and low in vegetables and fruit	Calcium-to-magnesium ratio in 100 g of food
Whole wheat	0.4:1	Bagel (white)	2.0:1
Oats	0.4:1	Pancakes	4.0:1
Wild rice	0.2:1	Doughnut	1.8:1
Blueberries	1.2:1	Cookies	13:1
Cranberries	1.4:1	Blueberry muffin	3.1:1
Apples	1.4:1	White rice	3.6:1
Hazelnuts	1.1:1	Macaroni	0.4:1
Walnuts	0.8:1	Eggs	4.6:1
Eggs	4.6:1	Chicken breast	0.5:1
Venison	0.3:1	Hamburger	0.5:1
Pheasant	0.6:1	French fries	0.2:1
Salmon	0.3:1	Onions	2.5:1
Trout	1.9:1	Orange juice	1.0:1
Oysters	0.8:1	Ice cream	4.0:1
Shrimp	1.4:1	Milk	7.0:1
Spinach	1.4:1	Yogurt (plain)	11.0:1
Turnip	2.0:1	Cheese (hard)	26.0:1
Average	**1.3:1** ca to mg	**Average**	**4.95:1** ca to mg

Data source: USDA food database, previously published in *Scientific Evidence for Musculoskeletal, Bariatric and Sports Nutrition*. 2006. Taylor and Francis (CRC Press) USA. pp 137–152

The above table illustrates the dietary shift in the ratio of calcium to magnesium even before we take additional calcium supplements, so widely recommended for postmenopausal women, into account. Excessive calcium intake from either foods or supplements or both will contribute to a magnesium deficiency[9] since calcium competes for absorption with magnesium.

Too much calcium and in all the wrong places

In addition to damaging mitochondria, the cell's energy-producing structures, especially when magnesium deficiency is present, excessive calcium may get deposited in the wrong places—kidneys, for instance, where it shows up as stones. The most frequent cause of recall after an abnormal mammogram is not breast cancer but calcification—small deposits of calcium in breast tissue that appear as white flecks on the mammogram. Calcification has become such a common problem seen on X-rays that some institutions doing mammograms check blood vessels in the neck at the same time; calcification will cause stiffening or hardening of arteries and veins, and reduce the flexibility of blood vessels. This, in turn, will increase the risk of heart disease, putting stress on the heart by impeding blood flow.

To prevent this buildup of calcium in blood vessels, we need another nutrient—vitamin K—which helps put calcium into bones and keep it out of blood vessels and other soft tissues like breast and kidneys.[10] Vitamin K may even reverse existing blood vessel calcification.[11] There is some suggestion that vitamin K may also strengthen bones, although how it does this is not yet clear, since it does not appear to increase bone density. However, a higher intake of vitamin K does appear to help prevent hip fractures in elderly men and women.[12] Vitamin K is found in green vegetables, and the amount (250 mcg a day) found to protect against hip fractures can be obtained from ½ cup of broccoli or a daily green salad.

Vitamin K was for many years banned in Canadian supplements and has only recently started to appear in the better multivitamins. This ban was the result of a mistaken idea that since vitamin K was required for blood to clot, taking vitamin K supplements would increase the risk of blood clots in healthy individuals. It does not, and vitamin K supplements are perfectly safe for most people.[13] The only people who need to avoid vitamin K supplements are patients taking certain oral anticoagulant drugs like warfarin. These drugs are given to people who have previously had a blood clot, or are at risk of blood clots because of abnormal heart rhythms. Warfarin works in these individuals to block the normal action of vitamin K, and taking extra vitamin K could reduce the effectiveness of the drug.

Blood pressure medication and magnesium

My client Kay had told me she had high blood pressure and was on two different diuretics to try to control it. Remember that blood pressure is controlled by tiny muscle cells (smooth muscle) that contract and relax the blood vessel walls. Contraction of smooth muscle cells pushes up blood pressure, but after each contraction the muscles need to relax again, an action facilitated by magnesium. Magnesium deficiency may cause sustained contraction of the blood vessel walls and increase blood pressure.[14]

As we saw in the chapter on sleep, the irony is that while raised blood pressure may be due to inadequate magnesium intake, many drugs used to treat high blood pressure, especially diuretics, further deplete magnesium. These drugs work by increasing the output of urine by the kidneys; this reduces the volume of blood circulating, which, in turn, lowers blood pressure. However, the extra fluid excreted by the kidneys contains minerals, including magnesium, as well as other water-soluble nutrients such as vitamin C.

The effect of diuretics on nutrients is well documented in the research literature, and should be compensated for by increasing the intake of the lost nutrients, including magnesium.[15] Unfortunately, most doctors are unaware of the nutritional implications of many prescription drugs, and this precaution is rarely taken. Since Kay was on two diuretics for blood pressure, I concluded that magnesium depletion played a role in the symptoms she was experiencing, including her nighttime foot cramps and post-gardening back spasms, as well as her constipation.

Resolving constipation with magnesium

As we know, the concentration of magnesium circulating in the blood is fairly constant. It is maintained in a narrow range by both the intestine and the kidney. When there is a high dietary intake, the kidneys sense this and filter out some of the magnesium, which is then excreted in urine, and when magnesium levels fall, the intestine increases its absorption from food. When the diet does not contain enough magnesium, blood levels are then maintained from bone or muscle stores. This is why blood tests for magnesium generally come back normal even when, as in Kay's case, she was taking drugs known to deplete magnesium and had physical signs of low tissue magnesium.

In taking patient histories, I sometimes hear about lifelong constipation that began in childhood. Sufferers report that their siblings and parents had the condition as well. Although the exact pathology of familial constipation is unknown, the clustering of chronic constipation in families suggests an underlying genetic cause.[16] We have already seen how magnesium needs are genetically determined, and it is interesting to speculate whether the same families who suffer from chronic constipation have other problems related to magnesium needs. Genetic or not, the situation still calls for extra magnesium, as it did in Kay's case. I made sure that Kay took just enough to relieve her constipation and not so much that she got diarrhea. Taking more magnesium than you need overrelaxes gastrointestinal muscle causing diarrhea, and the diarrhea in turn further depletes magnesium.[17]

I got Kay to start taking magnesium, increasing her intake in increments of 50 mg every three days. The small dose and the three-day interval between increases gives the body time to absorb the magnesium and build up tissue stores without loosening the bowels. As mentioned in the previous chapter, this is called titrating to bowel tolerance. Read the label on your magnesium because the type of magnesium used is also important. I use protein-bound forms of magnesium. Binding magnesium to a protein or amino acid (the building blocks of protein) mimics what normally happens in the digestive tract, where magnesium and other minerals are linked to protein before absorption. Use either magnesium taurate, magnesium glycinate or something called HVP (hydrolyzed vegetable protein) chelated magnesium. Chelated just means "attached to." Taken this way, magnesium is absorbed very reliably and is well retained in tissues.

Many supplements contain magnesium oxide or magnesium citrate, but their absorption and retention is hit-and-miss. Magnesium oxide needs stomach acid in order to be utilized by the body and as we age, we have less of that. In addition, many individuals are on proton pump inhibitors or other acid-suppressing medications. Magnesium citrate can stimulate the bowel to work quite efficiently, but it is rapidly excreted,[18] and I find that while it does solve the problem of constipation, it does not adequately replenish tissue stores. You may get diarrhea before there is any resolution of the other symptoms of magnesium deficiency. I explained to Kay that the type of magnesium she took was important, and so was building it up slowly, to avoid the runs.

While it's not possible to simply guess the correct magnesium dosage for everyone who has constipation, since it varies from person to person, titrating to bowel tolerance works well. Those who don't have constipation can benefit from magnesium gel, applied to the skin at night. Kay eventually got to the point of having two soft bowel movements a day. She was absolutely delighted with this. But more than that, when she got over her constipation, her tendency to spasm when she was kneeling to weed her garden also ended. Whether she was gardening or doing other physical activity, she felt much more comfortable and free in her movements. She continued her blood pressure medications, and had to pay close attention to her magnesium intake to counter their depleting effects.

The other day, I had a conversation with a 95-year-old woman who has been a client for some years. "I used to have a racing heart and irregular heart beat [arrythmia] that bothered me a lot," she told me. "But since I got rid of my constipation with magnesium, I don't have it any more. I was at the cardiologist recently and I said I got rid of my racing heart when I got rid of my constipation with magnesium. She said, 'Oh, yes. Magnesium can help.' But why didn't she tell me that at the beginning?" It's a question I am often asked. Doctors use the therapies they have been trained to use, and that generally means medications, not nutritional approaches.

The role of exercise

A sedentary lifestyle goes in tandem with constipation. Exercise can be both beneficial and harmful to the gastrointestinal tract.[19] Exercise causes a redistribution of magnesium in the body, drawing it out of storage sites in bones to meet the body's changing needs during increased physical activity. It is not surprising then, that regular mild-to-moderate exercise has been shown to reduce constipation.[20]

But more exercise is not better. Strenuous exercise may increase gastrointestinal signs of magnesium depletion such as nausea, vomiting, abdominal pain and even diarrhea. The diarrhea seems paradoxical, since magnesium deficiency is more often associated with constipation. It is a result of hyperexcitability of the nerves controlling the muscles of the gastrointestinal tract, and is usually accompanied by other symptoms of magnesium depletion, such as twitching of tiny muscles (fascic-ulation) and involuntary movements of large muscle groups in the limbs.[21]

One of my clients, a runner, told me she got leg cramps only when she was taking a break from her usual jogging routine. If leg cramps and muscle spasms were due to lack of magnesium, why would running correct this? This is an example of the numerous compensatory mechanisms the body uses to ensure that essential functions like the beating of the heart continue in the face of low tissue stores of magnesium. As my client ran, she would have released magnesium from storage sites such as bone into her blood, and this would have circulated to her leg mus-cles. However, when she was not running, she got leg cramps.

This client might have experienced serious trouble eventu-ally, since the compensatory effects of the running on her cal-cium-magnesium balance could begin to falter. Sudden death due to cardiac arrest is unfortunately not uncommon in elite athletes, and is rarely preceded by warning signs such as chest pains. While autopsy often reveals pre-existing heart problems, this is not always the case. Recent studies in women have shown that a higher dietary intake of magnesium protects against sudden cardiac arrest.[22] Don't ignore constipation. It not only affects your sense of well-being but has been linked to higher mortality rates, heart disease and insomnia. As we have seen in this chapter, once your doctor has ruled out any medical cause, treating it by natural means is not difficult. Be alert for com-panion symptoms such as leg and foot cramps, which indicate insufficient magnesium in your system. Try optimizing your magnesium intake, as described in Part 3 of this book, and you will find that all your symptoms will resolve.

10

Depression, Sadness, and Anxiety

▼

*Depression is the most unpleasant thing I have ever
experienced. . . . It is that absence of being able to envisage
that you will ever be cheerful again. The absence of hope.
That very deadened feeling, which is so very different
from feeling sad. Sad hurts but it's a healthy feeling. It is
a necessary thing to feel. Depression is very different.*

—J. K. Rowling, writer

MODERN LIFE may have brought greater prosperity
to more people than ever before, but it cannot be
said to have increased the total sum of human hap-
piness. The use of antidepressants and anti-anxiety medications has skyrocketed after their introduction in the late 1980s.
In 2007, the U.S. Centers for Disease Control and Prevention
looked at the 2.4 billion drug prescriptions written by doctors
in 2005 and found that the largest number, 118 million, was
for antidepressants. (Drugs used to treat high blood pressure

were the next most common with 113 million prescriptions.)

Severe clinical depression—despair, paralyzing numbness and complete indifference to everyday pleasures—should never be confused with normal sadness or mood swings and always requires medical attention. But even in the case of clinical depression, nutritional interventions can also be useful. While medications can stabilize mood, they do not cure depression and many have unpleasant side effects. Those side effects often stem from a failure to recognize that drugs used to treat depression can deplete nutrients, assuming those nutrients were part of the patient's diet in the first place. Replacing the missing nutrients can lessen side effects, and even increase the effectiveness of the drugs.[1]

Ongoing low-level sadness, known medically as dysthymia, does not interfere with everyday living, although it may handicap us enough to prevent us from achieving our full potential. Both sadness and anxiety are normal emotions and part of everyday life. Anxiety, for example, is entirely appropriate if we get a call from the taxman and we know we are overdue with our tax return. But sweeping anxiety for no particular reason or habitually low moods often signal nutritional needs that are not being met. The advantage of non-drug nutritional treatments for mood disorders and anxiety is that they produce lasting changes in brain biochemistry and long-term relief. In contrast to the possible negative side effects of mood-altering drugs, nutritional approaches will have side *benefits*, often improving sleep, focus and concentration as well as mood. If you find yourself more anxious and depressed with each birthday, look upon these symptoms as yet another red flag indicating possible nutritional problems.

The first time I spoke at a meeting of health care professionals about the idea that anxiety, depression and insomnia could simply be signs that the patient was not consuming enough of the raw materials needed for the brain to function properly, I feared that my message would be rejected. Without an adequate intake of certain vitamins and amino acids required for brain chemistry, it was impossible, I argued, to feel well. Since we knew that inadequate diets were common in North America, it was reasonable to assume that this may be the cause of a significant number of mood disorders health care professionals saw in their offices. Maybe before physicians prescribed an antidepressant, I told my audience, it would be better to start off by asking about the patient's diet, checking to make sure that the patient was consuming all the nutrients needed for the manufacture of the neurotransmitters dopamine and serotonin, the body's natural antidepressants.

This was a new idea for many of the doctors present, but it was based on a body of existing research. During the talk, I presented evidence that the typical North American diet was likely to be short of key nutrients needed to make serotonin and dopamine, and that the level of these two chemicals could be either high or low depending on the protein and carbohydrate content of an individual's last meal.[2] The levels could also be low if patients were short of essential vitamins and minerals, especially B vitamins and magnesium, needed as cofactors for the manufacture of neurotransmitters.[3]

After my talk, there were enthusiastic comments and questions. One doctor introduced himself to me at the coffee break. "Immediately after you finished speaking I called my wife," he said. "I told her, no wonder our daughter is having such emotional problems—she isn't eating properly." I left the conference feeling energized. I had got my message across about a subject close to my heart, and to a prime audience.

The link between depression and nutrition is now more widely recognized. In an article published in March 2010 in the *American Journal of Psychiatry*, Dr. Marlene P. Freeman writes:

"It is both compelling and daunting to consider that dietary intervention at an individual or population level could reduce rates of psychiatric disorders. There are exciting implications for clinical care, public health, and research."

The high cost of running a brain

Nutritionally speaking, operating a brain is an expensive process. Although it averages only 2 percent of total body weight, the brain uses about 20 percent of circulating oxygen, glucose and all the other essential nutrients. In other words, it needs 10 times more feeding than organs such as the heart or kidneys. And the harder you work your brain, the more nutrients, glucose, oxygen and protective phytochemicals it needs.

The brain is mostly fat, and must have the right kinds of fats for proper functioning and repair. Dietary fats and oils contain a combination of numerous different types of fatty acids, each with unique structures and biological functions. Saturated fats come mainly from animal foods. Examples include butter, lard, the fat found in meat, and in cream, milk and egg yolks. Although they play an important structural role throughout the body, brain included, saturated fats are not essential, since we can make all we need ourselves. Higher intakes of saturated fats are thought to increase the risk of heart disease, although this idea has recently been challenged.[4] Chemically, saturated fats are chains of carbon atoms attached to each other by a single bond. This makes them more stable in terms of storage and handling.

Unsaturated fats have one or more double bonds in their carbon chains. Fats are called monounsaturated if they contains just one double bond, and polyunsaturated if they have more than one. The double bonds are areas that are vulnerable to oxidation at room temperature, which is why unsaturated fats go rancid easily and therefore have a short shelf life. Polyunsaturated fats are found in whole grains, nuts, plants and plant oils, and seafood. Monounsaturated fats are found in olives and olive oil, avocados, and nuts such as cashews.

The polyunsaturated fats called omega-3 and omega-6 fatty acids are the two that are essential (EFAs). Since we cannot manufacture these fats ourselves, their concentration in the brain depends entirely on diet. Rich sources of omega-6s include corn oil, sunflower, safflower, soybean and cottonseed oil. Omega-3 fatty acids are found in fatty fish like salmon and sardines and in other seafood, including krill—small shrimp-like creatures that are a food source of omega-3 EFAs for the fatty fish that feed on them. Omega-3s are also found in algae, some plants such as flaxseed, and in nut oils.

More about balance

Both omega-3 and omega-6 fatty acids give rise to hormones called prostaglandins, important hormones that do not circulate in blood as do insulin or thyroxin, but act locally right in the cells that produce them. They can be either inflammatory or anti-inflammatory. Omega-6 EFAs increase the production of inflammatory prostaglandins, while omega-3 EFAs will block this effect. A diet that includes a high intake of omega-6 fats compared to omega-3s, the norm for modern Western diets, is therefore an inflammatory diet.[5] Studies of modern-day hunter-gatherers such as the Hadza of Tanzania and the San of the Kalahari suggest that ancient diets had a high intake of both omega-6 and omega-3 fatty acids in roughly equal proportions—about one-to-one.[6] However, today our omega-6 intake has increased while our omega-3 intake has decreased, and now the balance is between 10-to-1 and 20-to-1 omega-6 to omega-3.

This pro-inflammatory balance of essential fats undermines not only the health of our brains, but of all tissues and organs, and is an unfortunate consequence of official nutritional recommendations. Over the past decade or so, saturated and trans fats have both been vilified and substituting polyunsaturated omega-6 for them encouraged. As recently as 2009, the American Heart Association suggested that omega-6 fats should be increased to 5 to 10 percent of our daily energy intake and that this would benefit heart health. But when a thorough scientific review was done of all the studies of omega-6 fats and heart health, researchers found that, to the contrary, increasing omega-6 without consideration of the need to balance it with omega-3 was likely to *increase* heart disease, not reduce it.[7]

The importance of omega-3 fatty acids for brain health

Omega-3 fatty acids are highly concentrated in the brain. Symptoms of omega-3 fatty acid deficiency include fatigue, poor memory, mood swings or depression, as well as more serious psychiatric disorders like bipolar disorder and schizophrenia.[8] One reason omega-3 fats are important is that they are critical to the manufacture and release of neurotransmitters (chemical message carriers) from brain cells,[9] as well as to the functioning of the receptors, which are the docking sites for neurotransmitters. Two members of the omega-3 family of fats, docosahexaenoic acid (DHA) and eicosapentaenoic acid (EPA), are especially important. Found mainly in salmon, sardines and other fatty fish, EPA and DHA are not present in plant oils such as canola, or other plant-derived omega-3 supplements such as flaxseed oil. While it is theoretically possible to convert omega-3s from plant sources into EPA and DHA, humans are not very efficient at doing this and therefore vegetarians may be at risk of deficiency. Fish obtain their EPA and DHA from the microscopic algae they feed on, making omega-3 supplements derived from algae suitable for vegetarians.

DHA is the principal omega-3 fatty acid in the human brain. It stabilizes cell membranes and opens and shuts channels that allow electrical signals to move in and out of neurons. DHA makes up 15 to 20 percent of the total fatty acid composition of the frontal cortex,[10] the part of the brain responsible for decision making, consciousness and emotions. Studies have shown decreased brain DHA in patients with bipolar disorder or major depression.[11] EPA is important to neurological health as well, as it increases blood flow. It is a powerful anti-inflammatory and, when needed, can be easily converted to DHA.

Since most diets are likely to contain more than enough omega-6 EFAs, I recommend supplementing with omega-3 EFAs to achieve an omega-6 to omega-3 balance that is anti-inflammatory and more in line with our evolutionary past.

Trans fats

The fats we really want to avoid are trans fats. These artificially created fats were not a part of our diets until the 1960s. In 1902, a German chemist, Wilhelm Normann, discovered how to stabilize polyunsaturated fats and prevent them from going rancid by forcing hydrogen into them under pressure and at high temperatures. Using this process it was possible to convert polyunsaturated fats like corn oil and soybean oil, which were liquid at room temperature, into saturated fats that were solid at room temperature. These new hydrogenated fats had a longer shelf life and included margarines and shortenings. However, they were more difficult to work with for the home cook and baker, especially when refrigerators became common after the Second World War. Like butter, hydrogenated fats were hard when they came of the fridge.

If you only *partially* hydrogenated polyunsaturated oils you got an easier-to-use product. Partial hydrogenation decreased the number of double bonds and rearranged their configuration, making a solid fat that was not as hard at room temperature. Margarines could be made spreadable straight from the fridge, and cookies and snack foods were crispier and had more sensory appeal. Moreover, fats for deep frying could be used over and over again without going rancid. But partially hydrogenated fats contained new molecules called trans fats, not present in fully hydrogenated fats. The consumption of trans fats dramatically increased in the mid-1980s when the food industry was pressured to remove saturated fats, then thought to be a major cause of heart disease.

In the 1990s, researchers noticed that trans fats increased the risk of cardiovascular disease, type 2 diabetes and cancer, and although the exact mechanisms whereby this happens are still not clear, suspicion fell on the rearrangement of the fat molecule that is the hallmark of trans fats. In the brain, trans fats are molecular misfits and usurp the place of omega-3 fats in cell membranes. This can change the way neurons function, affecting the responses of cells to neurotransmitters including dopamine and serotonin. Once trans fats are in the brain, they can be difficult to dislodge. Not surprisingly, recent research has linked high intakes of trans fats to depression and the worsening of existing mental health problems.[12]

Many countries, including Canada, are looking at ways to reduce exposure to trans fats. In Denmark, trans fats have been virtually eliminated by law, but reductions elsewhere being made by the food industry are mainly voluntary. In the meantime, research continues to show that there is really no safe level of trans fats.[13]

Margarine: a healthier fat?

I never recommend margarine. Margarine can now be made with polyunsaturated fats, stabilized without hydrogenation. In a bid to entice us to keep using it, food scientists are busy adding new ingredients to margarine, for example, using it as a vehicle for plant compounds called stanols and sterinols that might bring down cholesterol (more on these later). It may not contain the high trans fat levels of previous generations of margarines, but it is still a manufactured, overly processed food, to be avoided if you want to eat a more natural diet.

Many margarines are made from canola or soybean oil. Canola oil comes from linseed, also known as rapeseed. Rapeseed is not an edible plant and its oil, linseed oil, was traditionally used as furniture polish and as a pesticide. Canadian plant scientists bred most of the toxins out of linseed to give us an oil initially called LEAR oil (low erucic acid rapeseed oil), but renamed in 1978 as the more consumer-friendly canola (from Canada and oil). However, small amounts of erucic acid still remain in canola seeds, and their oil has to be heavily refined to remove it before it is sold. Because the fats in it easily go rancid and develop an off taste and smell, it also must be deodorized. These processes involve heating the oil to high temperatures (300°F) and the use of chemical catalysts. During this processing, trans fats are produced, although Health Canada insists the levels are very low.[14] For the same reasons, soybean oil also contains low levels of trans fats. There are a number of websites that question the long-term safety of canola oil as a source of omega-3 fats, but so far there is not much research evidence to support these claims. If you want to avoid heavily processed food, I recommend using olive oil and a small amount of old-fashioned butter. Recent evaluations of natural saturated fats like those in butter and egg yolks have found no evidence of a link between saturated fat and heart disease in healthy people.[15] A little butter will do you no harm, especially if it is organic.

Serotonin and dopamine

Protein is another critically important macronutrient for the brain. Digestion breaks down protein into its basic building blocks—amino acids. These are then absorbed into the blood and used to manufacture our own body proteins. Two amino acids in particular, tyrosine and tryptophan, are required on a moment-to-moment basis to make the neurotransmitters dopamine and serotonin. Because we cannot store protein, we need a regular intake of the nutrient throughout the day so that these two amino acids will be available to synthesize dopamine and serotonin as we need it.

Dopamine is our true antidepressant neurotransmitter. When dopamine levels are high, we feel energetic, focused and in excellent spirits. When dopamine levels are low, we lack concentration and are indecisive. Dopamine is released in the brain as part of the dopamine reward pathway. When we engage in an activity such as eating or sex, dopamine neurons in the brain start firing in bursts. This so-called "burst firing" is perceived by the brain as pleasure. This is nature's way of ensuring we repeat experiences that are important for survival.

Dopamine also helps maintain the flow of sensory information—the sights, sounds and smells around us—into the brain. However, very high levels of dopamine cause us to be overwhelmed with information and have been linked to psychosis and schizophrenia. This is where serotonin enters the picture. One of its roles is to block sensory information from reaching the brain. High serotonin levels make us feel calm, sleepy, lacking in drive. When serotonin is high, we screen out the things that might worry us, which is the reason that serotonin is also considered an antidepressant.

Throughout the day dopamine and serotonin work in tandem to control mental functioning. Ideally dopamine should dominate during the working day, keeping you upbeat, focused and alert. But you also need enough serotonin to block unnecessary sensory "noise" to help you concentrate on what is important. In the evening, the balance should be reversed. Serotonin should rise to help us sleep, and dopamine, which keeps us alert, needs to take a back seat. To feel like a couch potato is fine at the end of the day when you are preparing for bed, but not after breakfast or lunch.

The importance of protein for breakfast and lunch

The building block for dopamine is the amino acid tyrosine, the most plentiful amino acid in protein-rich food. A high-protein meal will increase brain dopamine and allow more focus and concentration. For this reason, breakfast and lunch, the two most important workday meals, should always contain protein. The precursor for serotonin is tryptophan. Since it is the least plentiful amino acid in protein, we need a different strategy to get tryptophan into our brain: we need to eat something sweet or starchy to provoke insulin secretion and vault it over the blood-brain barrier. Otherwise, serotonin levels will rise very little no matter how much protein we eat.

Studies have shown that the type of breakfast we eat can have an impact on how we function later in the day. One study compared two different breakfasts—one high in carbohydrates, and the other high in protein. Volunteers were fed either pancakes and syrup with orange juice, or eggs, turkey bacon, cheese and grapefruit juice. The second meal was high in protein with only a little carbohydrate from the grapefruit juice. Later, the researchers tested the blood of both groups and found that after the high-carbohydrate breakfast, blood sugar levels rose sharply, followed by a rise in insulin. Under these conditions, tryptophan easily gets into the brain and causes an increase in serotonin. This in turn reduces focus and motivation, and increases daytime sleepiness, as happened in this study. The high-protein breakfast produced none of these effects.[16]

If you want to remain focused during the working day, remember to eat protein at breakfast and lunch, and get your carbohydrates from vegetables and fruit. At bedtime, of course, you want high brain-tryptophan levels to help you sleep; a sweet snack is now appropriate. Antidepressant medications (Prozac, Paxil, Zoloft) increase levels of various neurotransmitters by preventing their normal breakdown and reabsorption. That is why a popular class of antidepressants is called selective serotonin reuptake inhibitors or SSRIs. They help maintain an artificially high soup of seratonin in the brain. However, no drug has been developed yet that will help your brain make *new* serotonin. Only your diet can do that.

Aging and neurotransmission

Chronic low levels of neurotransmitters or low levels of the cofactors needed for them to function become more common with age. We have all heard of elderly people living alone who subsist on tea and toast. No wonder they sink into depression. The first thing, then, is to establish healthy eating patterns. But even if diet is adequate, there may be other deficiencies affecting brain function that are not supplied in sufficient amounts by diet alone as we age.

Vitamin D is one of these. Receptors for vitamin D are present throughout the brain, especially in the hippocampus, which is responsible for memory, and on dopamine neurons that make or respond to dopamine.[17] Those receptors are there for a reason. Mother Nature is not so capricious as to load the brain with vitamin D receptors if the brain did not require vitamin D to function.

People who feel depressed in winter but upbeat again as soon as summer returns exhibit the unmistakable pattern of vitamin D deficiency. With the use of supplements, it is possible to correct this condition, called seasonal affective disorder or SAD. A recent American survey of nearly 8000 young people aged 15 to 39 found depression to be common in those with circulating blood levels of vitamin D in the deficient range (less than 50 nmol/L) compared to those whose blood levels were 75 nmol/L or higher.[18] Low blood levels of vitamin D are common in the elderly, who synthesize vitamin D less easily from sunshine and generally spend less time outdoors.

Low vitamin D levels are also associated with pain, and chronic pain can cause depression. Fibromyalgia, a condition of widespread musculoskeletal pain, is frequently accompanied by anxiety and depression. But in some patients, fibromyalgia is simply undiagnosed vitamin D deficiency.[19] A physician friend of mine told me about a cruise she and a group of doctors took to the Galápagos Islands, in Ecuador. In Quito, the capital, they toured a large hospital with every kind of facility but no psychiatric department. At the end of the tour one of the doctors asked whether there was a psychiatric ward at the hospital. No, there wasn't. "So, is there a psychiatric hospital in the city?" the doctor asked. No, she was told, there isn't one.

The visiting doctors were astonished. But when you consider that Ecuador straddles the equator and Quito is at high altitude in the Andes where there would be maximum UV exposure year-round, you begin to understand the reason for this state of affairs. Studies have shown schizophrenia and other neurological diseases are rare at such latitudes.[20]

The stress response

Clients sometimes tell me that their low moods or depression began after a period of extreme stress. Stress can interfere with sleep, make us irritable, and affect how we function. One way stress does this is by depleting key nutrients involved in the generation and functioning of neurotransmitters.

Stress is common currency in our society. We exist today under conditions of stress unthinkable to our parents' and grandparents' generation. The impact of stress on health was first elucidated by the Hungarian-Canadian endocrinologist Hans Selye (1907–1982), arguably one of the greatest physicians and scientists of the twentieth century. Before Selye's day stress was an engineering term: the stress on a bridge was the total load it could carry without being damaged and Selye was the first to introduce the term into the medical vocabulary. To an engineer, it does not matter if the stress is one big load or multiple small loads—an overstressed bridge eventually starts to crack. Selye showed that the same was true of the human body: overload it and something has to give.

Selye first worked with animals (he had 15,000 in his Montreal lab) but later did human experiments. He showed that any change the body had to accommodate to could negatively affect health. Environmental toxins, extremes of heat and cold, overexertion all produced tissue damage that followed a predictable pattern. In one of his seminal papers, "A Syndrome Produced by Diverse Nocuous Agents" (1936), he wrote:

Experiments on rats showed that if an organism is severely damaged by acute nonspecific noxious agents such as exposure to cold, surgical injury, production of spinal shock (transcision of the cord), excessive muscular exercise or intoxication with sublethal doses of diverse drugs (adrenaline, atrophine, morphine, formaldehyde, etc.), a typical syndrome appears, the symptoms of which are independent of the nature of the damaging agent or the pharmacological type of drug employed, and represent, rather, a response to damage as such.

Selye injected his lab rats with chemicals or made them exercise without respite, and observed behavioural changes that we may notice in ourselves when we are stressed. They urinated excessively and their eyes watered and sometimes bulged out of their heads. If the stress was extreme and continuous, he saw a clouding of the lens of the eyes until the animals eventually developed cataracts. After the rats had been stressed for about 48 hours he dissected some of them and noted changes in their internal organs. He found that their adrenal glands had started to enlarge, sometimes to two to three times normal size, confirming that they were working harder. Sometimes the thyroid gland was also enlarged, suggesting that it, too, had had to work harder.

Other changes occurred indicating that the animals were not functioning well. Young animals stopped growing, and in mature animals, sex hormone levels dropped. Milk production stopped in those who were feeding their young. To Selye this meant one thing: the animals responded to stress by suppressing some biological functions to support others more immediately essential for survival. That was how they adapted.

The general adaptation syndrome he identified is the so-called stress response, also known as the fight-or-flight response.

Anything that perturbs us, any change we have to accommodate to, triggers this stress response and may have negative consequences. We tend to underestimate the variety of stressors that we are exposed to in our daily lives, from physical to emotional, social and medical. Excessive exercise, manual labour, extremes of temperature, transitions such as pregnancy, menopause, adolescence and advancing years are all major stressors. Aging is a stress, as we find ourselves progressively less able to do the things we used to do. When we have to lower expectations, when we face major life changes, we pay a price. Bereavement, retirement, financial difficulties, divorce are all social and emotional stressors.

Finally, we often fail to recognize the medical stressors that accumulate as we age. Infection is stress. Chronic pain brought on by arthritis, prolapsed discs or fibromyalgia constantly drain the body's nutritional resources. A bout of cancer that forces us to undergo chemotherapy is obviously stressful and usually acknowledged, but people are less likely to recognize that taking powerful daily drugs to control cholesterol, blood sugar or blood pressure is also a major stress.

Tyrosine supplements and stress

If stress is depleting us nutritionally and contributing to our risk of depression and anxiety, is there anything we can do to overcome it besides eating a good diet? Are there supplements we should consider?

One supplement that I use frequently in my practice is tyrosine, the building block for dopamine. Tyrosine is not one of the nine essential amino acids—it is what we call *conditionally* essential. That is, under certain conditions our nutritional needs cannot be met from diet alone. And stress is the condition that makes tyrosine essential. As we have seen, tyrosine is the most plentiful amino acid in protein food. We can nonetheless run short of it because it is in hot demand for many other important functional molecules that the body needs to operate besides dopamine. It is a building block for the adrenal hormones, adrenaline and noradrenaline, for the thyroid hormone thyroxine (recall that in Selye's lab animals, the organs most damaged by stress were the thyroid gland and the adrenal gland). It is also required for the synthesis of melanin, the colour pigment of hair and skin. As we saw in Chapter 5, the greying of hair frequently accompanies extreme continuous stress.

Tyrosine supplements seems to work best when neurons are firing fast due to stress.[21] They can counteract the effects of stress on mental and physical performance. Several studies have been conducted by the U.S. military in an attempt to find natural agents that would help personnel cope with combat stress. In one experiment in cadets undergoing intense training, tyrosine supplements improved memory and tracking tasks, reduced fatigue and blocked the expected rise in blood pressure due to stress.[22]

I use tyrosine widely in my practice. Clients who are athletes find it enhances endurance. A concert pianist takes tyrosine before performing and says it helps calm her nerves and focus on her performance. People who are chronically depressed or just have generally low moods can benefit from this supplement. One dose on waking, on an empty stomach, can be sufficient to switch one's mood and focus for the rest of the day, though some people find they benefit from a little more in the afternoon. Taking tyrosine too late in the day should be avoided, as it might interfere with sleep.

For working mothers, the busiest, most stressful time of the day is at the end, when they return home from work. The kids are back from school. Dinner has to be made, homework supervised, and kids put to bed. I often suggest a small amount of tyrosine just before they leave work and they tell me that by the time they open the front door in the evening, they find themselves surprisingly relaxed and able to cope more easily with the demands of family life.

Dopamine is involved in speech—we see this in Parkinson's patients who lack sufficient dopamine for fluent verbalization. When you are speaking, your brain uses up dopamine. If I have a client in a leadership position, say, the CEO of a large company, I suggest that he or she take tyrosine supplements every day, then take a little extra just before a major speech or big presentation. Thinking is hard work—it involves neurons firing constantly. If you are a lawyer facing a long day of arguments in court, a teacher who has to hold the attention of a class, a professor giving lectures, you could end up short of tyrosine.

Tyrosine, because it is a natural constituent of food, is considered very safe.[23] Taking it in purified form without the amino acids that accompany it when it is digested from protein-rich food makes it more likely to be used for dopamine synthesis than for making other body proteins. But if you want to experiment with tyrosine supplements, it is probably best to work with a knowledgeable practitioner to make sure you have all the other nutrients involved in dopamine metabolism. If you are taking one of the older antidepressants such as Nardil or Parnate, part of a class called monoamine oxidase inhibitors (MAIOs), tyrosine supplements are not recommended. Because tyrosine is the precursor for melanin (see above), supplements are also not recommended for anyone with a history of the skin cancer melanoma.

B vitamins, brain health and stress

The B vitamins are other cofactors needed for the production of dopamine and serotonin, as are magnesium and vitamin C.

All the B vitamins work together, and need to be taken in balance. For most healthy people, a multivitamin with higher levels of B vitamins than what is contained in the usual drugstore brands can supply these. The possible exception is vitamin B12. Most multivitamins now contain higher levels of folic acid, which is also needed for the manufacture of neurotransmitters, and many foods are also fortified with it. But folic acid and B12 work together, and when you use one, you need the other. B12 deficiency is much more common than previously thought. Higher intakes of folic acid can mask B12 deficiency, which can cause permanent neurological damage. Vegetarians are particularly at risk because B12 is found only in animal protein. Because the B12 in most multivitamins is fairly low compared to the amount of folic acid they contain, there have recently been calls to introduce B12 fortification of foods.[24]

Absorbing B12 from food is tricky. First, acid conditions are needed in the stomach to split the B12 from animal protein. Then it must be paired with the carrier protein intrinsic factor (IF) produced by cells lining the stomach before it is absorbed at the tail end of the small intestine. If B12 reaches this site without being bound to IF, it will not be absorbed. Most people make less stomach acid as they age, due to a deterioration of the lining of the stomach. And many will be taking drugs that totally suppress stomach acid.

Depression has been linked to brain shrinkage, especially in the elderly.[25] A recent study of brain health over a five-year period in healthy individuals aged 61 to 87 used brain scans to measure their brain volume at the beginning and end of the study, and checked their blood levels of vitamin B12 annually. At the end of the study, those who had the highest B12 levels were six times less likely to have brain shrinkage than those with the lowest B12 levels.[26] All the patients in both groups had blood levels of B12 well within normal range. I sometimes recommend a separate B12 supplement as well as a multivitamin with higher levels of B vitamins.

Vitamin C and mood

Despite the fact that vitamin C is needed for the conversion of dopamine to norepinephrine and for the production of serotonin from tryptophan, not a lot of attention has been paid to the effect of vitamin C on mood. But research at the Jewish General Hospital in Montreal in 2011 has confirmed that it, too, must be considered. Researchers randomly allocated patients hospitalized for a variety of conditions to receive either vitamin C (500 mg twice daily) or vitamin D (1000 IU twice daily). The patients' moods were assessed using a standard mood assessment questionnaire and their blood levels of vitamins C and D were checked before and after 5 to 10 days of supplementation.

A startling finding was that 56 percent of incoming patients were vitamin C depleted, while 81 percent showed inadequate vitamin D levels. Those who were given vitamin C not only experienced a clinically significant improvement in mood, but did so in a brief period of time. The vitamin D group reported no change in mood, probably because, as the researchers suspected, it takes up to three months for vitamin D levels to fully respond to supplements, and the study was too short to see an effect.[27]

Stress depletes the water-soluble vitamins C and B. These vitamins are often found together in products marketed as anti-stress supplements. A 2010 study from Newcastle-upon-Tyne in England tested the combined effect of these vitamins on the brain. Healthy males aged 30 to 55 were stressed by being made to do vigorous physical and challenging mental exercises before and after being given high doses of B vitamins, additional calcium, magnesium and zinc, as well as 500 mg of vitamin C. Stress levels were reduced and mood and cognitive performance underwent a big improvement after the men took the vitamin combination—evidence that, even in healthy individuals, proper nutrition can diminish the effects of stress.[28]

Is there a link between poor nutrition and dementia?

Unfortunately, most research is concerned with people who are already suffering from dementia. More long-term studies are needed of healthy older people to see who develops dementia and whether there is a link between dementia and prior nutritional status. Certainly, B12 deficiency is well known to cause one form of dementia, which can be reversed when B12 status is improved.

I worry about people who work their brain hard, but fail to support it nutritionally. The harder you use the brain, the better you have to feed it. I once had a professor referred to me who could no longer handle her teaching and research duties. Her cognitive function was so diminished that she had been asked to take early retirement. She was depressed, confused, and could not concentrate. Her diet was terrible and she claimed to have little interest in food. What shocked me was that this highly educated woman honestly believed that her brain could run all day on coffee and cigarettes. I advised her on diet and supplements, but ultimately was unable to help her—irreversible damage had already occurred.

Even a supply of brain-friendly vitamins and minerals may be of little use if dietary glycemic load is high. Let me explain. The brain needs a steady supply of glucose. If the glycemic load is high, blood sugar will spike, which will provoke insulin production. Blood glucose will then fall and the brain ends up unable to function because it is deprived of sugar once again. A diet high in sweet and starchy foods will ultimately lead to metabolic syndrome, which in turn predisposes one to depression.[29]

To provide the brain with a continuous supply of glucose, keep a watchful eye on your intake of starchy foods, and switch to eating plenty of what I call "smart carbs," meaning vegetables and fruit. This will supply not only the right amount of sugar for good brain function, but also the vital phytochemicals that are needed to protect the brain.

Magnesium and stress

Magnesium is also depleted by stress, and for a very good reason: survival could depend on it. Imagine you are a hunter-gatherer: you live in a calcium-poor and magnesium-rich nutritional environment. Almost everything you eat contains magnesium—fish, eggs, leafy greens, nuts and seeds, even the water you drink. But dairy products are not available, so calcium is scarce.

Here you are, this hunter-gatherer, totally relaxed (magnesium relaxes muscle), when suddenly you face a crisis: a child is drowning, or a sabre-toothed tiger appears. You cannot stay relaxed under these circumstances. The fight-or-flight mechanism must be activated, and you must tense up to run or to stay and fight. Your body releases adrenaline, causing tissue depletion of magnesium. This in turn allows increased muscle tension, especially in skeletal muscles. Where does the excess magnesium go? Out of tissues, through the kidneys and into the bladder. Now you have a bladder full of magnesium, and you want to pee. Remember Hans Selye's laboratory animals? One of the first changes he noticed in them after they were stressed was increased urination.

The same mechanism that once protected our ancestors and allowed them to cope with crises still operates today. Imagine that you are walking down a busy city street, and suddenly a gunshot rings out. Someone near you keels over in a pool of blood. You have just activated the fight-or-flight response. All around, people drop to the ground or run and hide. Tension rises in your muscles; your heart is pounding. Your bladder feels ready to burst and you think you may not make it to a washroom.

A hunter-gatherer would no doubt have rested and recovered his equilibrium once a crisis was over. But in today's world, we go from one stress to the next without sufficient recovery time. The many different types of stress to which we are subjected will deplete magnesium[30] and the resulting magnesium deficiency can manifest itself as depression and anxiety.[31] That is because magnesium is needed both for the manufacture of neurotransmitters inside neurons and their binding to other neurons once released. Rapid recovery from major depression has been reported in some patients after they received magnesium treatment.[32]

The case of the panicked mother

I saw the link clearly between stress, anxiety and magnesium deficiency when a young mother came to my office a few years ago. Her anxiety had increased after the birth of her third child and she was experiencing frequent panic attacks. She was now unable to look after her children, and her husband had to hire someone to care for them. I talked to her about what I thought might underlie her distress and explained that she would most likely need to change her diet and take supplements. Questioning revealed she was constipated, something she'd suffered from since childhood. Our conversation seemed to make her even more anxious, but she agreed to come back to see me again. After leaving my office, she called me from her car paralyzed with fear, in the grip of a terrible panic attack. Her husband had to come to get her.

We worked on her chronic constipation, and she started to improve. I remember her a year later, sitting cross-legged in one of the armchairs in my office, looking so laid-back that one could hardly believe she was the same person who'd come to me

12 months before. She asked, "Do you think all along my problems were due to magnesium deficiency?" Magnesium played a
role, I replied, but it was not the only problem. It was likely that
three closely spaced pregnancies were also part of the problem,
gradually depleting her of other nutrients as well (she had not
taken a multivitamin during pregnancy, only folic acid). She had
always had an anxious disposition, but it worsened after the second baby. The final straw was the third pregnancy.

She needed a comprehensive approach. We worked on her
low vitamin D intake and made sure she was consuming enough
omega-3 fats. Magnesium deficiency had certainly been a contributing factor to her condition, since she had experienced lifelong constipation and may have had a high genetic need for
magnesium—a need that would not have been adequately met
without supplements.

11

Colds and Flu

▼

*If I could live my life over again, I would devote it to proving
that germs seek their natural habitat—diseased tissue—rather
than being the cause of diseased tissue; e.g. mosquitoes seek the
stagnant water, but do not cause the pool to become stagnant.*

— Rudolph Virchow (1821–1902), German pathologist

MANY PEOPLE think of colds or flu the way they think of taxes and death—as something that cannot be avoided. But in my practice, I have seen proof over and over again that people who eat well and supplement their food with well-chosen vitamins and minerals will normally keep sniffles at bay and fight off the flu virus if they are exposed to it. If you dread the Canadian winter because you know you will be coughing and sneezing through it and taking days off work to nurse your sore throat, you need to ask yourself why you are so vulnerable to those common wintertime ills. Could your body be telling you something?

Children and young people have enormous reserves of vitality and recover quickly from illness, but this is less true of the elderly. As we age, our immune system ages too, a process called immunosenescence. Like other aspects of aging, immunosenescence is not inevitable. Paying more attention to nutrition is the key to keeping your immune defences strong.

The immune system: an owner's guide

The immune system is a complex, integrated system of organs and cells. Its job is to distinguish between self (good) and nonself (bad), defending the inside of our bodies against the outside world. It protects us against potentially dangerous micro-organisms including viruses, bacteria, moulds and fungi. It identifies and neutralizes toxins that could otherwise damage tissues. It also plays a key housekeeping role, getting rid of old or impaired cells and the debris that remains when cells are damaged. It attacks cancer cells, killing them or restraining them from runaway growth. Immune responses require the collaboration of many organs and cells: the bone marrow, circulating white blood cells, the spleen and the thymus.

The circulating immune cells, called white cells to distinguish them from the oxygen-carrying red cells, go about their everyday work silently. They produce proteins such as antibodies and interferon. Antibodies neutralize the effect of toxins and start the destruction of microbes. Interferon—a group of proteins—can block the ability of viruses to reproduce. At the same time, it is the release of interferon and other inflammatory molecules that produces a fever and makes your eyes hurt and your muscles ache when you have the flu. Both red and white cells begin life as stem cells in the bone marrow. When you have a routine blood test, the results will mention the number of white cells (leucocytes) per cubic millilitre currently circulating in your blood. It will also give you the numbers of several different subtypes of white cells: lymphocytes, monocytes, neutrophils, basophils and eosinophils, all of which play a role, sometimes many roles, in immune responses.

Some white cells such as monocytes and neutrophils are known as phagocytes. They directly gobble up microbes and foreign particles by a process called phagocytosis (from the Greek *phagein*, to eat or devour). Phagocytes are scavengers that constantly patrol tissues, seeking out the enemy. If they encounter invading viruses or bacteria, they rapidly engulf them, and then set about killing them. They do this by producing rapid bursts of reactive oxygen species (ROS), otherwise known as free radicals.[1] Other white cells, known as granulocytes, contain tiny packages of powerful chemicals that are released during immune responses. One of these—histamine—helps to dilate blood vessels, making it easier for immune cells to gain access to a site of inflammation.

Neutrophils are both granulocytes and phagocytes. Their granules contain chemicals that help dismantle and digest microbes once they have been swallowed up and killed. If your neutrophils are too low, for example, when you are having chemotherapy or radiation, the doctor may be concerned that you are not well equipped to fight infection and will not let you continue treatment until your neutrophil count improves. If they are too high, you may already have an infection, either one that is obvious like a sore throat, or hidden, and causing no obvious symptoms.

Lymphocytes make up about 15 percent of circulating white cells. Two types, the B and T lymphocytes, co-operate to produce a specific and long-lasting response to infection. From their immature state in the bone marrow, T and B lymphocytes (T cells and B cells) move to different organs to mature: B cells to the spleen, while T cells mature in the thymus—an often overlooked little gland in the neck that shrinks as we age. It's the B cells that make antibodies—Y-shaped proteins that bind to the infecting viruses or bacteria, preparing it for phagocytosis. However, B cells can't do this alone. They need the co-operation of T cells. Some of the T cells help the B cells make antibodies, and are called, predictably, T-helper cells. Others shut down the immune response once the invader has been destroyed. These are the T-suppressor cells.

Two different types of immune response

We classify immune responses into two types. The first and most basic is called natural, or innate, immunity. It is activated when we are exposed to a new threat we have never before encountered. The scavenger cells of the immune system use pattern recognition: they can identify novel strings or sequences of amino acids that are common to most microbes, whether they are bacteria, viruses, fungi or moulds. Since they are "non-self," that is, not part of our own tissues, the innate immune system is alerted to get rid of them. Innate immune responses are rapid and don't require a previous exposure to a particular bug to swoop in and attack it.

The acquired or adaptive immune response is more complex. It kicks in when innate immunity has failed to control an infection and its key players are the T and B lymphocytes. While maturing in the spleen, each B cell is genetically programmed to carry a unique receptor or recognition molecule on its surface. Somewhere among the array of circulating B cells there will be one with a receptor that is an exact fit for a molecule on the surface of an infecting virus. Like a key that slips easily into the correct lock, the two bind tightly together. This then triggers what we call clonal expansion—the B cell starts dividing rapidly, making copies or clones of itself. More and more copies of the B cell are made until there is a whole army of cells capable of responding to that particular virus. Then, with the co-operation of T cells, the B cells can begin to make antibodies specific to that virus.

Adaptive immunity takes time to kick in. But it leaves a lasting legacy of memory cells—long-lived lymphocytes that can respond quickly if the same virus or bacteria is encountered again, even years later. This is how immunization works.

What exactly is a cold?

Each winter we are bombarded with articles about "the common cold" and what you can do to minimize your chances of getting one. But what exactly is a cold? It is not a precisely defined disease, but simply a collection of symptoms caused by a range of agents—200 or more viruses, or sometimes, bacteria. Most of the research into the nutritional prevention or treatment of the common cold is unreliable, clouded by the failure to demonstrate that the research subject actually has a virus. Instead, researchers often use a checklist of symptoms. The assumption is that the subject has a cold if he or she has three or more of the following symptoms: sneezing, runny or stuffy nose, cough or sore throat. The problem here is that these signs are similar to the symptoms of allergy, although allergies are not contagious and not responsive to the same treatment. Unless researchers have actually isolated the virus that is supposed to be causing the infection, the research may not mean a lot.

Influenza is caused by a virus and comes on suddenly. While some of the symptoms like nasal congestion and sore throat may be similar to those of colds, flu is usually accompanied by fever, chills, exhaustion, headaches and body aches. Children might experience nausea and vomiting too, but these are not usually symptoms of flu in adults. Sometimes people talk of "stomach flu" when they have a gastrointestinal upset, which may be caused by food poisoning. That is not influenza. Most people are ill with flu for only a few days, but in others the illness can be much more serious, lasting weeks and even requiring hospitalization.

You might wonder why, if we get colds and flu every winter, our immune system doesn't remember previous exposures and react quickly to get them under control. The viruses that cause colds and flu are many and highly unstable; they change or mutate from season to season. The immune response you made to this year's flu may not protect you next year. This is why we are urged to get the flu shot annually, whereas for other viruses, polio, for example, one vaccination may protect for a lifetime.

Can you have flu but no symptoms?

The late 1970s and early 1980s were a time of intense focus on immunology worldwide due to the emergence of AIDS and the human immunodeficiency virus (HIV)—the virus that causes it. Suddenly there was increased public and scientific interest in this amazing protective mechanism we call our immune system, including a flurry of interest in how the immune system protects against colds and flu. These two mundane illnesses are the leading cause of absence from work and doctor visits. They not only disrupt daily life but also represent a considerable economic burden to businesses and health services.[2] If the transmission of colds and flu from person to person over the winter months could be contained, everyone would benefit.

Numerous research projects were undertaken in the 1980s, including one I found particularly revealing. This British study looked at flu transmission over the course of one winter among family members. Researchers observed 53 households, 26 of which eventually succumbed to the virus. The findings were surprising. Of 37 people who could be shown to have the virus,

12 had no flu-like symptoms—they were not ill at all.[3] The researchers made sure by swabbing the participants' noses that patients actually did have the virus, and that everyone in the same household had the same strain.

In a more recent study (2010) of viral shedding and flu transmission in Hong Kong, researchers found that 14 percent of infected household contacts had no symptoms of flu, even though they were shedding the virus.[4] And this is a consistent finding: you can have the flu, or at least the virus that is causing mayhem all around you, and yet be unaware that you have it. Such studies lead us to ask the following question: If you can have a virus, but appear to be healthy and symptom free, then what exactly causes the symptoms?

For the answer to that question we have to go back and revisit how the immune system reacts when exposed to a virus. As we have seen, phagocytes kill viruses by generating a barrage of reactive oxygen species (ROS) or free radicals.[5] However, like a blunderbuss that scatters shot in all directions, the free radicals are not precisely targeted: as well as killing the virus they damage surrounding tissue, including the immune cells themselves.[6] It is the intensity of this response that causes the symptoms of colds and flu—the sore throat and aching joints. And the more ROS damage to your immune cells, the harder you have to struggle to control the virus, and the longer those symptoms linger.

Alas, researchers who study how flu is passed from one person to another seem to have very little interest in individuals who have been exposed to the virus, carry that virus, yet have no symptoms. I believe this is a missed opportunity because these are the people we can learn from. How do they keep the virus under control and avoid the tissue damage experienced by other family members? Are they better nourished? Do they have higher circulating levels of antioxidants? Those are the right questions to ask.

The well-fed immune system

We have known for decades that an effective immune response depends on how well immune cells are fed.[7] An inadequate supply of key nutrients, including the B vitamins, vitamin C, zinc and the essential fats, especially omega-3 fatty acids, compromises the ability to fight infections. The opposite is also true: supplementing with key nutrients that the immune system particularly depends on can enhance immune function.[8] In the introduction to this book I recounted how I became aware of the nutritional requirements of the immune system, and used that knowledge to protect my family from colds and flu.

The immune system is a nutritional barometer, a highly sensitive indicator of how well nourished we are. When I develop a program for clients who regularly catch colds I expect their incidence of colds to diminish. I ask new patients how many colds they get in winter and how long they last. I keep a record of their answers and, after they have been on supplements for a while, I repeat the question. It is one of the ways I monitor how well clients are doing on supplements. They usually report a reduction in the number of colds they get, as well as their severity and duration.

I keep such records because I want to optimize their nutrition. If people regularly get colds, it alerts me to the fact that their nutrition is somehow falling short. Those who do eat well and take the appropriate supplements, in my experience, do not get colds or flu, or at least the symptoms that accompany them.

Antioxidants and immunity

Our tissues are protected from free radical damage by antioxidants—both vitamins A, C and E, and the minerals selenium, manganese and zinc. Phytochemicals—the colourful pigments of vegetables and fruit—are also antioxidants. We make a number of important antioxidant molecules ourselves, such as glutathione, uric acid, melatonin and coenzyme Q10, that is, if we have the right starting materials. Remember that tyrosine is the basic building block for coenzyme Q10, and is depleted by stress, as are the B vitamins and magnesium.

All these antioxidants work in different parts of our cells, and in different parts of the body. For example, fat-soluble vitamin E is important in protecting the membranes of cells, whereas vitamin C, which is water soluble, is active inside cells protecting the cell's nucleus and the mitochondria. Melatonin is active in protecting cells both internally and externally. It also stimulates the production of other natural antioxidants such as glutathione.[9] Lutein, one of the carotenoids, seems particularly important in protecting the eyes from free radical damage, whereas another carotenoid, lycopene, safeguards the health of the prostate. The important thing about antioxidants is their synergy: they work together, and enhance each other.

This is why taking large doses of single antioxidants—vitamin C, for example—is less effective than taking smaller doses of a wide range of antioxidants. Just as in soccer you need to build a strong team instead of relying on a single star player, so with antioxidants. Vitamin C is more effective if it is taken with vitamin E and selenium,[10] and also works synergistically with phytochemicals in vegetables and fruits.[11] Vegetables like beets, broccoli and red peppers have a high antioxidant capacity when tested in the laboratory.[12]

Consuming a wide range of antioxidants from both supplements and vegetables and fruits gets around one potential problem with antioxidants: in keeping down free radicals they can become mild free radicals themselves. Although these milder free radicals cause less tissue damage than the free radicals generated by activated immune cells, over the long term they are not entirely benign. Building a team of antioxidants protects against possible long-term harm. When taken as a team they recycle each other from their free radical or pro-oxidant form back again into antioxidants.

A good multivitamin, as described in Part 3, will provide a mixture of antioxidants, although you may need to supplement with extra vitamin C and E. And don't forget to load up your plate with colourful vegetables and fruits.

Vitamin C and the common cold

Many people swear that taking C when they feel on the verge of getting a cold keeps colds at bay. Vitamin C is an important antioxidant vitamin, and one that is deficient in a surprisingly large portion of the population. However, doctors are often skeptical that taking extra vitamin C achieves anything more than a placebo effect (a beneficial effect claimed by a patient after a fake or inactive treatment).

Most members of the animal kingdom can make their own vitamin C, using glucose as the starting material. Primates, humans included, have lost the ability to convert glucose into vitamin C because in primates, one of the four genes needed for the conversion is inactive. We therefore depend, like apes and monkeys, on our diets to obtain this essential nutrient. Guinea pigs, some fruit bats and a few birds are also incapable of making their own vitamin C, but most other species are efficient vitamin C factories, churning it out every day, particularly when stressed.

Animals that make their own vitamin C will make a large amount per kilogram of body weight compared to what is considered an appropriate daily intake for humans. A goat weighing 70 kg (150 lbs)—as heavy as an adult woman—will make more than 2 gm of vitamin C a day. Under stress, the same goat will increase its output from 2 grams to about 13 grams, more than a sixfold increase. Stress a rabbit, and it will make 25 times the vitamin C it makes when not stressed.[13] Indeed, rodents including rats and mice that can make vitamin C as needed are not suitable lab animals for cold and flu research since it is all but impossible to give them infections in the laboratory.

The daily allowance of vitamin C recommended by the U.S. Institute of Medicine and endorsed by Health Canada is 75 mg for adult females and 90 mg for adult males, regardless of height or weight. For a 100 kg (220 pound) man, that represents approximately 1.3 mg per kilogram of body weight daily. I believe that this greatly underestimates the amount of vitamin C such a person needs, particularly under stress. If we look at what we know about the daily needs of animals who cannot synthesize vitamin C, we find that a guinea pig kept as a pet requires a daily dose of 10 to 40 mg per kilogram body weight. That is 8 to 30 times higher than the dose considered sufficient for our 100 kilogram man. Monkeys in the wild consume daily intakes of vitamin C that are 10 to 20 times higher than our current RDA for men and women.[14]

A few years ago, the *Cochrane Review*, a respected source of scientific information, reviewed every research study on vitamin C and the common cold done since 1943 that used doses of 200 mg or more per day. The authors of the review wanted to see if they could come to a general conclusion about the impact of vitamin C supplements on the common cold.[15] The studies they included varied widely in their doses and in the duration of treatment. Some gave a single dose of the vitamin after a cold had started, whereas others continued to give patients vitamin C for days or weeks. Some studies used 200 mg, while others gave up to 2 grams a day, ten times as much. This diversity of approach presents a problem, as the effect of larger doses taken over a longer time may be obscured by studies using ineffective smaller amounts or shorter treatment periods.

The review found a consistent reduction in the duration of colds and the severity of symptoms in both adults and children at all doses studied. But there was no difference in the incidence of colds except in individuals under stress, either from exposure to extreme cold (skiers or soldiers exercising in Arctic conditions), or from heavy exercise (marathon runners). In these situations doses between 500 to 2000 mg did reduce the number of colds, as well as their duration and severity.

Despite these positive findings, the authors of the review insisted that the routine use of vitamin C could not be recommended, and this conclusion was widely reported in the media. "Vitamin C useless for preventing or treating colds," trumpeted the news agency Reuters at the time, a theme quickly picked up by the rest of the media. Media outlets did generally report that for people exposed to extreme physical exercise or extremely cold temperatures extra vitamin C might be useful, but concluded, as did the researchers, that this was the *only* type of stress where extra vitamin C would be of benefit.

Stress, as we have seen, includes not only physical but also medical (illness, surgery) and psychological stress. We can measure stress in humans by checking blood levels of cortisol, a hormone discussed earlier that rises when we are stressed. Ongoing high levels of cortisol are damaging to the body, raising our blood pressure and blood glucose. It also handicaps the immune system, making it less effective in fighting off infection. Studies have shown that everyday workplace stress, the kind most of us experience, increases blood cortisol levels.[16] One study exposed 120 healthy young adults to psychological stress consisting of mental arithmetic and public-speaking exercises. Half of them were given 3 grams of sustained-release vitamin C daily for 14 days, and the other half took a placebo. The researchers then examined the response of both groups.

Those who took the extra vitamin C felt less stressed, as measured by standard stress-response questionnaires, and also had lower blood pressure and cortisol responses.[17] This suggests that to prevent colds students and anyone who experiences workplace stress would also benefit from daily doses of vitamin C comparable to those given to the skiers and runners.

Vitamin D and immunity

When people say to me, "I think I'm pretty healthy," I always ask, How many colds do you get? "Oh, just the usual three or four in the winter," they reply. In my opinion, this is hardly a sign of robust good health. The first thing I want to know is whether they are taking vitamin D, and if so, are they taking enough.

Low wintertime stores of vitamin D, which are more common the farther north we live, increase our susceptibility to colds and flu. We get colds and flu mainly in winter because vitamin D is critical for activating innate immunity, the rapid response arm of our immune system that helps us deal with new infectious agents. Vitamin D is needed to activate T cells before they can do battle with pathogens. With too little vitamin D, the T cells remain sleepily unaware that an invasion of viruses has taken place.[18]

A Japanese study published in 2010 gave children 1200 IU of vitamin D a day in winter, while giving none to the control group. The researchers not only saw a reduction in the incidence of flu in those taking vitamin D, but also found that children with asthma did not need to use their puffers as often. If you have asthma and get flu, it can cause a flare-up of asthma symptoms that can be serious. Giving extra D to these children appeared to protect against such flare-ups.[19] A recent study in the United Kingdom (2011) in patients over age 45 found that the higher the blood levels of 25-hydroxy vitamin D, the body's storage form of vitamin D, the fewer upper respiratory tract infections occurred and the better the health of the lungs.[20] Other researchers have shown that blood levels of 25-hydroxy D of 95 nmol/L or higher can decrease the likelihood of wintertime lung infections by 50 percent.[21]

Zinc lozenges and colds: little and often

There has been a keen interest in recent years in using zinc lozenges, which are meant to be slowly dissolved in the mouth, to treat colds and sore throats. The nose and mouth are the areas of the body where airborne viruses first enter, and where the cold viruses mostly live and grow. Zinc deficiency makes us more susceptible to infection; it causes the thymus gland to shrink and the T cells that are maturing there to die.

The interest in using zinc lozenges for colds and flu apparently began with the accidental observation by researchers that a cold in a three-year-old with leukemia rapidly disappeared when she sucked a zinc pill she was given to prepare her for chemotherapy, instead of just swallowing it.[22] Clinical trials were then set up to see if this effect could be reproduced in other patients.

The benefits of zinc lozenges have been disputed in recent years. Some studies showed they were helpful, but others did not. However, a 2011 systematic review of all the controlled trials of zinc lozenges for the common cold carried out since 1984 explains why the results of studies have been so mixed: the doses used in some studies were too low. A total daily dose of 75 mg of zinc, taken as lozenges, does appear to shorten the duration of the common cold, but lower doses are not generally effective.[23]

As we age, absorption of zinc becomes more difficult. Inflammation depletes zinc, further reducing its circulating blood level. You use up zinc when you're fighting a cold.[24] One sign of this depletion is that our sense of smell and taste changes.[25] The relationship between zinc deficiency, taste and smell was first noticed in the 1960s in Egypt, in an area of the country where the soil was lacking in zinc. Some of the people who lived there had no sense of smell and could not taste food. Chances are you have experienced zinc deficiency. Think about how tasteless food becomes during and right after a bad cold, and how difficult it is to smell anything.

I have always been very respectful of zinc. Handle it with care. Too little zinc and the immune system will underperform, but take more than you need and you may suppress immunity. Not that taking excess zinc will have serious consequences, but it is unlikely to achieve the desired effect of nipping a cold in the bud. One sign of excess zinc is a metallic taste in the mouth.

There are low-dose lozenges of about 8 to 10 mg on the market and these are the ones I recommend. Some of them are flavoured with licorice or black currant, and when you take them, they taste pleasant enough at first. If after a while the lozenges start to taste unpleasant and heavily metallic, that is your clue that you now have taken sufficient zinc.

That is how I instruct people to take zinc: in small regular doses throughout the day, then to stop if the taste changes. Limit daily intake to no more than 80 mg, unless advised otherwise by your doctor, and only when you have a cold. Some people get enough zinc in a multivitamin, but others may need more. Food sources include pumpkin seeds, sunflower seeds, and best of all, oysters. Keep a tin of smoked oysters in the pantry and eat them when you have a cold coming on. Zinc from this food source is the most bioavailable and quickest to be absorbed.

Probiotics and the immune system

In our gastrointestinal tracts we carry an estimated 2 to 4 pounds of micro-organisms, a complex mix of beneficial and disease-causing microbes (pathogens) that we call our intestinal micro-flora. In the healthy gastrointestinal system the balance of good to bad microbes should ideally be 85 percent to 15 percent. The good bacteria, known as probiotics, contribute to our health by helping digestion, manufacturing B vitamins and vitamin K, and protecting us against infection. They help to keep bad micro-organisms from overgrowing by preventing them from binding to our tissues. When the balance of good and bad bacteria is altered, as it is when we take antibiotics, which indiscriminately kill both good and bad bacteria, the result can be an overgrowth of harmful bacteria and possibly of yeasts like Candida.

At the start of the twentieth century, Russian scientist and Nobel laureate Élie Metchnikoff was the first to suggest that to stay healthy we needed to maintain high levels of good bacteria in our gastrointestinal tract. In particular, he noted that in southeastern Europe, where fermented foods such as yogurt and kefir were consumed every day, people were healthier and lived longer. Modern research shows that taking probiotics, found in fresh yogurt, can aid immunity. Alternatively, we can take probiotics in capsules. These usually contain a range of different species, including *Lactobacillus acidophilus* and *Lactobacillus bulgaricus*, *Bifidobacteria* and *Streptococcus thermophilus*. Yogurts vary widely in quality, but with capsules, we know exactly how much probiotic support we are getting.

In a study done in 2010, a daily probiotic supplement was given to a group of 272 volunteers, while a control group received a placebo. The result was a 12 percent reduction of colds in the subjects who took lactobacillus. In the placebo group, 67 percent came down with cold symptoms compared with 55 percent of the group taking probiotics. That might seem like a small effect, but maintaining health is often a matter of combining many small protective measures.

I sometimes tell clients to take a probiotic capsule, open it and put it in about an inch of water to use as a mouth rinse just before bed, swishing it around their mouth after brushing their teeth, and then swallowing it. The immune system is weakest overnight and if we have a cold, we feel worse then. Supplements of probiotics are entirely safe since they consist of bacteria present in a normal, healthy digestive system.

Other foods that support the immune system

You may find your appetite is reduced as you age, and you want nothing more to eat than a cookie or a piece of toast and a cup of tea. But if you turn your back on protein-rich foods like fish and chicken, the health of your thymus will be severely compromised. Remember, we do not store protein and we show signs of protein malnutrition between one and three days after we stop eating it. When the body is deprived of protein the thymus gland shrinks, and there is a massive die-off of the T cells maturing in it. This will compromise future immunity and prematurely age the immune system.[26] In fact, a decreased desire for protein, often seen in the elderly, is another of the signs of zinc deficiency, which also has an impact on the health of the thymus. Zinc is required for protein digestion, and giving zinc supplements to patients who are avoiding protein-rich foods normalizes their appetite for it.[27]

Some people enjoy a fruit smoothie for breakfast. A smoothie should contain protein as well as fruits or vegetables. Whey protein supplements, but not other forms of protein like soy or hemp, contain lactoferrin, which can clump bacteria thus preventing them from binding to our tissues. Remember the phytochemicals found in herbs, spices, fruit and vegetables? They are natural antivirals, antifungals and antibiotics and if they are abundant in our diet give us an edge in fighting colds and flu.

Green tea contains the powerful antioxidant epigallocate-chin gallate (EGCG), and an extract of green tea has been shown to reduce the symptoms of colds and flu. Two or three cups of green tea a day is a pleasant and easy way to support immunity. Oil of oregano, available at health food stores, is another powerful anti-infectious agent, and in common with all natural antibiotics, it is also antiviral and antifungal. A few drops of oregano oil on the tongue at the first sign of a runny nose or sore throat may prevent a full-blown cold.

The gift of garlic

Garlic is as strong an antibiotic in the laboratory as penicillin or erythromycin and, like oil of oregano, it is also antifungal, antiviral, and even acts as an antihistamine.[28] As yet, no drug on the market does all those things. Garlic manufactures this cornucopia of natural pharmaceuticals to protect itself against the mass of infectious agents present in the soil in which it is growing, and when we eat garlic we can harness this plant chemistry to protect our own tissues.

It is important to know how to use garlic. The anti-infective agents in garlic such as allicin and alliin are produced only after the garlic is crushed or chopped and left in the air for five minutes or so. If you crush garlic straight into a hot frying pan little production of anti-infective agents will take place, since the enzymes needed to make them are destroyed by heat or acid conditions. Mince or crush garlic and leave it for five minutes before cooking with it or adding it to acidic salad dressings.

To treat a cold, crush four or five cloves of garlic into a small dish and add a little liquid honey to bind it into a paste. At the start of symptoms, take a small quantity of this paste, about enough to cover the nail of your baby finger. Place it on the back of your tongue and wash it down with a whole glass of water. The water is important because garlic can burn the esophagus if it lingers. The cold symptoms—a runny nose or watering eyes— will disappear within five or ten minutes, but return again, maybe in an hour or two. When they come back, take another dose of the garlic paste. You will find that as the garlic works its magic, the symptoms stay away for longer and longer periods between doses until eventually they are gone.

I had a friend who had been in poor health for some time, suffering from fibromyalgia. She was getting frequent colds even during the summer. She called me from her cottage and said, "I'm going to get another one of those awful summer colds. I feel terrible." I told her to make a garlic paste and take it as I have just described. Four days later, she left me a message. She said: "I think you might be a white witch. I can't believe how my cold just disappeared. That has never happened before." I assured her that I was no witch and that the garlic could take all the credit.

12

Weight Gain and Obesity

▼

"How long does getting thin take?" asked Pooh anxiously.
"About a week, I should think."

— from *Winnie the Pooh* by A.A. Milne (1882–1956)

M OST PEOPLE find themselves struggling to keep weight off as they age. The reasons for this are complex. The middle years represent a time of greater financial security, when people can afford to be more self-indulgent. They add wine to meals, which they perhaps conclude with a sugary dessert. They eat out more frequently. Despite attempts from health authorities to control them, portion sizes at chain restaurants in North America are increasing. A small order of McDonald's french fries comes in at 230 calories, but move to a large size and it will add 500 calories to your day's intake.

Our busy lives may also leave less time for exercise, and if we carry on consuming the same number of calories, over time extra pounds will accumulate. A gain of just one pound annually after the age of 45 will result in 20 extra pounds by the time we are ready for our first pension cheque. According to Statistics Canada, from the mid 1970s to 1990 there was little change in the caloric intake of Canadians. However, from 1991 to 2002, Canadians increased their daily consumption by a whopping 430 calories per person.[1] Most of the increase has been in the form of carbohydrates such as pasta, specialty breads, cereal- or potato-based snacks and soft drinks, all with a high glycemic index. In parallel with this jump in calorie consumption, the number of overweight and obese individuals has risen rapidly. In 2009, only 38 percent of Canadian adults were at a healthy weight, 37 percent were overweight and 24 percent were obese, with a higher proportion of men than women in the overweight category.[2]

Next to smoking, obesity is the most common cause of poor health, not only in older adults but in a significant percentage of younger people. Excess weight stresses all the organs of the body and paves the way for an array of chronic health problems, including type 2 diabetes, osteoarthritis, some cancers, cardio-vascular disease and stroke—the diseases of old age we would all like to avoid.[3]

Measuring the risk

Obesity is defined using the body mass index (BMI), a slightly more complicated formula for measuring body fat than simply looking at how much you weigh relative to height. Your BMI is your weight in pounds multiplied by 703 and divided by your height in inches squared. You can check your BMI on any of the many websites that have a BMI calculator. The BMI is divided into six categories according to the risk of health problems. A score between 18.5 and 24.9 is considered normal, the range in which people have a minimum risk of health problems. You are overweight if your BMI is in the 25 to 30 range. Over 30 you are considered obese. Obesity itself has three categories. A BMI between 30 and 34.9 puts you in Class 1; 35 and 39.9 is

Class 2; and over 40 is Obese Class 3. As BMI goes up through these rankings, the risk of disease increases from high, to very high, to extremely high.

Being underweight (BMI less than 18.5) is also a health risk, but only if it is due to an eating disorder or another serious health problem such as cancer. Some people appear to be lucky. They eat what they like and never gain weight. Their metabolic rate—the energy used to perform vital body functions while at rest—is higher than average, and this is probably genetically programmed.

As well as BMI, body shape can predict disease risk. If you are overweight, ask yourself if you are apple- or pear-shaped. Do you carry extra pounds around your waist or your hips? Fat that lies around the waist is called visceral fat, whereas fat that lies just under your skin—the type you can pinch—is subcutaneous fat. Visceral fat is harder to see since it is deposited in the abdominal cavity and around the liver, heart and other organs rather than on thighs and buttocks. It is visceral fat that carries the greater risk of diabetes, heart disease and other chronic conditions.[4] Middle-age spread should be avoided if you want to stay healthy. Measure your waist and hips. You are an apple if your waist circumference is larger than your hips.

Waist measurement alone is a reliable way of estimating the amount of visceral fat we carry, and whether it is likely to increase the risk of chronic disease. Men with a generally thin body type can have a large waist or beer belly; a spreading waistline is also common in postmenopausal women. For most men, a waist measurement below 40 inches puts them in the safe zone. For women, waist measurement should be 35 inches or less. For people of Asian, East Indian, or Central and South American background, a healthy waist measurement is smaller—under 35 inches for men and 32 inches for women. Waist circumference is a reliable indicator of disease risk only for those under the age of 65.

Why is visceral fat so bad?

The old idea that fat cells are just passive storage sites for excess calories has been superseded. We now know that fat cells are busy little hormone factories producing many different chemicals that regulate metabolism and affect the health of every part of the body, from heart to liver to brain. In a normal-weight person these hormones are helpful—they control appetite so that we do not overeat, help burn stored fat for energy and regulate insulin secretion to control blood sugar. But in excess, such fat cells are harmful. While subcutaneous fat may not be entirely innocent, it appears that visceral fat cells carry the greatest threat to health. The proteins they secrete constrict blood vessels, increasing blood pressure, insulin resistance and inflammation. The more visceral fat you have, the more inflammation is being produced in you body.

Visceral fat increases LDL cholesterol (the bad stuff) and lowers beneficial HDL cholesterol. After menopause, when the ovaries no longer manufacture estrogen, fat cells take over its production. Excess visceral fat produces an excess of estrogen, as well as other molecules known to increase the risk of cancer, such as insulin-like growth factors (IGF-1). This is one reason that overweight older women are at increased risk of postmenopausal breast cancer.[5] A high waist-to-hip ratio also increases the risk of dementia, especially in those over 65.[6]

Clearly we need to make every effort to try to prevent the accumulation of excess visceral fat, and to reduce it if we are overweight. The good news is that visceral fat is highly responsive to both diet and the right type of exercise. A Danish study tracked changes in waist measurements of 20,000 men and 20,000 women as well as the types and amounts of food they ate over a five-year period. More important than the total calories eaten was the source of those calories. A higher intake of calories from protein and from fruits and vegetables was associated with smaller increases in waist size.[7] Heftier waist sizes correlated with higher intakes of refined grains, white breads, pastas, rice, potatoes and sugar, as well as vegetable fat such as corn oils and margarine.

Strategies for weight loss

You will look in vain for a miracle diet plan in this chapter. What I try to do with my overweight clients is to help them understand that, first and foremost, the food they eat during any diet must be healthful and that weight loss alone should never be the goal. You could lose weight on a candy bar diet, provided it cut calories, but it will hardly improve your health. That said, many people eat good food, but too much of it, so that the first thing to do is reduce excess calories, especially from snacking. I was shocked to learn that many people today consume more calories between meals than at meals. Cutting out excess snacks is a good start.

But if you have a lot of weight to lose, the benefits of simply cutting calories may be exaggerated. The usual rule of thumb, used by many weight-loss programs, is that if you cut 500 calories from your current daily intake you will lose a pound of body weight every week. If this were true, a man weighing 300 pounds would disappear altogether in about six years.[8] What happens is that metabolism slows down as we lose weight, and eventually plateaus. Weight loss stops.

All about balance

Calories do count, but as mentioned above, the source of those calories matters even more. During weight loss diets the balance between the carbohydrates and protein in your diet will affect not just the amount of weight but also where you lose it. In one study, researchers compared two different diets: a carbohydrate-heavy diet with a protein-rich diet. The caloric content for both diets was identical. Both groups lost weight, but researchers found that the high-protein diet was more satisfying and improved weight loss. And more body fat was lost on the high-protein diet, whereas more muscle was lost on the higher-carbohydrate diet.

Carbohydrates and protein have different effects on appetite. Protein increases satiation—the feeling of satisfaction and fullness we feel after eating—because it takes longer to digest. It thus helps to curb appetite. Since it takes more energy to process protein, your metabolism increases. On the other hand, a diet rich in starchy carbohydrates such as bread, potatoes, breakfast cereals, cookies and desserts can stimulate appetite. Sweet and starchy foods trigger high blood sugar after being consumed. As we have seen in previous chapters, a spike in blood glucose is followed by high insulin levels. Insulin removes glucose from the blood into storage cells. The effect of this is twofold: first, the sugar is stored as fat, increasing potential weight gain; second, blood sugar drops, which has consequences for the brain.

The brain depends on a constant influx of sugar to function and if blood sugar falls, the brain will signal that it needs feeding. "Eat something," the brain will dictate. "Go get me a candy bar, another slice of toast, a cookie. Just get me some sugar." Of course, if we do eat more sugar or starch, starch being sugar in disguise, the cycle will repeat itself. When the brain is running low on glucose, good judgment flies out the window. We specifically crave high-calorie foods and are less likely to turn to fruit, for example. As our brain glucose levels drop, so does our impulse control.[9]

The secret to ending cravings for high-calorie foods is to make sure the brain never runs out of glucose. This can be achieved by eating low-glycemic carbohydrates, vegetables and fruits; they break down gradually, and provide the steady input of sugar the brain needs. At the same time, they provide health-giving phytochemicals. Eat the vegetables and fruits in their entirety, lightly cooked or raw. When we juice fruits and vegetables we effectively burst open the cells releasing the sugar inside. Fruit juice, even when it is home-squeezed, will trigger too fast a rise in blood sugar and should be avoided. Vegetable juice is acceptable, especially if it is made from vegetables that grow above ground, since it tends to be lower in calories and sugars.

Similarly, whole grains that are pulverized or ground into fine particles are quickly digested into glucose. Grains, therefore, should be consumed in their natural state or only minimally processed. A wheat berry salad, for which grains of wheat are cooked whole, is sustaining because it pushes up blood sugar more slowly than a slice of bread made from finely ground flour, even if the flour is whole wheat. Try taking a slice of your usual whole wheat bread and squeezing it. If you can easily roll it into a sticky ball, then it is bad for you. Regardless of what good ingredients went into making it, the bread will quickly turn into sugar once you eat it.

When my clients learn to eat a low-glycemic load consistently, they are astonished that their cravings for sweet, starchy foods disappear. Recently a young man brought his father, whose eating habits the younger man was trying to improve, to see me. The young man said he had so reformed his own diet over the last two or three years that lettuce now tasted sweet to him. Of course, there is sweetness in lettuce; it's just that most of us cannot taste it. As you adapt to a natural diet based on minimally processed food, your taste buds become more sensitive to the natural sugars in food. This in turn can reduce your craving for sugar. When you can taste the natural sugar in milk, why would you need to add sugar to your coffee?

At your annual physical, you will usually have a test to determine if your blood sugar is normal. Your doctor may also check your long-term control of blood sugar by testing hemoglobin

A1c (HbA1c). Whereas a random blood sugar test is a snapshot of blood sugar control on the day your blood sample was taken, HbA1c provides a bigger picture and is a measure of whether blood sugar has been properly controlled during the previous three months—less of a snapshot and more like a movie. If your blood test results indicate your HbA1c is above the top limit of normal, your blood sugar has not been well controlled.

Insulin resistance and metabolic syndrome

For insulin to remove glucose from blood and facilitate its storage in cells, it must first attach to its own specific receptor on the cells, the insulin receptor. Over time, unrelenting spikes of insulin cause cells to become desensitized to it; they become, in other words, insulin resistant. They do this by reducing the number of surface receptors that can bind insulin. Once insulin receptors start to disappear, you are in trouble: now when you eat sweet or starchy food, insulin has difficulty keeping blood sugar in check. You are insulin resistant if you have high insulin *and* high blood sugar at the same time. The pancreas responds to this situation by pumping out more and more insulin. Eventually the insulin-producing cells become exhausted, and then you are diabetic. Insulin resistance is associated with excess visceral fat, but whether insulin resistance causes this is unclear. What is clear is that losing weight, particularly around the belly, will reduce both visceral fat and insulin resistance.[10]

What makes insulin resistance such a dangerous condition is that insulin is our storage hormone not only for sugar; it is required to store all nutrients in all the organs, including amino acids and minerals such as potassium, magnesium and phosphorus. Insulin resistance can therefore have devastating effects on many body tissues. Not only is it a risk factor for type 2 diabetes, it also predisposes us to Alzheimer's disease (AD) and dementia. AD is sometimes referred to as diabetes of the brain because the ability of the brain to use glucose is compromised when cells cannot respond to insulin, so that brain cells can literally starve.

Insulin resistance may be part of metabolic syndrome, also known as syndrome X. Metabolic syndrome is actually a collection of conditions in the same individual. If you have a high waist circumference, elevated cholesterol and blood sugar levels, plus high blood pressure, you have metabolic syndrome. Metabolic syndrome is a gateway disease, paving the way for the development of all chronic diseases. It is sobering to learn that, according to recent estimates, one in five Canadian adults has metabolic syndrome, and the incidence almost doubles in those between 70 and 79.[11]

Not all sugars are created equal

Table sugar is a disaccharide, meaning that it is composed of two sugars: one molecule of glucose and one of fructose. Glucose will trigger the release of insulin, but fructose will not—it is largely metabolized by the liver. For this reason, pure fructose has been considered a safer sugar for diabetics. Lately we are hearing a lot about fructose because cheap, high-fructose corn syrup (HFCS) has become the food industry's sweetener of choice. Despite its name, HFCS is only 55 percent fructose; the rest is glucose. Like sucrose, HFCS will therefore stimulate insulin release. Fructose occurs naturally in vegetables and fruits, and is not in and of itself unhealthy. The HFCS in processed food has, however, pushed the general intake of fructose to extremely high levels. It has been estimated that the hunter-gatherer diet would have included about 15 grams of fructose per day, from vegetables and fruit. Today, poor diets heavy in processed foods may provide as much as 70 to 75 grams of fructose daily.

When high amounts of fructose enter the liver, the liver converts part of it into a saturated fat called palmitate, which increases the risk of heart disease by causing a rise in triglycerides and LDL cholesterol. Fructose is also thought to be the main cause of fatty liver disease. Recall that Morgan Spurlock, the documentary filmmaker who ate fast food exclusively for a month, had the liver of an alcoholic by the end of his experiment. He was drinking milk shakes and pop daily and developed a condition called NASH (nonalcoholic steatohepatitis). NASH is becoming more common in young people who are hooked on fast food. It has even been found in China, where children are drinking more pop and eating hamburgers on top of their traditional diet. Overweight 10- and 11-year-olds there may eventually be candidates for liver transplants at an early age. Fructose presents no problem in small amounts. It becomes a danger only in large quantities that overwhelm the liver.

What about sugar substitutes? Can they help us control weight?

Unfortunately, the answer is no, and they may even make things worse. Both animal and human studies show that a diet containing artificially sweetened drinks often leads to more calories being consumed later on in the day. When we consume glucose, we instinctively reduce subsequent calorie intake to compensate. However, when we consume novel chemicals that taste sweet but have no calories, that instinctive brake on overconsumption stops working. A famous cardiovascular study of several generations of residents of Framingham, Massachusetts, that began in 1948 and is still going on, has found that drinking diet soda was more strongly linked to metabolic syndrome than the consumption of regular soda.[12]

At Purdue University, West Lafayette, Indiana, a group of researchers has been trying to understand the relationship between zero calorie sweeteners and weight control. They found that when they fed rats low-fat yogurt sweetened with an artificial sweetener, the rats ate more and gained more weight than did a second group of rats that were fed yogurt sweetened with sugar. The second group appeared to compensate for the extra calories by eating less of the freely available laboratory chow.[13] Artificial sweeteners may not, therefore, aid weight loss and may, in fact, have the opposite effect. Most zero-calorie sweeteners are man-made chemicals, and are best avoided for that reason. Consumed over long periods, they could be toxic.[14]

Natural sweeteners that have no calories do exist. One of them is stevia, a very sweet leaf that has been used for centuries in both South America and China. I sometimes recommend stevia for those who are trying to wean themselves off sugar. Stevia appears to have many health benefits, such as helping to control blood sugar and blood pressure. It may also have anti-inflammatory, anti-tumour, anti-diarrheal, and immunity-enhancing properties.[15] But like other zero-calorie sweeteners, stevia, if consumed regularly, could encourage overeating.[16]

Other factors that affect appetite

In the regulation of appetite, one important and often overlooked factor is a sound night's sleep. While we sleep, hormones that control glucose metabolism and regulate appetite are set for the following day. The best researched of these hormones are leptin and ghrelin.[17] High levels of circulating leptin signal to the brain that the body has sufficient energy, and appetite can now be suppressed. Low levels signal that energy expenditure should decrease and appetite increase. If we do not get enough sleep to generate the required leptin, the resulting low levels of this hormone can turn us into supersnacking couch potatoes the next day. Similarly, ghrelin, a hormone produced by cells in the stomach, plays a role in stimulating appetite, as well as promoting effective storage of food consumed. The actions of both these hormones, when they are disturbed by inadequate sleep, thus promote weight gain.

Skipping meals is another factor in weight gain. Many people who take great care planning dinner put almost no thought into breakfast and lunch, or pass on one or another of those meals. Breakfast skipping not only influences our performance at work and school, but leads to increased appetite and, over time, weight gain. Regular breakfast consumption, on the other hand, is associated with better school performance in children,[18] particularly if the breakfast is high in protein. When adolescents who had been skipping breakfast were divided into three groups, with one group asked to eat a high-protein breakfast (one containing 50 grams of protein), the second a lower-protein breakfast (18 grams), and the third to carry on as before skipping breakfast, the group that ate the high-protein breakfast experienced reduced appetite and calorie intake later in the day, unlike the group that ate a lower-protein breakfast or no breakfast at all.[19] In older adults, eating irregularly is one of several risk factors for insulin resistance and metabolic syndrome.[20]

The volume of food we consume also has an effect on satiety and appetite later in the day. In one study, three groups of men were given yogurt shakes 30 minutes before lunch. All the shakes contained the same nutrients and the same calories but were whipped up to have different volumes. The men were given either 300 mL, 450 mL or 600 mL shakes and were then tested to see how full they felt, how satisfied, and how hungry they still were. The findings: the men felt much more satisfied after the highest-volume drinks, though they contained no more calories than the smallest shake; and the higher the volume of their shake, the fewer the calories they subsequently ate at lunch, though they were permitted to eat as much as they liked.[21]

An easy way to create the sensation of bulk is to drink a large glass of water about 20 minutes before a meal. It will fill you up a bit and you might eat less. Plenty of fruits and vegetables will also, of course, bulk up your diet. Soups are an excellent addition to any diet. Taken at the start of a meal, they expand the volume of food eaten through the simple addition of water.

Can weight loss ever damage your health?

The assumption is often made that if excess weight puts you at risk for disease, then losing weight automatically makes you healthier. But how you lose the weight is extremely important. If you have a lot of weight to lose, you may benefit from joining a support group or having a weight-loss consultant check up on you every week. To maintain motivation and morale, people often turn to dieting organizations that demand you weigh in every week. By the time you finish reading this book, I hope you will be able to evaluate the health impact of any diet you are given, because damaging your health by dieting is a real possibility.

I'm particularly against too-rapid weight loss. Psychologically it gives people a boost to be able to say they have shed 10 pounds in one week. But if you do that, you may be losing muscle and not the fat you really want to lose. If the diet you are using causes hair loss, constipation, headaches or is low in protein or vegetables and fruit, you can be sure it is not healthy. Other complications of rapid weight loss include gallstones[22] and electrolyte imbalances that could be life threatening.

The other concern I have about rapid weight loss is the precipitous release of stored environmental toxins, known as persistent organic pollutants (POPs), into the bloodstream.

Approximately 80,000 new toxins have been introduced since the end of the Second World War. They are called persistent because they do not break down, either in the environment or in our tissues, but are stored in our fat cells and released into circulating blood when fat cells break down. They are also known as xenobiotics—environmental toxins with health consequences. Xenobiotics are found in personal care products like soaps, body lotions and perfumes, and in food as preservatives, artificial colourings, flavourings and stabilizers. They leach from plastic water bottles and food wrap. They are found in conventionally raised food as residues of pesticides, fungicides and herbicides.

Many of these chemicals have been linked to cancers as well as diabetes and heart disease, and we know they can target tissues such as breast and prostate when they are released into circulating blood. In one study, serum levels of six common environmental pollutants were found to be about 50 percent higher in those who reported large weight losses over a decade, compared to those who gained weight during the same period.[23] It is possible to detoxify from xenobiotics, but our ability to do so depends on a high vegetable intake.[24] Fruits and vegetables will switch on genes in the liver that are required to make enzymes involved in detoxification. Any potential negative health effect of rapid weight loss will be compounded if the diet of choice limits vegetable and fruit intake as, for example, the Atkins diet does.

Any weight loss program that promises rapid weight loss is, in my opinion, a bad idea and likely to have a negative impact on health. Far safer to take a year to lose 20 pounds, and eat lots of fruits and vegetables to stimulate detoxification, than lose it in two months on a very limited selection of foods.

Getting the right amount of exercise

In Canada, only 5 percent of the population actually manages to accumulate the recommended 150 minutes of moderate exercise a week. As in other developed countries, the average person in Canada may be spending more than nine hours a day in a sedentary occupation, possibly in front of a computer screen. And when he or she comes home, leisure time is spent in front of the TV. We must make time for exercise if we want to remain healthy. The British statesman Edward, Lord Stanley (1826–1893) put it best: "Those who think they have not time for bodily exercise will sooner or later have to find time for illness."[25]

If you go to a gym and use, say, the elliptical trainer or the treadmill, you will get a readout telling you the number of calories you have burned over the course of your 30-minute workout. Every activity burns calories and many websites now exist to help you calculate the energy expended by activities such as swimming or cycling or climbing stairs—the Exercise Expended Energy or EEE, sometimes also referred to as Exercise Expended Calories (EEC). You can check, for example, whether two hours spent strolling will give you the same benefit as 30 minutes of brisk walking.

I have already discussed telomere length as a reliable biomarker for healthy aging. The longer our telomeres are, the younger our body age. One study that looked at telomere length and EEE found that too much exercise had the same detrimental effect on telomere length as too little, and that moderate exercise that burned between 1000 and 2400 calories per week was best. Those who burned less than 1000 calories had shorter telomeres; those who clocked in more than 2400 EEEs also had telomeres that were shorter. Extreme forms of exercise appear to be stressful.

I have older people in my practice who take up marathon running or other strenuous exercise regimes and find that they end up with health issues related to the extreme exercise—a painful knee or a torn rotator cuff. Then, of course, they are forced to stop exercise altogether, at least for a while.

I record my weight every day because I have a slow basal metabolic rate and gain weight readily. Then I track how many hours I sleep because I want to avoid short sleeping when my work schedule gets hectic. The third thing I record is how much exercise I have done each day, and how many calories I have expended doing it. Looking at my exercise diary for one randomly chosen week, my records show that I exercised five times. Not bad, you say. On Monday I did 30 minutes of low-impact aerobic exercise on an elliptical trainer, burning 210 calories. The next day I did 50 minutes on the elliptical and on a rowing machine. Wednesday I had a day of rest. I did 45 minutes of moderately paced swimming on Thursday. On Friday I spent an hour with a Pilates trainer, and that's fairly intense, although not aerobic. Saturday I did nothing, and on Sunday I walked briskly for 40 minutes. My total EECs for that week was 1425, quite low but within the recommended range. I try to aim for the top end of that range, about 2000 EEEs.

The benefits of exercise come not only from the calories burned while you are doing it, but also afterwards. As you exercise and become more toned and fit, you replace fat with muscle and that speeds up your metabolic rate. Muscle burns calories at a faster rate than fat cells so that if you gain muscle mass, your body will burn more calories simply to maintain itself. The benefits from a good workout can last up to 24 hours. It's not over when it's over. We need many different types of exercise to stay healthy. Studies show that visceral fat is the first to go with aerobic exercise.[26] Weight-bearing exercise is important in the prevention of osteoporosis, while stretching is important if we want to stay flexible and keep our balance as we age. In fact, all three types of exercise—stretching, strengthening and aerobic—should be part of your regular weekly routine.

Why we have a tendency to overeat

When our earliest ancestors were hunter-gatherers, food was scarce and they had to eat whenever they had the chance. Ancient man would have had to eat often in order to survive because what he was eating most of the time—berries, roots, leafy greens, fruits—was low in calories and therefore low in energy. Since hunting and gathering food was hard work, hunter-gatherers burned those calories as fast as they were taking them in. They would therefore have to rest and conserve energy whenever possible. And what might have made us stop eating? The best guess currently is that we stopped when we had a surfeit of health-giving phytochemicals.[27]

Those two instincts, to eat constantly and to rest when we have eaten enough, are still part of our genetic makeup, but instead of carrying a survival advantage, they are now working against us. The work we are doing is generally not exhausting physical labour, but we still have the instinct to rest from it when we can. Today our lives are sedentary while much of the food so readily available around us is calorie dense and nutrient poor. We cannot go back to foraging for our food, but we can learn general principles from the past. One is to make plants the bulk of our eating. Plant-based foods are lower in calories and they also bring with them an abundance of protective phytochemicals. If they displace the more energy-rich, nutrient-poor processed foods from our diet, that can only be good for our health.

If we can look at the pattern of eating of existing hunter-gatherer tribes, in which obesity is rare, we find that diets include two to three times more fibre, twice the monounsaturated and polyunsaturated fats, and four times as much omega-3 fats than what is found in the modern Western diet.[28] Contemporary hunter-gatherers also eat two to three times more protein, and 30 to 40 percent less saturated fat than is found in the standard American diet. If you compare the Western diet and the prudent or Mediterranean-style diet, the latter wins hands down for maintaining weight. A multitude of studies indicate that people who eat more fruits and vegetables, more omega-3 fats, and fewer refined carbohydrates and sugar are not only healthier, they are slimmer.[29]

Vitamin D and weight

Excess vitamin D whether from sunshine or supplements is absorbed by fat cells, making it unavailable to the body for use. People who are obese or overweight generally have lower circulating blood levels of 25-hydroxy D, the storage form of vitamin D.[30] Recent studies have shown that when you lose a significant amount of your total body weight—15 percent or more—blood levels of vitamin D go up as stored vitamin D is released from fat cells into the blood. The greater the weight loss, the more marked the surge in vitamin D levels.

Metabolic syndrome is more likely to develop in older people who have lower circulating levels of vitamin D.[31] Some researchers believe that it is very hard to control our weight without sufficient vitamin D. Vitamin D in turn may control insulin secretion and prevent insulin resistance and metabolic syndrome. The link between vitamin D and weight gain is intriguing but not proven. More research is needed.

Mindful eating, smaller plates

Numerous clients come to me because they want to improve their health with a good diet and supplements; some also happen to be overweight. I put them on the sort of diet included in Part 3 of this book. It is a very simple approach to changing the way they eat, making sure that the largest component of every meal is vegetables and/or fruits, that there is protein at each meal and a small amount of good fat. A modest portion of high-quality, unrefined grains is also included. In countless cases people come back six months after starting the program and say: "I'm delighted, I've lost 10 (or 15) pounds." This has happened without their necessarily focusing on weight loss, only on improving diet and practising restraint with regard to food.

Portion size matters. Both my mother and father were overweight—not obese, but certainly heavier than normal. When I think back now, I see that we were eating way too much food. My mother thought everyone should have second helpings unless they were unwell. And her second helpings could be as big as the original serving. We probably consumed twice the calories at a sitting than we actually needed. These days I have banished second helpings from my dinner table.

Another trick that can help if you need to lose a little bit of weight is to use smaller dinnerware—a salad plate instead of a dinner plate for the main course. The bigger the plate, the more people will eat. On a smaller plate, you will eat smaller meals with less sense of deprivation. We eat with our eyes. Recent studies show that we are satisfied with less if we look at the food closely before eating, enjoying its smell and colour even before lifting a fork to our mouth. Pay attention to the act of eating and you will eat less. Chew and swallow one mouthful before taking the next bite. The reverse is also true: you consume more when you eat mindlessly. Eating in front of the TV, not sitting down to a meal, bolting down your food will lead to less satisfaction and more overeating.

13

Cholesterol and Hypertension

▼

A man is as old as his heart.

— Sir William Osler (1849–1919), physician

O UR NUMBER-ONE TASK as we age should be to keep our heart young because a sick heart robs us of energy and dynamism as nothing else can. High blood pressure (hypertension) and elevated cholesterol (hypercholesterolemia) are risk factors for cardiovascular disease, and both grow more common as the decades go by. This fact is often interpreted to mean that such changes are inevitable and part of the normal aging process. But is this really so? Both are considered lifestyle diseases, due to a large extent to inadequate diets, lack of exercise, cigarette smoking and stress. And both respond well to changes in lifestyle.

When your doctor tightens a blood pressure cuff on your arm, he or she is measuring the force blood flow is exerting on the walls of large blood vessels. Normal blood pressure is 120/80.

The top number is the pressure (systolic) in a blood vessel at the moment the heart is pumping blood, and the lower number (diastolic) is the pressure between beats, when the heart is at rest. If the first number is high, the increased pressure will put a strain on the blood vessel walls, on the heart and also on the kidney, where the blood is filtered. High blood pressure has been considered a risk factor for heart disease since the 1920s.

Cholesterol, a waxy fat-like substance, is of more recent interest to doctors and researchers. It is a necessary component of cell membranes and the precursor for hormones including testosterone, estrogens and progesterone. In the skin, a derivative of cholesterol is needed to make vitamin D. Cholesterol is an essential part of myelin, the insulating material of neurons. It is needed to make bile acids for the digestion and absorption of fats, and for absorption of fat-soluble vitamins in the small intestines. The healthy body manufactures cholesterol as needed, primarily in the liver and intestines, but also in the brain. In fact, 25 percent of the body's cholesterol is produced in the brain.[1]

While cholesterol is essential to the body's health, problems arise when the body makes too much cholesterol, which can then get deposited in the arterial walls. Researchers began in the 1950s to link elevated cholesterol levels to heart disease. Arteries—the blood vessels that carry blood away from the heart to other tissues—need strength and elasticity. When cholesterol is deposited in them they become narrowed and rigid, which impedes the passage of blood and limits the supply of nutrients and oxygen to organs. The buildup of cholesterol plaque is called atherosclerosis, or hardening of the arteries. Plaques may also break away from the blood vessel wall, causing blood clots that can block the artery.

According to Statistics Canada, 40 percent of Canadians aged 20 to 79 have unhealthy cholesterol levels.[2] Narrowed blood vessels push the heart to work harder, and lack of elasticity in the arteries causes blood pressure to rise. It should be no surprise, then, that high blood pressure and high cholesterol tend to be found together in the same individuals.

Know your numbers

You have high blood pressure if your reading is 140/90 or higher. Anyone with a reading consistently that high would be medicated. Slightly higher than normal values in the range of 121 to 139 (systolic) and 81 to 89 (diastolic) are now considered pre-hypertensive, an early warning that blood pressure problems are around the corner. Given that anxiety can raise blood pressure temporarily, it is important to be relaxed when having your blood pressure checked. Some people suffer from "white coat syndrome" and become overly tense when faced with a doctor. Waiting a while until you feel calmer, or having the cuff applied by a nurse, may result in a more accurate reading.

When you have your cholesterol measured, the results usually include readings for a series of different fats—a lipid panel—all of which are used to estimate your risk of atherosclerosis. To travel through the blood, cholesterol is encased in proteins, making what is called a cholesterol complex. These complexes are categorized according to their density: high density lipoproteins (HDL-C) are called "good" cholesterol, while low density lipoproteins (LDL-C) are known as "bad" cholesterol. In some cases, very low density lipoproteins (VLDL) are also measured. Total cholesterol is the combination of all these types of cholesterol. You will also be given the ratio of total cholesterol to HDL, a number obtained by dividing the total cholesterol by the good cholesterol. For example, a person with a total cholesterol of 5 mmol/L and an HDL-C of 1.5 mmol/L has a ratio expressed as a single number, in this case 3.33. The desirable ratio is 4.11, but the lower the number the better (see Table 1).

Table 1
Healthy levels of lipids in blood

Total Cholesterol (TC)	less than 5.2 mmol/L (20–79 years)
Triglycerides	less than 1.7 mmol/L
LDL-C: Low density lipoprotein-cholesterol or "bad" cholesterol	less than 3.4 mmol/L
HDL-C: High density lipoprotein-cholesterol or "good" cholesterol	higher than 1.0 mmol/L (men) higher than 1.3 mmol/L (women)
TC/HDL-C: Ratio of total cholesterol to HDL-cholesterol	less than 4.11

*Adapted from "Heart health and cholesterol levels of Canadians, 2007–2009." http://www.statcan.gc.ca

Although we call LDL-C bad cholesterol and HDL-C good cholesterol, these terms are probably misnomers. LDL-C is the circulating form of cholesterol needed to make sex hormones (estrogen, progesterone, testosterone) and becomes a problem only if it is too high and damaged by oxidation. Infection, poor diet, or high levels of inflammatory molecules circulating in the blood can all result in oxidation. HDL-C, the so-called good cholesterol, is a cholesterol scavenger, removing LDL cholesterol from arteries and ferrying it back to the liver for destruction. Low HDL-C is cause for concern, and improving HDL-C levels is an important goal in the fight against heart disease. The ratio of good to bad cholesterol is another important measure, although not usually given in lipid panel results; you will have to work it out for yourself. If your HDL-C is 1.2 and your LDL-C is 3.6, your ratio would be 0.3, which is good.

The lipid panel also includes triglycerides. These high-energy fats are needed to provide energy for cells and, like cholesterol, they are essential. They get their name from their structure—three fatty acid molecules attached to one molecule of glycerol. Triglycerides are present in all cholesterol complexes but highest in very low density lipoprotein (VLDL). High circulating levels of triglycerides are a risk factor for heart disease and stroke, and also increase the risk of fatty liver and inflammation of the pancreas. The triglycerides the doctor measures come either directly or indirectly from diet. They are the main form of fat found in plant and animal foods, but they are also manufactured by the body itself from excess calories, particularly after a high-carbohydrate meal. Triglycerides rise if we eat too much, smoke, fail to exercise, drink too much alcohol or are overweight.

C-reactive protein predicts heart disease risk

People who are about to go for a physical often ask me what other tests might be useful for identifying heart disease risks. C-reactive protein (CRP) is one I suggest. This test measures inflammation, and while it is not specific for heart disease, studies suggest it is as good or better at predicting who is at risk of heart disease as cholesterol levels.[3] CRP is elevated in any condition where inflammation is high; therefore, do not have it tested if you have a cold or other infection. Other conditions where CRP is high include autoimmune diseases such as rheumatoid arthritis, chronic obstructive pulmonary disease (COPD), diabetes and obesity. The test is sometimes written as hs-CRP, which stands for high-sensitivity C-reactive protein. You can estimate your risk using Table 2.

Table 2
C-reactive protein and cardiovascular risk

Low risk   hs-CRP level lower than 1.0 mg/L
Average risk   hs-CRP level between 1.0 and 3.0 mg/L
High risk   hs-CRP level over 3.0 mg/L

Data taken from the Canadian Cardiovascular Society's position statement: "Recommendations for the diagnosis and treatment of dyslipidemia and prevention of cardiovascular disease."[4]

If your CRP is high, vitamin C supplements can bring it down. A recent study from the University of California, Berkeley, showed that 1 gram (1000 mg) of vitamin C daily lowered CRP levels by 34 percent in two months in otherwise healthy non-smoking adults.[5] Vitamin C is required to repair and replace damaged collagen, a molecule that makes up 25 percent of the connective tissue of blood vessel walls. A person suffering from scurvy will find it impossible to maintain collagen, and his or her blood vessels will weaken. Higher intakes of vitamin C–rich foods such as strawberries are associated with lower levels of CRP.[6]

In the 1950s, Canadian researcher Dr. G. C. Willis showed that atherosclerosis occurs mainly in the large blood vessels near the heart, in the arteries most exposed to severe mechanical stress. He noted that atherosclerosis was not necessarily permanent. When he followed the same individuals over time, he could see from X-ray evidence that plaques (cholesterol buildups) could get bigger or smaller, often quite rapidly. He therefore reasoned that under certain conditions arteries could repair themselves.[7] Willis knew that guinea pigs do not develop atherosclerosis unless you deprive them of vitamin C. Like humans, guinea pigs are one of the few animals that cannot make their own vitamin C. But atherosclerosis can be quickly repaired in these animals by returning vitamin C to their diet.[8] Willis gave his human subjects daily doses of 500 mg of vitamin C and observed the disappearance of plaques in at least some of the patients.[9] The dose of vitamin C Willis used was quite low. To make it comparable to the amount used in the guinea pig studies, he would have needed to give his human subjects 5 grams (5000 mg) a day, so the fact that he saw any improvement at all in his patients is remarkable.

I have been concerned for a long time that we greatly underestimate the intake of vitamin C needed for good health. For prevention I usually recommend 2 grams a day—the safe tolerable upper limit of vitamin C.

Drug treatment of dyslipidemia and high blood pressure

Only 10 percent of the cholesterol measured in your blood comes from diet. The rest you have made yourself. An enzyme called HMG-CoA reductase fine-tunes cholesterol production, switching supply on when we need it and off again when we have made enough. Elevated cholesterol therefore suggests a malfunction of this mechanism.

A class of drugs called statins, already mentioned in connection with sleep, will switch off cholesterol production by blocking HMG-CoA reductase. This is not necessarily a good thing since cholesterol is needed for cell membranes and the manufacture of hormones. Statins can bring down LDL cholesterol—the bad stuff—but have only a modest, if any, effect on triglycerides or HDL-C. A recent international study looked at patients on long-term statin therapy and found that 75 percent of the 910 patients enrolled in the study failed to meet targets for one or more elements on the lipid panel.[10]

There can be serious side effects from these drugs, too. Statins can cross the blood-brain barrier, and shut down cholesterol synthesis in the brain. Cholesterol is, however, critically important for a healthy brain. Some studies have shown links between statin use and depression, particularly in the elderly.[11] Another problem is muscle weakness and pain, which 10 to 15 percent of patients on statins experience. A small proportion of these will go on to develop a serious form of muscle damage called rhabdomyolysis. Your doctor can monitor for this by testing for another enzyme, creatine kinase (CK), which may be elevated when muscle damage occurs. However, damage can also occur even when CK is not elevated.[12] The muscle weakness, pain and damage that statins sometimes cause are due to their blocking the synthesis of coenzyme Q10 (CoQ10).[13] This naturally occurring enzyme is a powerful antioxidant, protecting cell membranes from free radical damage. It is also required by all cells to produce the energy that they need to function.

Although the pain and weakness are usually felt in skeletal muscle, the lungs and heart are also affected. The muscles that control these organs have high energy needs, since they must keep working at all times. If you have been warned that you may be at risk of heart disease, you will have probably been advised to start exercising. However, strenuous exercise also induces muscle damage, adding to the depletion of CoQ10 caused by statin therapy—a double jeopardy. Exercise-induced muscle damage can be offset by taking CoQ10 supplements.[14] In my opinion people who take statins require CoQ10 supplements, particularly if they exercise. Many doctors now suggest CoQ10 to their patients. (You will find more information on this supplement in Part 3.)

Use nutrients instead of drugs

Rather than keeping HMG-CoA reductase permanently switched off with drugs, with their attendant possibilities of serious side effects, we should try to understand why cholesterol production is out of control in the first place. Magnesium is needed to control the on/off function of HMG-CoA reductase, and if adequate amounts of magnesium are present in tissues, then cholesterol production will be properly regulated. But when magnesium levels are low, this enzyme can turn off or get stuck in the "on" position. Both animal and human studies have shown a strong link between dietary intake of magnesium and heart disease: the lower the intake of magnesium, the more likely atherosclerosis will develop.[15] The late great magnesium researcher Mildred Seelig pointed out that in controlling production of cholesterol, the actions of magnesium closely parallel those of the statin drugs.

Magnesium is necessary to activate enzymes needed to lower LDL-C and triglycerides, as well as to raise good cholesterol (HDL-C). Low levels of magnesium increase oxidative stress. Remember that the most damaging form of cholesterol is oxidized cholesterol. In animal studies chronic long-term magnesium deficiency increases oxidative stress and cell death, and decreases telomere length—a hallmark of unhealthy aging.[16] Mildred Seelig concluded that anything statins could do, magnesium might do as well, perhaps even better.[17] And without the risk of damaging side effects. The difference between drugs and nutrients is that drugs will bring down cholesterol even in healthy individuals with normal cholesterol levels. Magnesium will instead normalize cholesterol.

Blood pressure medication can create a vicious cycle of nutrient inadequacy. Diuretics (water pills) flush water out of the body, blocking the kidneys from recycling fluid and nutrients back into the circulation. This reduces circulating blood volume, thus reducing the pressure in blood vessels. At the same time diuretics flush out valuable nutrients including water-soluble B vitamins, vitamin C and all of the minerals, including magnesium, needed to relax the blood vessels. Some researchers believe that continued depletion of multiple nutrients by such drugs eventually leads to heart failure.[18]

Other drugs work by interfering with the nervous impulses to the heart, slowing it down. One class of drugs, called calcium channel blockers, stops calcium from entering the muscle cells of the heart and blood vessels, causing them to relax. But magnesium, sometimes called "nature's calcium channel blocker," does exactly the same thing.[19] To put it another way, calcium channel blockers are only needed when magnesium is deficient. As we age we take an ever-growing list of prescription medications and since many of those are known to deplete magnesium, it is not surprising that many older people find their control of both blood pressure and cholesterol synthesis diminished.

Niacin and HDL cholesterol

Niacin (also called vitamin B3) has been shown to lower LDL-C cholesterol, and is the only agent known to consistently raise HDL cholesterol, reducing the risk of heart disease.[20] It is praised even on medical websites, where it is usually (and erroneously) referred to as a drug rather than a nutrient. In fact, it works far better than most drugs, not only slowing the progress of atherosclerotic plaques but, in one study, reducing the incidence of cardiovascular events by approximately 90 percent compared to a placebo.[21] Niacin deficiency used to be a problem in North America, especially in poor communities on monotonous and inadequate diets. But today cereals are fortified with niacin, and serious niacin deficiency is no longer common. The body can also make niacin from the amino acid tryptophan, but since it takes 60 mg of tryptophan to make 1 mg of niacin, the process is wasteful, and may result in a relative tryptophan deficiency. Depletion of tryptophan may in turn lead to depression.[22]

One problem with niacin is that a short time after you take it, your skin may become red and itchy. A niacin flush is harmless, and usually passes in 20 to 30 minutes, but some people find the sensation disconcerting. The amount that causes flushing varies from one person to another, but few people flush as a result of the 25 to 50 mg contained in multivitamin or B-complex formulas. Occasionally people get a partial flush—their skin looks blotchy—and have been known to show up at the emergency room thinking they are having an allergic reaction. A partial flush passes, too, and is entirely harmless. If you want to try niacin to reduce cholesterol, work with your doctor or other qualified health care practitioner. The amounts required may be high, and since some forms and doses of niacin can be hard on the liver, periodic blood tests are needed.

Diet and cholesterol: Peter's story

Peter came to me with his wife, who had been a client of mine for years. Peter had been healthy until recently, when suddenly his cholesterol went up (dyslipidemia). His doctor wanted him to take medication for the condition, but because he had seen his wife's health improve markedly under my care, he decided he would first like to try diet. The doctor agreed but assured him he was unlikely to be successful. "I have never seen cholesterol come down with diet alone," he told Peter.

Because dyslipidemia is thought to be caused primarily by a high-fat diet, especially one high in saturated fats, the usual advice to people with elevated cholesterol is to cut out fat and all cholesterol from food. A careful reading of the scientific literature, however, shows that such a diet has little impact on heart disease. A recent review that looked at the outcomes of all clinical trials using low saturated-fat diets found no evidence that saturated fat was the villain in heart disease. The researcher conducting the review wrote that "there is insufficient evidence to conclude that dietary saturated fat is associated with an increased risk of coronary heart disease, stroke or cardiovascular disease."[23] No wonder Peter's doctor was skeptical. All his other patients had been told to go on low-fat diets and he had never seen them work.

I told Peter I would like him to try a low-carbohydrate Mediterranean-style diet, which had been shown to decrease triglycerides and LDL cholesterol.[24] I recommended that he cut out sugars completely and dramatically cut back on starches, keeping his intake to one small portion with each meal. That was hard for him because he loved candy and desserts. I told him he could eat eggs and a little dark chocolate, which pleased him, and that he could have a moderate intake of fat, especially from olive oil and fatty fish. All cereals had to be whole grain. And he could include a daily glass of wine if he wished. I also suggested that he work hard at increasing his daily vegetable and fruit intake. These foods contain phytochemicals with known antioxidant and anti-inflammatory properties. The Mediterranean diet is associated with very low rates of heart disease and is especially rich in tomato-based dishes containing protective lycopene.[25] I assured him that this diet would be satisfying and that he would soon lose his taste for candy and desserts.

Five months later, Peter's lipid panel was normal. His HDL (good) was high and his LDL (bad) in the normal range, and so was his total cholesterol. Seeing such good results, the doctor said: "I don't know how you did it, but congratulations," and he shook Peter's hand. Actually, Peter's doctor was right. His cholesterol had not come down on diet alone because he was already taking supplements. We had worked to optimize his vitamin D. He took a daily multivitamin and some extra vitamin C. He optimized his magnesium intake and took a fish oil supplement. But it was changing his diet to limit sugar and starch that was the final step he needed to take to improve his health.

Other supplements that help control blood pressure and cholesterol

When I first started to get interested in vitamin D, I was astonished to discover that both cholesterol and blood pressure are lower in the summer months and higher in winter. Since then studies have shown that low circulating levels of 25-hydroxy D increase arterial stiffness, which would increase blood pressure in the months with little sun.[26] Although the mechanisms whereby vitamin D might affect cholesterol are unclear at the moment, low levels of 25-hydroxy D are associated with high total cholesterol, LDL-C and triglycerides.[27] These emerging studies lend credibility to the suspicion that seasonal variations in blood pressure and cholesterol are related to sun exposure and therefore vitamin D status.

The right fats are important for heart health, too, but the role different types of fats may play in preventing or promoting heart disease is a matter of ongoing controversy.[28] However, several facts are emerging that everyone can agree on. We know that trans fats are bad and need to be eliminated from the diet.[29] There is growing acceptance that omega-3 fatty acids from fish or fish oil supplements help prevent cardiovascular disease in healthy individuals, improving the heart's electrical activity and vascular tone, stabilizing atherosclerotic plaques and controlling blood pressure.[30] And we are beginning to see that saturated fats, especially those that come in foods containing other beneficial nutrients, like egg yolks, are not so bad after all. We do not want too much saturated fat in our diet but need not fear it in moderation.

The new kids on the nutritional block are phytosterols, the sterols and stanols, plant-derived fats similar in structure to cholesterol. Plant sterols and stanols occur naturally in small amounts in many grains, vegetables, fruits, legumes, nuts and seeds, and they were probably high in the diet of our ancestors. Sterols and stanols lower LDL cholesterol, and manufacturers have started adding them to foods. You can now get stanols or sterols in margarine spreads, orange juice, cereals and granola bars. I have even seen sterol- and stanol-fortified yogurt. The U.S. Food and Drug Administration (FDA) allows health claims for them. There is some concern that at higher intakes sterols and stanols could block absorption of the fat-soluble vitamins A, D, E and K. If we eat nuts and seeds and whole grains, and use olive oil, we should get enough phytosterols, but I am dubious about taking large amounts as supplements or in fortified foods since we have no long-term studies about their safety.

Ultimately, there is no one nutrient that will magically protect the heart, any more than there is just one that will boost brainpower. We need to pay attention to them all.

Sodium, potassium and blood pressure

Mentioned in an earlier chapter, the Dietary Approaches to Stop Hypertension (DASH) diet is an experimental diet shown to reduce blood pressure. It features high intakes of fruit, vegetables, legumes and nuts; moderate amounts of low-fat dairy products; and low amounts of animal protein and desserts. Sodium is restricted on this diet to about 1800 mg daily. A regular Western diet contains about 3400 mg. DASH has been shown to reduce blood pressure even in those with normal blood pressure.[31]

Clients who suffer from hypertension typically ask me if they have to cut out all salt. First, I tell them that most of the salt they ingest is likely to be in commercially produced foods. If they cut out processed foods and eat a diet as close to nature as possible, they will be ingesting less sodium. Second, I explain the relationship among four key minerals that work closely together to control blood pressure—sodium, potassium, calcium and magnesium. Together, I explain, they control the balance of minerals inside and outside cells, relaxing and contracting the smooth muscle cells in blood vessels that regulate blood pressure. Magnesium and potassium are generally found inside these cells, while calcium and sodium are found outside. Magnesium blocks calcium from getting into cells (remember nature's calcium channel blocker?), and potassium does the same job for sodium.

If magnesium levels drop in cells, calcium rushes in, causing muscle cells to contract and push up blood pressure. If potassium is low inside cells, sodium can rush in, and again, blood pressure rises. But keeping potassium inside cells requires a great deal of energy (ATP), which, as we have seen, requires adequate tissue levels of magnesium. Thus, a deficiency of either potassium or magnesium will increase blood pressure. If you are eating a phytochemical-rich diet (meaning 8 to 10 servings of vegetables and fruits daily) you are unlikely to be low on potassium. But magnesium is another matter. If magnesium is low, both sodium and calcium can get into the cell and push up blood pressure. Researchers have estimated what our intake of sodium, potassium, calcium and magnesium would be if we ate a natural diet. Such a diet would exclude processed foods, and would consist of approximately two-thirds plant-based and one-third animal-derived food. Based on 2100 kcal per day, such a diet would have contained about 500 mg of sodium, about 7400 mg potassium and about 800 mg of magnesium.[32]

This is very different from the intake and balance of those critical minerals today. Now the average North American consumes about 1½ teaspoons or 3400 mg of salt a day, but only about 40 percent of the recommended intakes of potassium and magnesium, which in any case are low compared to ancestral diets. Governments are working to raise consumer awareness about the hazards of a high salt intake and encouraging the food industry to restrict the salt they add to food. But without salt food tastes bland. Salt substitutes have been developed that add flavour to food and bring down blood pressure.[33] These salt substitutes have a lower sodium content and are enriched with potassium and magnesium. If we really want to have an impact on high blood pressure and heart disease, a far better strategy than merely restricting sodium chloride would be to encourage the use of salts containing magnesium and potassium both at the dinner table and in processed foods.

Phytochemicals and the French Paradox

The French famously eat more saturated fats from butter, cheese and eggs, yet have lower rates of heart disease. Could this be because of the wine that accompanies their meals? In animal studies, a phytochemical called resveratrol, present in wine, particularly red wine, has been shown to protect against heart disease.[34] However, you would have to drink gallons of wine daily to duplicate the doses given to laboratory animals in these studies. Resveratrol is present not only in red wine but in many types of berries, red and purple fruits, peanuts and beets, and also (in lower amounts) in white wine, but the quantities typically consumed are considered too low to account for the French Paradox. The alcohol itself could also offer protection and so could a more convincing phytochemical candidate called proanthocyanin that is present in grapes and grape seeds. Proanthocyanins are powerful antioxidants, with 20 times the antioxidant activity of vitamin E and 50 times that of vitamin C. They bind to collagen in skin and in blood vessel walls, supporting and stabilizing it and keeping blood vessels flexible and elastic.[35] People living in areas of the Mediterranean region with the highest concentrations of proanthocyanins in the local wine have the greatest longevity.[36]

Can people who modify their diet and take supplements go off prescription medications?

The most satisfactory use of diet and supplements is for prevention. I would never advise my clients to stop medications without their doctor's encouragement, if they are already taking them. Even those on medications can benefit from eating a balanced diet and taking certain supplements. I often see people on three or four different medications for blood pressure, yet their blood pressure is still not well controlled. Then my focus is on making sure that their supplement regime compensates for any nutrient depletion caused by their medication. Once you have optimized diet and supplements, and made some necessary lifestyle changes—quitting smoking, exercising regularly and reducing stress where possible—it might be appropriate to discuss with your physician how to modify your drug regime, perhaps taking a drug holiday from statin drugs while watching what happens to your cholesterol and blood pressure. Lifestyle changes really are important. Nutrients cannot work optimally when handicapped by an unhealthy lifestyle.

14

Memory Problems

▼

Memory is identity. You are what you have done; what you have done is in your memory; what you remember defines who you are.

— Julian Barnes, English novelist
(in *Nothing To Be Frightened Of*)

A T ANY STAGE of our lives memory can briefly fail us. We can forget a loved one's birthday or where we left the car keys. As a child, I was terribly absent-minded. At the dinner table, if I had to wait my turn to speak, I would forget what I wanted to say and if sent on an errand, I would forget what I had been sent for. Often I would forget where I was going and end up elsewhere, so that someone had to come find me. An avid reader, I promptly forgot the title of the book I had just read, or its plot. Luckily, we are not stuck with the brain we were born with, and later my memory improved.

Individuals differ in their powers of recall, and normal memory lapses need not concern us. But what about the experience that strikes in late middle age when we want to introduce a close friend to someone we have known for years and suddenly blank out on the name? Or we walk from the living room to the kitchen to fetch something, then stand there, baffled by what it was we needed? Or we cannot recall the title of the film seen only last night? Or we stop in mid-sentence unable to summon a word that is (or was until a second ago) part of our vocabulary? Such "senior moments" may worry us when they strike, but we usually recover in short order. They are not necessarily red flags that you are progressing down the road to dementia. The name, the word, the title will reappear if you set aside your anxiety about them.

What is the difference between normal forgetfulness and a change in brain function that alerts us and those around us that something is very wrong? The primary difference is that age-related memory loss is not disabling—we can carry on a normal life, we can get to work, we can read, follow the plot of a film or play and find our way home. Abnormal memory loss, on the other hand, interferes with work and social relationships, diminishes the ability to perform necessary chores such as cooking or shopping, or stands in the way of activities one used to enjoy. If you were a formidable Scrabble player and suddenly can't put a word together, if you go out and suddenly do not know where you are, those are indeed red flags: you should see a doctor as soon as possible to rule out serious medical reasons for such problems. The good news is that once illness is ruled out, those senior moments can be prevented or at least made less frequent. Memory does not need to deteriorate with age.

Memory failure is rarely the reason people come to see me. The subject usually comes up incidentally when we are talking about health in general. I will ask, how is your memory? The answer I regularly receive from middle-aged clients is that it's not as good as it used to be. But I am often taken aback when 30- to 40-year-olds make the same admission. Both my older and younger clients are surprised to find that such problems may be related to nutrition. Research is beginning to show that memory problems associated with normal aging can be slowed or even reversed by providing the right chemical environment for better brain function.[1]

The hippocampus

The South African biologist, author and adventurer Lyall Watson (1939–2008) observed that "if the brain were so simple we could understand it, we would be so simple we couldn't." This assertion certainly applies to memory. Many different regions of the brain are involved in memory, and the contribution each part plays in the formation, storage and retrieval of information is still poorly understood today.

One area of the brain that has received a lot of attention from neurobiologists is the hippocampus. In 2003, scientists at Harvard and NYU identified the key role of the hippocampus in learning and remembering the sights, smells and sounds that help create our long-term memory for facts and events.[2] Named after the Greek word for seahorse, whose shape it resembles, the hippocampus is involved in the transfer of information from short-term memory to long-term memory, as well as the retrieval of that information when we need it—think of it as a sort of central hub for processing the import and export of data. The hippocampus is also the locus of our ability to navigate in space. In people with Alzheimer's disease, damage occurs to the hippocampus before any other part of the brain, which explains why Alzheimer's patients wander and get lost.

The hippocampus may deteriorate with age for a number of reasons. Growth factors that normally protect and repair brain cells and stimulate brain cell growth decline with age.[3] Estrogen is involved in learning and spatial memory, causing some women to experience memory problems after menopause, when estrogen levels decline. Another reason for deterioration of the hippocampus is cardiovascular disease. If blood vessel walls stiffen and lose their elasticity, blood flow to the brain could decrease, and the passage of oxygen, glucose and essential nutrients into the brain becomes more difficult.[4] A buildup of cholesterol plaques, too, will impede blood flow; high LDL cholesterol and low HDL cholesterol have been linked to poorer working memory in middle age.[5] If blood is thicker than normal it will flow more slowly, carrying oxygen and nutrients at a reduced rate, and will have a greater tendency to clot, leading to infarcts— small areas of dead tissue in the brain that result from the interruption of local blood supply. Higher blood viscosity has also been linked to declining memory as we age.[6]

Overproduction of the stress hormone cortisol affects several regions of the brain, but the effect is greatest on the hippocampus. The stress response shunts glucose away from the brain to muscles, leaving the hippocampus energy deprived and therefore unable to make new memories. This may explain why people often cannot recall the details of very traumatic experiences. Since cortisol interferes not only with the formation of new memories but also with the retrieval of long-term memory, stressful situations make remembering much more difficult. Next time you blank out over someone's name, ask yourself if you were particularly stressed at the time. Fortunately, such cortisol-induced memory malfunctions are short-lived, and normal memory function is restored later. Chronic stress over a lifetime, however, is a different matter, and a risk factor for the development of Alzheimer's disease and other forms of dementia.[7]

Lack of sleep takes its toll on memory, as well. In a previous chapter, we talked about the importance of getting REM sleep in order to consolidate memories and newly learned information. As pointed out earlier, people disturbed during REM sleep will not remember what they learned the previous day. The longest period of REM occurs at the end of our night's sleep, and if we regularly rise at 5 a.m. to go to the gym before work, and then go to bed after midnight, we may be setting ourselves up for a gradual decline in our ability to retain new information.

Beefing up the hippocampus

Like other organs in the body, the brain is continually renewing itself. Cells in the hippocampus can be stimulated to divide and form new cells. Brain games have been devised that will specifically stimulate this renewal and enhance memory.[8] An interesting example of how learning may affect the hippocampus comes from a study of London taxi drivers, who have to learn how to get to and from every little back street in one of the world's largest cities. After two to three years of training, they must pass a test before they are licensed to drive one of London's famous black cabs. When researchers examined the brains of the drivers who had passed this test, colloquially known as "the knowledge," they found an increase in the size of the hippocampus.[9]

Exercise, especially aerobic exercise, can also bulk up the hippocampus. A study in adults aged 55 to 80 examined the effect of walking around a track for 40 minutes three days a week for one year. At the beginning of the study, all participants were given standard memory tests, and it was established that those with the largest hippocampus performed better on them. The test subjects were then randomly divided into two groups. Researchers found that after one year, the walkers had increased the size of their hippocampus and improved on memory test scores, whereas continued age-related shrinkage was seen in the controls, who instead of walking, were assigned a stretching routine.[10] These discoveries clearly show that we are not stuck with the brain we were born with, but can improve it and its capacity to remember at any age.

The amazing neuron tree

The brain cells most familiar to us are neurons, the main players in the nervous system. Neurons in the part of the nervous system outside the brain—the peripheral nervous system—collect information from inside and outside the body, and send it to the brain and spinal column, the central nervous system. There the neurons calculate what to do about the information, then transmit impulses back to the organs, telling them how to respond. Neurons tell muscles when to contract or relax, instruct glands to release their hormones, and control digestion, blood pressure and heart rhythm.

The structure of a neuron resembles a tree. The main trunk, along which electrical signals are transmitted, is called the axon. The thicker the axon the faster signals travel. In some neurons the axon is protected by an insulating layer, myelin, rather like the bark that protects a tree. Signals travel much faster along these myelinated neurons. From the crown of the tree (the soma) grows an elaborate network of branches. These branches are the dendrites, and the branching process is called arborization, from the Latin *arbor*, for tree. At the other end of the neuron—the root end or axon terminal—are projections similar to the dendrites, but not nearly as complex in their branching. Both dendrites and the root-like terminal projections end in tiny protrusions called synapses. This is where neurons connect with each other and signals are passed on, one nerve cell to another. Physical exercise stimulates the growth of new dendrites.[11]

The more interconnectedness there is between neurons, the better our brains function. Because each neuron may be connected to thousands of others, messages can travel through multiple pathways in the brain, and one neuron may even send multiple signals along different pathways simultaneously. Like a well-maintained tree, dendrites and the connections between neurons need frequent pruning. Neurons in regular communication strengthen their connections, while connections that are seldom used will disappear. Vigorous mental activity stimulates arborization, particularly when it involves doing something novel and complex, such as learning a new language, dance routine or musical instrument.

The other brain cells

Neurons are not the only cells in the brain—between 70 and 90 percent of cells in the brain are glial cells. Glial cells take their name from the Greek for glue, because in the past their main role was thought to be supportive. They were considered simply packing material between the neurons, holding them in place. Far from being mere bystanders however, glial cells are now recognized as essential, performing such vital functions as feeding, protecting and detoxifying neurons. Indeed, glial cells are sometimes referred to as nursemaid or housekeeping cells. As the saying goes "while neurons do the thinking, glial cells keep house." They do this by forming a transportation network to pull glucose, oxygen and other nutrients into the brain. Competent security guards, as well, they form the blood-brain barrier that prevents bacteria and other noxious agents from passing from the blood into the brain. Specialized glial cells, called microglia, act as scavengers, digesting and removing dead and dying cells and other debris.

Other glial cells—the oligodendrocytes—wrap themselves tightly around the axon where their fatty outer membrane insulates the neurons and forms the myelin sheath, much like the insulation on the electrical wires in your house. This allows electrical signals to flow efficiently and quickly. The insulating envelope of myelin needs constant maintenance and repair. In people who suffer from multiple sclerosis, the myelin sheath is not maintained, with devastating effects on motor skills and memory.

Nutrition and memory

Since we know that the brain has heavier demands for nutrients than any other organ in the body, poor nutrition cannot help but affect brain health. And because cells in the brain and spinal column send signals that control the activity of every other organ, loss of functional brain cells in turn affects the health of all other body parts. Stem cells have been found in the brain left over from fetal development that are capable of developing into new glial cells or neurons, and this finding has spurred research into how to coax these cells to grow, with the hope that normal brain function and memory may be restored, if lost. But even with all the exciting discoveries about the brain over the past couple of decades, little attention is paid to preventing memory loss in the first place, and understanding its nutritional roots.

The neurotransmitters involved in memory that have been most studied in relation to diet are dopamine, norepinephrine, serotonin and acetylcholine. Since we do not store neurotransmitters, our ability to manufacture these chemical signals depends on a meal-by-meal intake of their precursor molecules.[12] The amino acid tyrosine, as already noted, is the precursor molecule for dopamine and norepinephrine. These two neurotransmitters keep us focused, alert and upbeat, and play a key role in working memory. Dopamine seems to play a particular role in our remembering emotionally significant information—whether something we did angered, saddened or pleased someone, for example.[13] You can improve word recall and speech by increasing tyrosine in your diet.[14] Dopamine is further metabolized in the body into two other neurotransmitters: epinephrine and norepinephrine, which are important for memory retrieval, especially spatial memory—remembering directions, or where you parked the car.

Epinephrine and norepinephrine (also called adrenaline and noradrenaline, respectively) are short-term players, called on to deal with stress and keep us focused and alert in an emergency. Because chronic stress continuously shifts dopamine farther along the metabolic path towards adrenaline and noradrenaline, more tyrosine is needed by the brain to ensure sustained dopamine synthesis. I consider aging a stress, and most of my older clients agree that it is. Usually I recommend that they try tyrosine supplements, and if they report feeling less stressed and fatigued while taking them, I suggest they continue on them indefinitely. In any case, those who do benefit from tyrosine supplements do not want to give them up.

I will always remember a young man who came to me because he had been feeling very low for a long time, though not low enough for him to be considered clinically depressed. He did not want to take prescription drugs, and eventually I put him on tyrosine. He came back to see me about a month later and asked if I thought tyrosine could affect the way he worked. I asked what he had noticed. "Well, I'm the world's worst procrastinator," he said, "and I go off and do other things and get distracted very easily. Now I'm going into my office and I'm really focused and getting everything done in an orderly way." I told him that that's exactly what tyrosine could do.

Serotonin is also needed for learning, especially in situations where there are high demands on memory.[15] The precursor molecule for serotonin is the essential amino acid tryptophan, the least plentiful amino acid in protein foods. Circulating levels in the blood depend on protein intake, but getting tryptophan into the brain is no easy feat. Eating something sweet or starchy before bed, as we saw in Chapter 8, can help raise brain serotonin and help with sleep, which in turn benefits memory.

Acetylcholine a.k.a. the brain's memory manager

Acetylcholine, the most abundant neurotransmitter in the body, is probably the one you are least familiar with. It is responsible for sending messages from neurons to muscles, telling them when to move and when to stop moving. In the brain, acetylcholine is required for memory, and referred to popularly as the brain's "memory manager." When Alzheimer's disease strikes, neurons in the hippocampus that respond to acetylcholine are among the earliest casualties. The receptors or docking molecules in the brain for acetylcholine also bind nicotine, and many people who smoke complain that when they stop smoking, their memory loses some of its sharpness. In those cases, it is especially important to help them understand which nutrients can optimize acetylcholine production and reduce their dependence on the memory-enhancing effect of cigarettes.

The precursor or building block for acetylcholine is a fatty substance called choline, often classified as a B vitamin. Although it was officially recognized as an essential nutrient by the U.S. Institute of Medicine in 1998, I consider choline to be the forgotten fat. Choline is crucial in a mother's diet during pregnancy. Animal studies confirm that the amount of choline given to a pregnant animal dictates how good the memory of the offspring will be, and the effect seems to last even into old age. Summarizing animal experiments documenting the relationship between pregnancy, choline and memory, Professor Steven Zeisel from the University of North Carolina, a noted choline researcher, wrote: "The mother's dietary choline during a critical period in brain development of her infant influences the rate of birth and death of nerve cells. These changes are so important that we can pick out the groups of animals whose mothers had extra choline even when these animals are elderly. Thus, memory function in the aged rat is, in part, determined by what the mother ate."[16]

What an extraordinary idea—our mother's diet while carrying us may be influencing our memory, for better or worse, 50 or more years later.

The two richest dietary sources of choline are egg yolks and liver, once consumed regularly in most household. In recent years, intake of these foods has declined because choline-rich foods are also higher in cholesterol. A surprising number of people have been told by doctors and dieticians not to eat eggs, driving down choline consumption steadily with potentially disastrous effects on fetal development and on the aging brain.[17]

Table 1

Choline content of food in commonly eaten portion sizes

Food	Serving size	Choline content (mg)
Liver (beef)	3½ oz	532
Eggs	1 large	282
Atlantic cod (cooked)	3 oz	71
Beef (trimmed of fat)	3 oz (cooked)	62
Shrimp	3 oz (canned)	60
Salmon	3 oz	56
Soy beans (edamame)	½ cup	33
Broccoli (cooked)	½ cup (chopped)	31
Tofu (firm, full fat)	3½ oz	28
Cauliflower (cooked)	½ cup	22
Peanut butter	1 tablespoon	10

Note: adequate intake is estimated at 550 mg per day for men and 425 mg for women. The tolerable upper level of intake is 3.4 g per day for men and women.

I ask my clients to keep a diary of what they eat and bring it to each visit. I am saddened whenever I see egg white omelette listed as a breakfast item. Not only is the precious choline discarded with the yolk, but so are valuable vision-protecting nutrients such as lutein, which help prevent macular degeneration (see Chapter 6 for more about eggs). While I have never thought there was a good reason for demonizing eggs, liver from factory-farmed animals is a different matter. The liver is the clearing house for toxins, which accumulate there more than in other parts of an animal. Liver from factory-farmed livestock may contain pesticides, antibiotics and other environmental toxins. But organic liver from naturally raised animals and chickens is available, and that is what I recommend.

When I was a child, liver with bacon and onions was served for dinner once a week, and it was delicious, but many of my friends turn up their noses at liver, which is an acquired taste. Most people, however, can enjoy eggs. For those who are allergic to eggs or dislike them, I recommend a choline supplement for memory support. The majority of such supplements are derived from soy, and can be used by anyone with egg allergies. Phosphatidylcholine is one well-absorbed supplemental form, and comes in standard-dose capsules, three of which are roughly the equivalent to one egg yolk. Some people consume phosphatidylcholine as lecithin granules sprinkled on food or stirred into smoothies. One tablespoon of lecithin granules contains about 250 mg of choline.

Another choline supplement I use in my practice is called citicoline. Also known as CDP-choline, this supplement has been around since the early 1980s and is used in Europe for cognitive problems, especially after head injuries or stroke. It has recently become available as a supplement in North America, where its potential for memory protection as well as brain repair after trauma is being explored.[18] I put anyone having early senior moments on citicoline, and the majority find that their memory problems disappear. These are people who are already on a sound diet and have been taking a basic supplement regime, including a multivitamin with good levels of B vitamins, magnesium, vitamin D and omega-3 fats. This basic regime is often enough to resolve small memory issues. I add in citicoline only if shortfalls in memory persist after about six months on a basic supplement regime. In research studies, up to 2000 mg a day has been used, but I usually find 500 mg citicoline taken twice a day is sufficient. Since there are genetic differences in individual requirements for choline,[19] the dose that works for one person may not work for another. Some people may find lower doses effective.

Connie (not her real name) was a university professor who began to notice problems with word recall at meetings and while she was teaching. She ate well, was physically active and for several years had been taking a core supplement regime. When she started to complain of memory problems I suggested she add citicoline. She began taking 500 mg twice a day, with breakfast and dinner, and after a few weeks found that this worked really well. However, to meet her individual needs and find her ideal maintenance dose, I suggested that she gradually reduce her intake. Recently she was in my office. "I know exactly how much I need," she volunteered. "If I take 500 mg in the morning and 250 mg in the evening I am fine. But if I reduce to 250 mg twice a day it is not enough." This is a good illustration of biochemical individuality. For choline, as for vitamin D, iron, magnesium and many other nutrients, there is no one size fits all.

Glutamate and GABA:
red and green lights for nerve cells

Some neurotransmitters are excitatory and generally stimulate neurons to fire, while others are inhibitory. Glutamate is the most common excitatory neurotransmitter, while gamma-amino butyric acid (GABA), like serotonin, can put the brakes on. Glutamate is found in food as a component of protein, and is naturally present in mushrooms, scallops, cheeses, especially Parmesan cheese and tomatoes where it imparts a characteristic and appealing savory taste. You may know glutamate in the form of one of its salts, monosodium glutamate (MSG), which is widely used as a flavour enhancer, particularly in Chinese food. MSG is responsible for "Chinese restaurant syndrome"—the numbness, dizziness and headaches that some sensitive people experience after eating Chinese food.

Glutamate plays an essential role in the hippocampus. When it binds to its receptors it triggers motor neurons, the nerve cells that convey messages from the brain to muscles and glands to fire. Synapses in the hippocampus that respond to glutamate are thought to be important for memory storage. However, ingesting an excessive amount of glutamate is not a good thing since overstimulation of neurons by glutamate leads to a cascade of biochemical events that ends in the death of nerve cells. This potential for glutamate to become toxic when glutamate levels rise too high is thought to be central to the development of degenerative conditions involving learning, memory and movement, including Lou Gehrig's disease (ALS), Parkinson's disease and Alzheimer's.[20]

Hyperexcitation occurs whenever we are stressed (or distressed); for example, if we are constantly dealing with tight work deadlines, coping with bereavement or divorce, or watching our life savings disappear during a stock market meltdown. To prevent damage from hyperexcitation we need inhibitory neurotransmitters, and here GABA enters the picture. The main role of GABA is to regulate neuronal excitation and damp down excessive activation of the central nervous system. If you do not drink coffee yet feel as if you have just had three double espressos, you are short of GABA. If you go to bed with a head buzzing with ideas and then cannot calm down enough to sleep, you are short of GABA. GABA can relieve anxiety, ease tension and re-move the mental blocks that sometimes happen to overactive minds. Alcohol and anti-anxiety medications such as Valium interact with GABA receptors; that is how they produce their calming effect. A better option than drugs or alcohol is to take GABA itself, which is available as a supplement and works very well without the risk of dependency. In my practice I often sug-gest chewable lozenges containing 100 mg each—a tiny but often effective dose. Just chew one whenever you feel that three-espresso buzz or are overwhelmed by work.

Vitamins and minerals for memory support

It goes without saying that all the vitamins and minerals needed as cofactors to manufacture neurotransmitters must be available to the brain at all times. In particular, we need magnesium, B vitamins and vitamin D. Lower circulating blood levels of 25-hydroxy D—the storage form of vitamin D—are associated with memory impairment in older individuals.[21] You need to have a blood test for 25-hydroxy D to determine whether or not you are in the danger zone (see Part 3). Vitamin C is needed for dopamine synthesis, and if you are short of vitamin C you may have difficulty manufacturing it. Older people who take sup-plements of vitamins C and E have a lower risk of developing Alzheimer's disease.[22]

Also needed are the previously discussed long-chain omega-3 fats: EPA and DHA. Clinical trials have shown improved mem-ory and learning in individuals with mild cognitive decline after they were treated with DHA.[23]

One group of vitamins that seem particularly important for memory is the B vitamins. The B vitamins were once thought to be a single vitamin. Later this "B vitamin" was found to contain a number of distinct compounds that were chemically unrelated to each other but often occurred in the same foods, probably because they worked together. The B vitamins have names and most of them are numbered, but not consecutively (there's no B4, for example) according to the order in which they were discovered: thiamine is B1, riboflavin is B2, niacin is B3, pantothenic acid is B5, pyridoxine is B6, and then we skip to B12 (cobalamin) and folate. Because many of the B vitamins work together they are often taken together as a B-complex supplement. A well-formulated multivitamin will have high concentrations of B vitamins, often five to ten times the RDA. This is one of the criteria I use when deciding which multivitamin to recommend to a client (see Part 3).

All of the B vitamins are important for memory. B vitamins are water soluble, and since they are depleted over the course of the day, they need to be regularly replenished. One way to know if you are really short of B vitamins is to have a blood test that measures homocysteine. If you'll recall, homocysteine is an amino acid formed during normal metabolism. It is toxic and damages tissues and blood vessels; in healthy people it is rapidly removed from the circulation. However, this process requires several B vitamins: B2, B6, B12 and folate. When they are in short supply, serum homocysteine increases.[24] Homocysteine levels increase with age, and high levels are associated with increased risk of heart disease and dementia. The test for homocysteine is not covered by government plans, but I recommend to all my clients that they request it when they're having their annual physical, even if they have to pay for it. Laboratory values considered normal are below 14 micromoles per litre but the lower the better. I use research suggesting that the appropriate cut-off point to aim for is 8 mmol/l or less.[25] If it is higher, taking a B-complex should bring it down.

The dementia that is curable

Vitamin B12 plays many roles in brain health, but in particular it helps maintain the myelin sheath, the insulation around nerve fibres. Physical signs of B12 deficiency include fatigue and weakness as well as peripheral neuropathy—tingling, numbness and pain in the hands and feet. Meat and dairy products are the main dietary sources of B12, making vegetarians especially at risk of deficiency. Absorption of B12 depends on the presence of acid in the stomach, and the decrease in acid secretion that occurs with aging may explains why B12 deficiency is more common in the elderly. Acid-suppressing drugs like tagamet and ranitidine, and newer antacids called proton pump inhibitors such as Nexium, will make it difficult to absorb dietary B12, and with the widespread use of these drugs today it is possible that B12 deficiency is much more common than we think.[26]

B12 deficiency can also cause what is called B12 deficiency dementia. It's a pity that this form of dementia often goes undiagnosed because it is one dementia that is potentially curable.[27] A serum B12 evaluation is another blood test worth asking for, especially if you are showing any signs of memory impairment or experience tingling sensations in your hands or feet. The results, when they come back from the lab, will tell you the amount of B12 you have in your blood and whether it falls into the range that the lab considers normal. However, recent publications show that what is currently considered normal for serum B12 may well be inadequate for good brain function. Most labs quote anything above 133 picomoles per litre (pmol/L) as perfectly fine. A serum B12 test below the normal range is serious and needs immediate treatment. But even levels in the normal range may be insufficient for optimal brain health.

One of the measurable signs of brain deterioration is brain shrinkage that can occur with age. When researchers measured brain volume in men and women 65 and older and again four to five years later using magnetic resonance imaging (MRI), they found that those with the lowest serum B12 had the greatest brain shrinkage, and this was linked to poorer cognitive performance.[28] They also measured homocysteine and found that higher levels of homocysteine, which may reflect deficiencies of other B vitamins, not only B12, were also associated with mental decline and brain shrinkage. What was notable about this study was that the blood levels that were associated with mental decline and brain shrinkage were well into the normal range. This suggests that our normal range for B12 is incorrect.

In my practice, I like to see high B12 blood levels. Current laboratory values do not include an upper limit but reported case histories show that blood levels between 1000 and 2000 pmols/L are associated with clinical improvement in memory and word recall.[29] You need to address B12 deficiency early, since full-blown neurological damage from B12 deficiency may, according to some estimates, take up to 20 years to become obvious. Older people often report a surge in energy after being given B12 shots. If you do not want injections, supplements are available that bypass the problem of absorption from the intestines, and maybe just as effective as shots. Methylcobalamin is the form of B12 supplements that I favour. Sucked as a lozenge, the B12 is absorbed from the mouth directly into the bloodstream.

Taking acidophilus and other probiotics may also increase B12 in the body. Good bacteria were a traditional source of B vitamins. Today, we are overexposed to antibiotics, both as prescription medication and through the food chain, killing off many of these good bacteria. Factory-farmed animals and farmed fish are usually treated with antibiotics to enhance growth and control the infections that would otherwise be rampant in the cramped conditions in which they are raised. We are therefore exposed to antibiotic residues in food today more than ever before, and together with overprescription, this is considered a major factor in the development of drug-resistant strains of bacteria—superbugs like methicillin-resistant *Staphylococcus aureus* MRSA and *Clostridium difficile* (*C. difficile*). Antibiotic overuse may also be a factor in declining levels of B vitamins.

The anti-inflammatory diet

Inflammation can damage any organ, but the delicate structures of the brain are especially vulnerable. Cortisol, the stress hormone released during the fight-or-flight mechanism, has an anti-inflammatory effect, but in excess, it increases inflammation.[30] As we have seen, the stress response shunts glucose away from the brain, leaving the hippocampus energy deprived. We need to manage stress, especially chronic stress. Use whatever methods work best for you: practising meditation, getting a massage, going for walks, listening to music.

Once again, the key to an anti-inflammatory diet is to make vegetables and fruit the bulk of your food intake. Their colour pigments are antioxidants, high levels of which can protect the brain from free radical damage. Higher intakes of cabbage and antioxidant root vegetables such as carrots have recently been shown to be associated with memory preservation.[31] Cabbage, like other cruciferous vegetables such as broccoli, cauliflower and Brussels sprouts, helps us to detoxify from man-made chemicals that pervade our environment. Even if you buy organic foods and don't smoke, these pollutants are hard to avoid completely, and high levels have been linked to memory disorders.[32]

Just as important for damping down inflammation are the omega-3 fats, which are in short supply in the modern Western diet. An anti-inflammatory diet that supports brain health will include salmon, trout, and tree nuts such as walnuts and almonds. Complement these with salads made from tomatoes, red and yellow peppers and green onions. Include powerful anti-oxidants found in berries, chocolate powder and dark chocolate. Add a glass of red wine and you have a tasty diet that is anti-inflammatory and detoxifying. Always bear in mind the glycemic load of your meals: for the brain to function, it needs a steady supply of glucose best provided by vegetables, fruit and whole grains.

We come back again and again to two basic rules of diet, rules so consistently supported by research that it would be foolhardy to disregard them: First, we need to eat a plant-based diet, chock full of colourful phytochemicals, as well as a diet with a low-glycemic load; second, exercise—both mental and physical—cannot be ignored if we want to preserve memory. Neurons create new connections when we are exercising or learning new skills.

3

The Protocols

15

Food for Health

▼

*My definition of Man is, 'a Cooking Animal.' The beasts
have memory, judgement, and all the faculties and passions
of the mind in a certain degree, but no beast is a cook.*

— Samuel Johnson (1709–1784), English lexicographer,
in *The Journal of a Tour to the Hebrides with Samuel Johnson*
by James Boswell

*I*T IS EASY to be confused about diet when faced with an
onslaught of advice from all sides about what to eat and
what not to. Government-issued eating guidelines are
frequently out of date and unhelpful. Yet eating nutritious and
well-balanced meals is not difficult. We have more science to
guide our choices now than ever before, although eating to com-
ply with that science is a radical departure from current meal
patterns in North America.

Two threads run through the research literature that links diet
to the chronic diseases of aging: First, we are not eating enough
vegetables and fruit; and second, our diets contain too much
sugar and starch. Several diets have been shown to be effective in
extending disease-free life expectancy. The diet of the Okinawans

in Japan, the DASH diet, or modern versions of the diet of our hunter-gatherer forebears, are all high in vegetables and fruit, and lower in total calories, sugar and starchy carbohydrates. Eating this way takes some getting used to and demands a new and different way of meal planning.

These diets have something else in common: They are delicious. I find that most people who adjust their eating to this healthier pattern find that their desire for processed food simply vanishes, and they begin to appreciate natural tastes and aromas. The in-built capability of our taste buds to direct us to health-giving foods that allowed our ancient ancestors to survive re-asserts itself and we begin to enjoy food as never before.

Ten rules for healthy eating

1. Have three well-balanced meals a day

Many people I see subsist on two meals a day because they mistakenly believe that this approach will control their weight, or because they are too busy to stop and eat. Three well-spaced meals a day are required for proper control of our metabolism and appetite. Skip one, and you will end up consuming more calories later in the day.[1]

Properly balanced meals are heavy on vegetables and fruits, light on starch and contain modest portions of protein and good fats. Each meal should be similarly structured. Use your hands to visualize portion sizes and the balance between the different food groups. Dinner, for example, should include:

- a palm-sized serving of high-quality protein (fish, chicken, meat, eggs, yogurt, cheese)
- the same-sized portion (or less) of minimally processed starchy carbohydrate (whole grain bread, brown rice, whole wheat pasta)

- two handfuls of vegetables and/or fruit
- a thumb-sized amount of fat (see list below)

Such a meal might include a salad to start, several servings of vegetables with the main course, and berries or other fruit for dessert. It will contribute at least five servings towards your daily tally of vegetables and fruits. If the protein is a 6-ounce salmon steak, the starch might be ½ cup of brown rice. Or skip the rice or other starchy carbohydrate altogether for a few weeks if you want to kick-start a weight loss program. Legumes (peas, beans and lentils) contain fibre, phytochemicals and vegetable protein, and although their glycemic load is lower than most whole-grain breads or brown rice, legumes are starchy. Consider them part of your starch allowance.

Fat may already be present in egg yolk, cheese, salmon or perhaps as olive oil in salad dressing or sesame oil in a stir-fry. Select from the list of foods below containing good fats, reserving the foods containing less healthy fats for very occasional treats. Provided your diet is generally low in added saturated fats, a little bit of butter on cooked vegetables is not unhealthy and will help with the absorption of phytochemicals.

Foods containing good fats

Whole grains
Nuts and seeds
Seafood (shrimp, lobster, crab)
Cold-water fish (salmon,
    sardines, trout)
Lean organic meat
Olive oil; flaxseed oil
Avocados
Tofu (full fat)
Omega-3 eggs

Foods containing bad fats

Hydrogenated margarine
Red meat, unless grass-fed
Cured meat (sausage, salami)
Commercial salad dressings
Potato chips
Corn chips
Fried and deep-fried foods
Pastries, muffins, cookies
Ice cream, some candy

Structuring meals this way will automatically reduce their calorie content, and help control your weight. Do not overeat at any meal; leave the table feeling 80 percent full. This will allow you to digest each meal properly before eating again. Daily treats can include a glass of wine and a small amount (1 to 2 ounces) of dark chocolate. The chocolate should have 70 percent or higher cocoa content to avoid causing a spike in your blood sugar.

2. Never skip breakfast or lunch

Apart from the negative effects on metabolism, skipping breakfast or lunch makes it impossible to meet your daily quota for vegetables and fruits. Eat breakfast within 30 minutes of waking. Your body has been using nutrients overnight for maintenance and repair and consequently needs to fuel up again as soon as you are awake.

Structure breakfast the same way you structure other meals. First, choose your protein—an egg, some yogurt or cottage cheese. Second, think about how to add fruits or vegetables: maybe a large ripe field tomato with an egg, or a plate of fruit with cottage cheese or a bowl of fresh berries with plain yogurt. Third, if you like, add a small amount of minimally processed starch. Add a slice of whole-grain toast spread with almond butter or low-fat cream cheese to your egg and tomato. If you like cereal, top your fruit and yogurt with a tablespoon of crunchy granola or other whole-grain cereal. A bowl of cereal all by itself is not a good start to the day. Most ready-made cereals have a high glycemic load. Last, think about fat. The yolk of your egg will provide some, and yogurt or cottage cheese should be at least 1 percent fat.

A fruit smoothie is a good beginning to the day, provided you add a little fat and protein in the form of yogurt or protein powder. Protein powders available from health food stores are predigested into amino acids, and these are rapidly absorbed and utilized by the brain. I prefer whey protein, which appears to have beneficial effects on weight control compared to other protein powders, such as soy.[2] But because it does not stay long in the digestive system, predigested protein may not satisfy you for as long as the solid protein contained in an omelette or boiled egg.[3]

How bagels and muffins acquired a reputation as a healthy breakfast is difficult to understand. A large bagel is approximately 350 calories, the equivalent of 23 cubes of sugar! And a low-fat blueberry muffin from your favourite coffee shop tops 430 calories, the equivalent of 29 cubes of sugar! Can you imagine trying to eat 20 or more cubes of sugar? Even those with the sweetest tooth would find it difficult, and most people would gag after two or three.

In a busy workplace, finding time to eat lunch can be a challenge. But it is essential if you want to stay productive during the afternoon and sustain your focus and concentration. Be especially careful of starchy carbohydrates at lunchtime; they will raise serotonin levels, leaving you feeling sluggish and sleepy. For this reason, sandwiches are not the best choice for lunch, unless they are open faced on one slice of slow-to-digest bread such as pumpernickel. You will need protein such as eggs, cottage cheese, chicken or fish to increase brain dopamine so that you can work effectively during the afternoon.

If you eat at a food court, a julienne salad and a can of vegetable juice is a good foundation for a high-energy afternoon. It will provide you with four to five servings of vegetables and protein in the egg and turkey breast. If you bring lunch from home, leftover stir-fried chicken and vegetables from last night's dinner can be next day's lunch. Or try making a lower-calorie version of a chicken or egg salad wrap, substituting yogurt for mayonnaise and a large lettuce leaf for the wrap.

If you find yourself on the road at lunchtime, pack a container of easy finger food—cherry tomatoes, carrot, pepper and celery sticks—to munch as you go. Roll up chicken or turkey slices spread with a little low-fat cream cheese and Dijon mustard for a complete meal on the go.

3. Keep healthy snacks at hand

Allow four to five hours to elapse between meals to permit full digestion of the last meal before you eat again. But if you go more than five hours, you are likely to need a snack. This is when blood sugar drops. A brain deprived of glucose makes bad food choices, and you will end up raiding the cookie or candy jar. Smart snacking can keep energy levels high throughout the day.

Consider snacks as mini-meals and structure them similarly to your main meals. Ideally, they should contain protein, at least one serving of vegetables or fruit, and a little good fat (see list on page 241). In a pinch, a caffè latte made with 1 percent milk and no added sugar will keep you going for an hour or two. The milk provides protein and lactose, the natural milk sugar; the 1% milk contains enough fat to absorb phytochemicals from the coffee. Other snack suggestions:

- hard-boiled egg and a glass of vegetable juice
- hummus and cut-up vegetables for dipping
- a handful (about 1 ounce) of almonds or walnuts
- an apple or pear with a small piece of cheese
- small carton of cottage cheese with a handful of cherry tomatoes
- fruit smoothie with added whey protein

Before bed, have a small sweet snack. A glass of milk and a whole-grain cookie is good preparation for a sound night's sleep.

4. Load up on vegetables and increase fruit intake

Canada's Food Guide has recently increased its recommendations for vegetables and fruits from a low of five a day (vegetables and fruit combined). Five a day, which became a mantra for dietary advice for the last decade or so, was only ever appropriate for children 2 to 6 years. For adults between the ages of 19 and 51, a daily intake of 7 to 8 servings of fruits and vegetables for women and 8 to 10 for men is now recommended. Inexplicably, however, Canada's Food Guide also suggests that over the age of 50 we can reduce our intake, and that seven servings a day is ample for both men and women. This advice makes absolutely no sense. We do not have reduced requirements for vitamins, fibre and phytochemicals as we age; we need instead to maintain or even increase vegetables and fruits in our diet.[4]

It is sometimes suggested that we cut our consumption of corn, carrots and bananas because they have a slightly higher glycemic load. However, their fibre, vitamin and mineral, and phytochemical content is high and this makes them a desirable part of a well-balanced meal. Do control the amount of white potatoes and bananas you eat. One banana is the equivalent of 8 teaspoons of sugar and is quickly digested. Eat half mixed with other fruit, and put the other half in the fridge for later. Fruit juices raise blood sugar quickly and I discourage them; one large glass of orange or apple juice contains the same amount of sugar as a can of Coke—about 10 teaspoons. Instead, eat the whole orange or apple. Vegetable juice has a lower glycemic load and can be a useful way to bump up intake. Use a juicer that retains all the fibre.

For optimal health I suggest aiming for 10 to 14 servings a day of fruits and vegetables combined, with the emphasis on the low-calorie leafy greens, berries and citrus fruits. To achieve this, you have to get into the habit of counting the number of servings you have consumed each day as you go along. Keep the vegetables and fruits diary at the back of this book for a week. Do it from time to time until you become aware of how many portions of vegetables and fruits you are consuming each day. Then try to raise your intake.

5. Go easy on starchy carbohydrates—even whole grains

Whole grains do provide more fibre and this slows down their digestion, but a lot depends on how they are prepared. If they are overprocessed, as in instant oatmeal, or pulverized, as in the milling of flour to make bread, they convert too rapidly into sugar. Bread labelled whole-grain may be made largely with white flour, with only a small amount of whole-grain flour added. Look at the ingredients on the packet: if they include unbleached flour avoid that brand. Unbleached flour is, in fact, white flour. Old-fashioned dark rye bread is slower to digest.

6. Watch your protein intake, especially if you are a vegetarian

As we age, we need to prevent loss of muscle mass and maintain physical strength. This requires that we eat protein every day, since the nutrient cannot be stored in the body. Protein needs go up with increased physical activity, and rise dramatically following surgery or when we are fighting a serious infection. The best way to consume protein is in regular small portions throughout the day as part of all meals and snacks.

Animal proteins—meat, poultry, fish, eggs, milk and cheese—are complete proteins, that is, they contain all the essential amino acids, the ones we cannot manufacture ourselves. Apart from soy and tofu, vegetable sources of protein such as nuts, seeds, legumes and grains are incomplete proteins and vary in how many essential amino acids they contain. You can certainly mix and match different sources of vegetable protein to make meals that contain all nine essential amino acids. For example, grains are low in one essential amino acid, lysine, while legumes are low in methionine. A combination of grains and legumes, therefore, should provide all the essential amino acids.

If you are a true vegetarian, and eat no animal products at all, your diet needs careful planning to provide all the amino acids in a timely manner. Vegetarian diets are generally lower in the scarce amino acid tryptophan. Good sources include cashews, pumpkin seeds and peanut butter. Vegetarians may also miss out on the extra tyrosine in animal protein needed to maintain good dopamine levels, which help us focus and improve mood and concentration. A 6 ounce chicken breast contains 950 mg of tyrosine, compared with 395 mg in a cup of cooked lentils, or 190 mg in a cup of cooked brown rice.

A good vegetarian diet—one that is high in fibre, vegetables and fruit, nuts and seeds—is heart friendly and protects against type 2 diabetes.[5] Conversely, one that is high in refined starchy carbohydrates and sugar provides the perfect environment for disease to take root. Avoiding meat will not keep you healthy if you replace it with lots of potatoes, ice cream or bread.

7. *Eat organic when possible*

Organic food is food produced without added man-made chemicals, the persistent organic pollutants (POPs) we have previously discussed. These chemicals interfere with normal hormone function, and have been implicated in the development of insulin resistance, diabetes, obesity and thyroid disease. They may increase the risk of cancer and, in children, they have been implicated in learning problems and attention deficit disorder.[6]

Organic food is usually also free of genetically modified ingredients. In North America, the most common genetically modified crops—corn and soy—are specifically designed to tolerate high levels of pesticides.

The main source of exposure to pesticides is conventionally grown grains, fruits, fruit juice and vegetables, and this exposure can be detected in urine. One study in children in Seattle, Washington, replaced conventionally raised foods with the same foods that were organically grown. Five days later the levels of several commonly used pesticides dropped to undetectable levels in the children's urine, but reappeared again when non-organic foods were reintroduced.[7] While the effect of POPs on health is controversial and no one knows exactly how pollutants change human physiology, I believe it is better to err on the side of caution and avoid them where possible.

Each year the Environmental Working Group (EWG)—a U.S.-based not-for-profit organization dedicated to protecting public health and lobbying governments on health and safety issues—puts out two lists of vegetables and fruits they call the Clean 15 and the Dirty Dozen. The Clean 15 are those conventionally grown fruits and vegetables the EWG consider safest because they are lowest in pesticides, whereas the Dirty Dozen are those they recommend we buy organic. You can visit the website www.ewg.org and sign up for the "Shoppers Guide to Pesticides in Produce."[8]

We do not know whether organic foods are any more nourishing than conventionally grown foods. This is not an area that has been well researched and the evidence is contradictory. One study compared organic to conventionally farmed oranges and showed that the organic fruit had a higher content of antioxidants, phytochemicals and vitamin C than conventionally grown oranges.[9] Other studies showed that the phytochemical content of vegetables is sometimes similar and occasionally higher in organic compared to non-organic green vegetables. Researchers speculate that the phytochemical content increases the more a plant is exposed to insect predators.[10] Remember that phytochemicals are the plants' protection against enemy attack. Perhaps plants grow lazy when we spray them with pesticides, and reduce their own natural output of protective phytochemicals.

While the cost of eating organic is often higher than similar conventionally produced foods, costs are coming down as demand increases, and sometimes the difference in price is only marginal. In any case, even if you can't afford organic food, that should not deter you from increasing your vegetable and fruit intake. The proven benefits of a diet rich in phytochemicals trumps concerns about pesticide residues every time.

8. Consume alcohol in modest quantities

Over the past 20 years, compelling research from countries throughout the developed world has shown that moderate alcohol intake reduces the risk of many chronic health conditions, from heart disease and stroke, to dementia and diabetes. But keep your daily intake of alcohol modest—excessive intake increases the risk of all chronic illnesses.

A recent study carried out by researchers at the University of Calgary analyzed 84 previous studies of the relationship of alcohol to heart disease and stroke. It found that men and women who consumed up to 14.9 grams of alcohol a day—a little more than one standard drink—had a 14 to 25 percent reduction in heart disease, or death from any cause, compared to those who never drank. But drinking larger amounts increased the risk of stroke, as well as death from any cause.[11]

What is a standard drink? In North America, it is a 12 ounce serving of beer, 5 ounces of wine or a 1.5 ounce shot of 80-proof liquor like gin, rum, vodka or whiskey. No consensus exists on whether women should drink any alcohol at all, since some studies have shown an increase in breast cancer with alcohol intake at any level, while others have found no increase at one drink or less per day. According to the American Cancer Society, there is a very tiny increase in the risk of breast cancer in women who consume one standard drink per day, but a 50 percent increase at two to five drinks per day when those drinkers are compared to women who do not drink at all.

Modest alcohol intake appears to benefit the brain. Men and women followed for seven years who had moderate regular intakes of wine but no other forms of alcohol performed better on all tests of mental processing, whereas women who drank no alcohol showed mental deterioration over the same period.[12] Thus, while regular low intakes of alcohol do appear to benefit health, moderation is key. If you do not already enjoy the occasional glass of wine or beer, there are no compelling reasons to start. If you do drink, try adopting the "10, 3, zero" rule as now endorsed by Health Canada. This means drinking no more than 10 drinks in a week, no more than three drinks on any day, and keeping at least one day a week alcohol free.

9. Exercise regularly

For our hunter-gatherer ancestors, diet and exercise were inextricably linked. To survive, they would have been constantly on the prowl for food, expending large amounts of energy in the process. The food they gathered would have been nutrient rich but low in calories, and when they did not have to hunt or gather, they would have rested to conserve energy.

Today we still have the same instincts. We are preoccupied with food, but the food we eat is often low in nourishment and high in calories, while the only energy we expend to obtain it is the energy needed to push a cart around the supermarket. When the fridge is full, we still prefer to rest, opting for the couch rather than a walk or a bike ride. This combination of an energy-rich, nutrient-poor diet and sedentary lifestyle has created the perfect storm, setting the stage for a rapid rise in the chronic diseases of aging.

Telomere length, which as we have seen predicts biological age, is dramatically affected by exercise, which appears to stimulate our bodies to produce proteins that stabilize telomeres. This in turn prevents the shortening that generally accompanies aging, and improves predicted lifespan. The amount of energy we use on a weekly basis for exercising is important; both under-exercising and overexercising have been shown to shorten telomere length.[13]

To be at the top of that range you will probably need to work out at least five days a week. Brisk walking—walking as if you are in a hurry—for 30 minutes seven days a week will get you into the lower end. Aerobic fitness is beneficial to brain health, too, reducing the rate of brain shrinkage that occurs with age.[14] You do not have to be a marathon runner. In fact, although usually taken to be evidence of excellent health, such prolonged and extreme exercise can have adverse effects on joint and heart health, and has been associated with sudden death.[15] There are many sites on the Internet where you can calculate how many calories you expend through regular exercise.

Strength training is important as we age, and works together with an adequate intake of high-quality protein, vitamin D, antioxidants and omega-3 fatty acids to improve muscle strength, reduce the accumulation of fat and even improve immunity.[16] To maintain flexibility we also need to stretch, and supervised stretching programs have been shown to improve posture and gait as we age.[17] If you want to look and feel younger, good posture and a fluid and easy walking style are vital. Walk whenever you can. Do yoga or Pilates, and, if it's in your budget, work with a personal trainer to develop your own stretching and strengthening routine. If we want to age well, there seems to be no alternative but to mimic as best we can the walking, running, bending, stretching and lifting that was part of the everyday life of our hunter-gatherer and farming forebears.

10. Become a "cooking animal"

The best way to reduce the cost of good food and make sure your meals are healthy is to cook them yourself. If you are not already a competent cook, you need to learn to be at home in the kitchen. A host of courses are available to teach basic cooking skills. Check out your local school or community college. You may find courses for couples or ones where the whole family can learn to cook together.

The food you cook need not be complicated. Recipes should be quick to prepare and include fresh, natural ingredients, herbs and spices. Look for cookbooks that limit the number of ingredients in each recipe to five or fewer. I encourage clients to make their own cookbooks. Get a scrapbook and snip recipes from magazines and newspapers that conform to the healthy-eating rules outlined here. If you already cook, you may need to let your baking skills lie fallow, using them only on special occasions. For everyday eating, leave out desserts altogether or serve fruit at the end of the meal. While it is fun to make a cupboard full of jellies and jams, these are too much of a temptation; admittedly, they include lots of phytochemicals, but jams are usually way too high in sugar. Instead, freeze seasonal fruits for the winter months. Soft fruit like raspberries and strawberries can be puréed and frozen in ice cube trays, and used for smoothies, or added to yogurt.

I often hear complaints that it is impossible to eat in a health-ful way if your work or lifestyle involves eating out frequently. But here you have to make choices, too. While it is difficult but not impossible to eat a balanced diet at food courts, regular restau-rants increasingly cater to their customers' requests. Choose eating establishments where the food is fresh and the portions modest. Or, if you know in advance that the portions are large, plan to have a salad to start and share an entrée with a compan-ion. Do not be afraid to ask for substitutions—two vegetables instead of vegetables and rice, for example. Many restaurants are happy to oblige.

The proof that you are eating well and keeping your metab-olism humming is that you will feel energetic and upbeat, your weight will stabilize, and overall you will feel less stressed and much happier.

16

Building a Core Supplement Regime

▼

Vitamins are like seat belts. Wearing a seat belt doesn't give you a license to drive recklessly; it just protects you in case of an accident.

—Jeffrey Blumberg, Professor, Human Nutrition
Research Center on Aging, Tufts University

IF YOU HAVE NOT taken supplements previously, you may not notice any particular benefit when you first start. But after a while you should begin to feel increased stamina, less irritability and have fewer colds—evidence that you are now healthier than you were before you began to take them. If you were constipated and have slowly increased your magnesium until you are as regular as clockwork, take this, too, as a sign of improved health. That extra magnesium is not only boosting digestive health but also can have multiple other benefits, such as improved mood, better control of blood pressure and sounder sleep.

The real benefit of supplements, however, goes deeper than simply feeling well; they could be making you less vulnerable to serious health problems. Suppose you have inherited a bad gene, perhaps the colorectal cancer or breast cancer gene. These genes can lurk in our DNA like time bombs waiting to explode. But bad genes do not have to be activated: adequate levels of vitamins and minerals can keep them in check. Even if you do not have such a genetic inheritance, failure to supply the essential nutrients needed for the day-to-day repair and maintenance of your body could still make you susceptible to many chronic diseases associated with unhealthy aging, including heart disease and diabetes.[1]

Telomere length, which at the moment is the best indicator we have of our biological age, depends very much on optimal nutrition; the longer our telomeres are, the better we are aging. Telomeres are longer in those who take supplements, including multivitamins, B vitamins, antioxidants, vitamin D and omega-3 fats. Rather than take single supplements, it therefore makes sense to increase the intake of all these nutrients. This is the approach advocated in this book.

The supplements I recommend are divided into two groups. I usually start a new client on a basic supplement program or core regime, one from which any healthy individual can benefit. It includes a good multivitamin; individualized vitamin D intake, determined by a blood test; omega-3 fats; calcium and magnesium in the proper balance; additional antioxidants (C and E). The core regime does not cover the additional nutrients a person may need when sick or under chronic stress. Nor does it provide total insurance against depletions caused by pharmaceutical drugs. If you regularly take prescription medications it is important that you do not stop them unless advised to do so by your physician. It is also important that you seek the advice of a pharmacist or other knowledgeable health practitioner who can suggest how to compensate effectively for any nutritional depletions your drugs cause.

The second group contains additional supplements that may not be needed by everyone but are helpful in specific situations. They should be used with the core regime because their effectiveness can be compromised if you are short of basic nutrients. For example, you may see little benefit from taking tyrosine if you are short of some of the nutrients required to convert it into dopamine, such as vitamin C, the B vitamins and magnesium. Extravagant claims are made for supplements from natural food sources, but they are not always superior. While some synthetic supplements are less effective (for instance, vitamin D2) or to be avoided altogether (some forms of vitamin E), other synthetic vitamins including C are perfectly fine since they are chemically identical to the vitamins found in food. In this case, the body will respond in exactly the same way to synthetic and natural forms.

Some definitions

Some of the terms used when discussing appropriate and safe intakes of nutrients can be confusing. They include the following:

Estimated average requirement (EAR): Health Canada defines the EAR as "the amount of a nutrient that is estimated to meet the requirement of *half of all healthy individuals* in a given age and gender group." While EARs may be some use to health planners trying to assess population intakes, they are not at all helpful to us as individuals, since we have no way of knowing if we are in that 50 percent for whom the EAR is adequate.

Recommended Dietary Allowance (RDA) or **Recommended Nutrient Intake (RNI)**: RNIs were introduced in Canada in 1938 and are the equivalent of the Recommended Dietary Allowance (RDA) in the United States. The RDA is the amount of a nutrient needed to maintain good health in most people of a particular age or gender. It applies to healthy people only, and not to those with pre-existing health conditions or those recovering from trauma or surgery, whose needs will be higher. The RDA is not calculated to take into account nutritional depletion caused by heavy exercise or manual labour, or by medications.

Dietary Reference Intakes (DRI): These are the most recent set of dietary recommendations established by the Food and Nutrition Board of the Institute of Medicine (IOM), a body that oversees recommendations for Canada as well as the United States. DRIs are a complex combination of older existing methods for making recommendations and are used for counselling individuals and groups. The DRIs are updated from time to time and will eventually replace RDAs.

Adequate Intake (AI): Where the IOM feels there is insufficient scientific evidence to calculate a DRI for a nutrient, it sets an "adequate intake." The adequate intake is the amount of a nutrient that meets or exceeds the amount needed to maintain a particular body function. For example, over time choline deficiency will cause liver damage, so the adequate intake for choline is set at the amount needed to prevent liver damage.

Upper Tolerable Limit (UL): This is the highest daily intake of a nutrient that is likely to present no risk of adverse health effects in most individuals. According to Health Canada, at intakes at or below the UL the risk of adverse effects is close to zero, but beyond the UL the risks increase.[2]

Should we aim for RDAs or ULs?

The Recommended Dietary Allowance (RDA), although adequate to prevent the main deficiency diseases such as rickets, beriberi or scurvy, is probably inadequate for preventing chronic diseases such as heart disease, diabetes or dementia. This is because the latter conditions are thought to result from less than adequate intakes over prolonged periods, often decades.[3] The upper tolerable limit (UL) for any nutrient is many times higher than the RDA and has a built-in safety factor to account for individual variations in needs. It has been set so that at this level of intake there is little likelihood of adverse reactions. This is very reassuring, and makes taking vitamins at these higher levels much safer than, for example, taking a daily baby aspirin, which can cause damage to the lining of the gut, peptic ulcers and even gastrointestinal bleeding.[4]

Of course, nothing in life is entirely risk free—even the reckless overconsumption of water can be fatal.[5] So, while we know that intakes of essential nutrients at the upper limit are considered safe for unsupervised use, I believe it is always better, when possible, to follow the guidance of a nutritionally knowledgeable physician or other qualified health practitioner such as a naturopath when taking higher than RDA doses. He or she can also decide whether blood tests are necessary, and supervise increases or decreases in your intake as needed.

The table below shows both the daily RDA and, where there is one, the UL for some of the nutrients discussed in this book.

Table 1
*Comparison of the adult recommended daily intake (RDI) and
upper limit of intake (UL) for selected essential nutrients. No upper
limit is set where no evidence exists of toxicity at higher intakes*

| Nutrient | Dietary Reference Intakes (DRI) | | Upper limit (UL) |
	Adult Male	Adult Female	
Vitamin A	3,000 IU	2,300 IU	10,000 IU
B-vitamins:			
Thiamine (B1)	1.2 mg	1.1 mg	None set
Riboflavin (B2)	1.3 mg	1.1 mg	None set
Niacin	16 mg	14 mg	35 mg
Pantothenic acid (B5)	5 mg	5 m	None set
Pyridoxine (B6)	1.3 mg *(up to 50 yr)* 1.7 mg *(over 50 yr)*	1.3 mg *(up to 50 yr)* 1.5 mg *(over 50 yr)*	100 mg
Vitamin B12	2.4 mcg	2.4 mcg	None set
Folic acid	400 mcg	400 mcg	1 mg (1000 mcg)
Biotin	30 mg	30 mg	None set
Vitamin C	90 mg	75 mg	2000 mg
Vitamin D *Assuming minimal sun exposure*	600 IU *(up to 70 yr)* 800 IU *(over 70 yr)*	600 IU *(up to 70 yr)* 800 IU *(over 70 yr)*	4000 IU
Vitamin E **(alpha tocopherol)**	22 IU	22 IU	1000 IU
Choline (AI)	550 mg	425 mg	3500 mg
Calcium *From diet and supplements combined*	1000 mg *(19-50 yr)* 1000 mg *(51-70 yr)* 1200 mg *(over 70 yr)*	1000 mg *(19-50 yr)* 1200 mg *(51-70 yr)* 1200 mg *(over 70 yr)*	2500 mg *(19-50 yr)* 2000 mg *(51-70 yr)* 2000 mg *(over 70 yr)*

Magnesium	400 mg *(19-30 yr)* 420 mg *(over 30 yr)*	310 mg *(19-30 yr)* 320 mg *(over 30 yr)*	350 mg from supplements. *No upper limit* *from diet.*
Zinc	11 mg	8 m	40 mg
Omega-3 **fatty acids** (total)	1.6 g	1.1 g	None set
EPA + DHA	No recommendations		None set

Source: The Linus Pauling Institute Micronutrient Information Centre, Oregon State University. http://lpi.oregonstate.edu/infocenter/

The following are core supplements I recommend in my practice:

1. Multivitamin and mineral supplements (MVMs)

If you take only one supplement, make it a multivitamin and mineral supplement. Since all nutrients are required by all tissues all the time, a well-formulated MVM, which contains a little bit of everything, is an insurance policy against low intakes of any single one and provides important cofactors that can enhance the effect of other supplements.

As we have seen, regularly taking a multivitamin can protect telomere length, and some studies have shown a reduction in the incidence of cancer and heart disease with regular use. However, there are also contradictory studies on the benefits of multivitamins, and it is unlikely that maximum benefits can be obtained in one single formulation. For example, MVMs do not provide much calcium, magnesium or vitamin C because these nutrients are bulky. Vitamin E is also usually present in only tiny amounts, as natural forms of the E vitamins are oily and spoil the consistency of pills or capsules. Although some MVMs contain 1000 IU of vitamin D, most do not. All these nutrients are best taken as separate supplements.

Do not buy multivitamins that are not separately formulated for men and for women, or for those under or over 50. Formulas for men and postmenopausal women do not generally contain iron, although men of all ages and some postmenopausal women may need to take iron supplements, as directed by their physican. MVMs for older men contain extra nutrients needed for prostate health, and those for older women, nutritional support for menopause and after.

As a general guide your multivitamin should contain:

- **Generous amounts of B vitamins**. B vitamins are water soluble and need to be replaced every day. Many generic multivitamins contain only the RDA of the B vitamins, and these levels may not be optimal. Look at the amount of B6 in an MVM. A moderately potent one will contain about 25 mg, nearly 20 times the RDA. Higher than RDA levels of B6 have been shown to protect women against heart disease.[6] The more potent MVMs contain B vitamins at or near the UL where set.
- **A full spectrum of vitamins and minerals**: Look to see if your multivitamin contains less-well-known trace minerals such as molybdenum. Some MVMs do not yet contain trace minerals that have only recently come to the attention of researchers—strontium, for example, which can help support bone health—but look for them in the near future. The presence of vitamin K is a good indicator of an MVM that has recently been reformulated according to the latest research. Vitamin K supports bone health and protects against calcium being deposited in the wrong places—blood vessels, brain, kidneys or breast tissue, for example. But until recently it was not permitted in multivitamins sold in Canada.

- **Minerals that are reliably absorbed**: How efficiently we absorb and use minerals, their bioavailability, depends on many factors, including the health of the gastrointestinal tract and the way in which the vitamins and minerals are formulated. Some mineral formulations require acid in the stomach in order to be absorbed, and these include oxide or carbonate forms. The elderly or anyone taking antacids regularly will not absorb these forms reliably. Chelated minerals (from the Greek word meaning "claw"), in which minerals are attached to a carrier protein or amino acid, are well absorbed by most people, even the elderly and those taking antacids. Krebs cycle salts (citrate fumarate, gluconate) are also well absorbed.

Most MVMs are one-a-day formulations and are best taken with breakfast. Occasionally, the daily dose is divided into two or three, to be taken throughout the day. This is thought to enhance absorption and may sustain blood levels longer. If you are taking such a product, make sure to take all of the daily dose, as recommended by the manufacturers.

Be careful of overlap between your MVM and any other supplements you may be taking for specific conditions such as eye or bone health. These often contain a range of vitamins and minerals and are almost, but not quite, a multivitamin. Take time to add up the amounts of each nutrient present in both formulations and make sure the total does not exceed the daily upper limit for that nutrient. If it does, seek the advice of a qualified health practitioner before continuing to take both.

2. *Optimizing intake of vitamin D*

Very few foods *naturally* contain vitamin D. Salmon and other fatty fish, liver, and egg yolks from chickens fed extra D in their food are those that do. Cod liver oil, a rich source of vitamin D, has been used in Europe to prevent rickets since the seventeenth century. Because in the past vitamin D deficiency was considered a public health issue, some foods including milk products, margarine and certain cereals are fortified with vitamin D. But the amount of vitamin D in these foods is low. For example, you would have to drink about 10 glasses of milk a day to obtain the 1000 IU recommended for healthy bones by the Canadian Osteoporosis Society.[7]

Suspect vitamin D deficiency if you are suffering from a reduction in muscle strength or unexplained stiffness, muscle or bone pain, especially if you are over 70 or have dark skin. Back, hip and leg pain, walking awkwardly with a waddling gait, difficulty going up and down stairs or getting up out of a chair are common manifestations of vitamin D deficiency. Other recently recognized signs of vitamin D deficiency are a pronounced body sway when standing upright, reduced grip strength and difficulty walking a straight line. Supplementing with vitamin D can improve all these signs of vitamin D deficiency.[8]

The upper limit for vitamin D intake in North America is now set at 4000 IU a day, which is considered safe for unsupervised consumption by anyone nine years and older. To put this dose in perspective, 30 minutes of midday summer sunshine in Toronto or Vancouver, wearing a bathing suit and no sunblock (which blocks vitamin D synthesis) would generate 20,000 IU of vitamin D.[9] Thus, 4000 IUs represents the equivalent of six minutes of unprotected sun exposure.

After you have been taking vitamin D for three to six months, have your doctor test your blood levels of 25-hydroxy D—the storage form of vitamin D—to make sure that the supplements you are taking are having the desired effect. Doctors who do check for 25-hydroxy D are often surprised at the low levels of some of their patients, even those who have been taking supplements as recommended. The same intake of supplemental vitamin D will not raise blood levels of 25-hydroxy D to the same degree in everyone.[10]

Vitamin D3 or cholecalciferol is the naturally occurring form that is present in most supplements, and is identical to the vitamin D made in your skin when you are exposed to UVB radiation. Vitamin D2 or ergocalciferol is a synthetic form that is sourced from irradiated mushrooms. Vitamin D2 is much less effective at raising blood levels of 25-hydroxy D and has a shorter duration of action compared to vitamin D3.[11] Vegetarians who prefer to use D2 or physicians who occasionally prescribe it should be aware of this and may want to monitor blood levels. Vitamin D3 comes in pill form or as drops. Both forms are effective and should be taken with food, preferably the largest meal of the day, for best absorption.

The normal range for 25-hydroxy D quoted by most Canadian laboratories is 75 to 250 nmol/L (30 to 100 ng/mL in the United States). You might wonder where in that range it is desirable to be—at the lower end of the normal range, in the middle, or nearer to the top? We do not know yet, although the evidence suggests that higher levels are needed for cancer prevention, for example, than for bone health. Our human ancestors evolved as a tropical species, where vitamin D levels would have remained high and stable year-round—between 100 and 200 nmol/L (40 to 80 ng/mL). These are the blood levels to which our physiology is presumably attuned. I believe it is prudent to align our D levels today with those of our ancestors. Indeed, if these higher levels were harmful, natural selection would have caused humans in tropical and subtropical regions to die out.[12]

Once you achieve a desired blood level of 25-hydroxy D it is important to keep that level stable. Upswings in vitamin D either through sun exposure or supplement use are followed by a steady drop when sunshine is no longer available or if you reduce or stop your supplements. Some researchers now believe our biology is not well adapted to the large fluctuations in vitamin D that occur in northern climates, and that the swings in blood and tissue levels of this critical nutrient put us at higher risk of diseases such as cancer, compared to those living nearer the equator, who have stable year-round 25 hydroxy D levels.[13]

During the summer months, or if you are on a sunshine vacation, I think you can skip your vitamin D any day that you get 15 to 20 minutes of sun in minimal clothing—say, by a pool or on a deck—and resume taking it on days when you have no sun exposure. Whether you take vitamin D supplements or not, testing vitamin D as part of your annual physical is a good idea.

3. Omega-3 fats

The omega-3 fats, along with omega-6, are the essential fats; the body cannot manufacture them and a regular intake from diet or supplements is necessary if we are to stay healthy. Both are "good" fats, but the balance between them is critically important. An excess of omega-6 fats is generally considered inflammatory, whereas omega-3 fats are anti-inflammatory, which may be why omega-3s are so important for protecting the health of the heart, eyes and brain. There is presently little concern about deficiency in North American diets of omega-6 fats, which are found in eggs, meat and cooking oils including corn, cottonseed, sunflower and safflower. On the other hand, omega-3 fats, found mainly in seafood, are in short supply, especially in those not eating fatty fish regularly. This has resulted in an excess of omega-6 relative to the amount of omega-3 fats we are consuming.

Traditional Mediterranean diets contained a 4 to 1 ratio of omega-6 to omega-3 fats, and ancestral hunter-gatherer diets may have contained a balance of 1 to 1, or 1 to 2. Current diets in North America are skewed towards a much higher intake of omega-6 fats and contain anywhere between 14 to 25 times more omega-6 than omega-3. A lower ratio of omega-6 to omega-3 fats is essential if we are to reduce the risk of many of the chronic diseases of aging (cancer, arthritis and cardiovascular disease).[14] Even in healthy young individuals, supplementing with omega-3 fats has been shown to decrease inflammation and anxiety.[15] If you want to increase your intake of omega-3 fats from food, you need to consume at least two servings a week of fatty fish such as sardines or salmon.

Since many people do not like fish or are concerned about pollution in our fish stocks, use supplements only to increase omega-3 fats and let diet take care of the omega-6s. Two types of omega-3 supplements are available: those that come from marine sources like fish, krill and algae, and plant-based supplements that come from flaxseed, canola oil, soybeans, pumpkin seeds and walnuts. The plant-based sources contain the short-chain omega-3 fat alpha-linolenic acid (ALA) and do not contain the long-chain omega-3 fats eicosapentaenoic acid (EPA) and docosahexaenoic acid (DHA) that are so important for brain and cardiovascular health. These are found exclusively in marine sources.

Some animal species such as chickens are good at converting ALA into DHA. Chickens fed flaxseed produce about 75 mg of DHA per egg. The human body, on the other hand, is very inefficient at elongating ALA into DHA and EPA, and so supplements of fish oil become necessary if you are not eating fatty fish regularly. Make sure that any supplement you buy is certified free of such environmental pollutants as mercury, PCBs and dioxin. When the fish oil is distilled to remove pollutants, the fishy taste is often reduced and natural flavourings such as citrus are added. You should aim for supplements of fish oil to give roughly 750 mg EPA and 500 mg DHA per teaspoon per day. A good method of taking it is to stir it into yogurt or unsweetened apple sauce. If you take fish oil in capsule form, be sure to take the correct number of capsules to deliver that dose. Many people take only one capsule, when they may need two to four capsules daily to deliver the same amount as contained in a teaspoon of liquid oil.

Fish oil is a blood thinner, and in healthy people this is a great benefit, reducing the risk of stroke. However, those taking anti-coagulant drugs like warfarin should not take fish oil without consulting their doctor; the dose of anticoagulant may need to be altered. Because of its blood thinning effect, stop omega-3 fats ten to 14 days prior to surgery, and resume as soon as possible afterwards.

4. Calcium and magnesium

Calcium and magnesium work together to regulate how muscle cells contract and relax—calcium is required for contraction, while magnesium is required for muscle cells to relax again. Signs that calcium and magnesium are not balanced are apparent from problems with skeletal muscle: cramps and charley horses, restless legs, or sore, tense muscles. Palpitations or arrhythmia may be due to the magnesium needs of the cardiac muscle not being met, while headaches and blood pressure problems may be due to imbalances of calcium and magnesium in the smooth muscle cells that line blood vessels. Asthma or shortness of breath and frequent urination may all be due to a relative lack of magnesium in the smooth muscle cells of the lungs and bladder, respectively. The most common sign of imbalance, however, is constipation. This is because peristalsis, the wave of muscle activity that moves food through the digestive system, cannot work effectively when magnesium is in short supply.

Calcium is one nutrient that is not at all difficult to obtain from food. Check your daily intake from food using the calcium diary at the end of this book (Appendix B). If you find that you do not meet the RDA for your age and gender, then add in a supplement of calcium, preferably protein bound (see Table 1, p. 260) to bring you up to the RDA. Magnesium supplementation is trickier, as magnesium stores are easily depleted by stress. If you do not have any of the symptoms of magnesium deficit noted above you will probably benefit from a little extra magnesium anyway. Consider taking 100 mg of a protein-bound form before bed, when it will relax you and help with sleep. In my practice I find magnesium glycinate works very well.

If you do regularly have several of the signs of magnesium deficiency, and especially if you are chronically constipated, it is better to very gradually increase your magnesium intake from supplements in small doses, until you are no longer constipated—titrating to bowel tolerance. Start low with 100 mg of magnesium glycinate, taurate or protein chelate before bed. Then increase by ½ a pill (50 mg) every three days until you achieve one to three soft but formed bowel movements a day. Talk to your doctor before you do this, and rule out any medical reason for constipation.

Too much magnesium will over-relax the bowel and cause loose stools or diarrhea. This must be avoided since it will deplete your store of magnesium and defeat the whole purpose of the exercise. Once you find your optimal dose, which varies from one individual to another, maintaining that dose will keep bowels working well. It should also help get rid of any other symptoms of magnesium deficiency. Magnesium gel is another form of magnesium and can be applied to and absorbed by the skin. It contains magnesium chloride from sea water. Squeeze a 25 cent–sized blob onto the palm of your hand and rub it into inner arms or legs. Used like this, magnesium will enter the bloodstream and relax tense muscles in about five minutes.

Apply before bed for restless legs or difficulty sleeping or at any time during the day to relax tense shoulders.

5. *Antioxidants*

Both vitamin C and vitamin E are antioxidants, and together with the selenium, manganese and zinc contained in your multivitamin and the phytochemicals from the fruits and vegetables in your diet, boost defenses against free radical damage. Vitamin C is also required for immunity, collagen repair and replacement, and to manufacture the mood-enhancing neurotransmitter dopamine. I therefore advise using it at the upper level rather than the RDA. Use the time-released form twice a day, which will maintain steady blood levels. Vitamin E and C should be taken together, since vitamin E can help recycle your vitamin C and extend its life.

Vitamin E taken regularly may protect against heart disease, stroke, dementia and some cancers, but be sure to take a supplement that contains all eight forms of vitamin E found in nature—the four tocopherols (alpha, beta, delta and gamma) and the four tocotrienols (alpha, beta, delta and gamma), as all appear to have different benefits.[16] Taking them all together in one supplement is therefore the most logical approach since some of those benefits will be missed by taking just one alone, for example, alpha-tocopherol. Make sure to avoid the synthetic form of alpha-tocopherol and any supplements containing it. It will be labelled as dl-alpha tocopherol.

Vitamin E is a blood thinner, and like the omega-3 fats, it is useful for healthy people in preventing blood clots. However, like fish oil, it should be stopped 10 to 14 days prior to surgery, and can be resumed immediately afterwards. It is not suitable for those taking anticoagulant medications like warfarin, unless they are advised by a physician that it is safe to do so.

6. Probiotics

Dysbiosis is a term used to describe a state in which the balance of beneficial and harmful micro-organisms in our intestines is tipped in favour of the harmful ones. Taking probiotics shifts the balance in favour of the beneficial microbes. Signs of dysbiosis include flatulence, bloating and irritable bowel syndrome (IBS). Probiotics—the good bacteria—make a number of important nutrients, including B vitamins and vitamin K. They help us detoxify from drugs, hormones and cancer-causing chemicals. They protect us from an overgrowth of disease-causing organisms such as candida (yeasts) or *E. coli* and produce substances that reinforce the health of the gut wall, making it more disease resistant. Probiotic-containing yogurts are now widely available, and if they are a regular part of your diet, it may not be necessary to take a supplement. Look for yogurts that contain live or active bacteria and a range of probiotic strains.

If you do not eat yogurt, you need to consider a supplement. Choose one that contains between 5 to 10 billion bacteria per capsule and includes multiple strains, since different people respond to different species. The best supplements include several species of Lactobacilli, such as *Lactobacillus acidophilus, Lactobacillus bulgaricus, Lactobacillus rhamnosus* or *Lactobacillus casei*, as well as other species like *Streptococcus thermophilus, Bifidobacterium bifidum* and *Bifidobacterium longum*. Most supplements need refrigeration, which leads to a greater likelihood that you will forget to take them. However, enteric-coated supplements, designed to resist the acid in the stomach, are stable for many months out of the fridge. They are readily available and well suited for travelling.

Good bacteria in the gut are easily killed off by stress and poor diet; thus, they need regular replacement. If you are healthy, take one capsule just before bed, since the immune system is weakest overnight. If you are taking antibiotics, add an additional capsule earlier in the day but not at the same time as you take your antibiotics. Continue taking two daily for at least one month after finishing the antibiotics, then reduce your dose to one at night. If you have a lingering stuffy nose or sinus congestion, it may be helpful to take your evening probiotic as a mouth rinse. Simply open a capsule into a small glass of warm water. Mix, then swish vigorously around the mouth for about a minute, then swallow the mouth rinse. Add more water to the glass to capture any remaining bacteria, swish and swallow again.

Although probiotics may reduce gas and bloating caused by overgrowth of bad bacteria, some yogurts intended for therapeutic use contain very large numbers of bacteria (50 billion or more in a small tub), and these may themselves cause gas and bloating at the recommended daily dose. If this happens, reduce the amount you are taking until you feel comfortable.

7. *Tyrosine*

The amino acid tyrosine is the basic building block or precursor for a number of neurotransmitters active in the brain, including dopamine, adrenaline and noradrenaline. Tyrosine is also needed to make the enkephalins—the body's natural painkillers—and two other important chemicals: melanin, the major pigment of skin and hair, and the hormone thyroxin. Research studies have shown that mood, intellectual and physical performance, as well as sensitivity to pain, are all altered by the level of tyrosine in the daily diet.[17] Under conditions of stress, tyrosine may be used up to make neurotransmitters such as dopamine, noradrenaline and adrenaline faster than the diet can provide. Tyrosine supplements have therefore been found to be beneficial in reducing depression[18] and offsetting some of the adverse effects of stress.[19]

For tyrosine supplements (usually labelled L-tyrosine and available in 500 or 600 mg capsules) to be effective, they need to be taken on an empty stomach. Try taking 1500 to 2000 mg on waking and wait 30 minutes before eating. You can take an extra 1000 to 1500 mg again in the middle of the afternoon, again on an empty stomach (at least two hours after eating). An additional 1000 to 1500 mg may be helpful taken just before a stressful event—perhaps a theatrical performance or athletic competition. Always wait 30 minutes after you take it before eating. Plasma levels peak two hours after ingesting tyrosine. Experimental studies in human subjects have used up to 7 grams per day or 100 to 150 mg/kg body weight without adverse effects.[20] However, in my experience, most individuals get a good result with a daily dose of 1500 to 3000 mg in total.

Because tyrosine is also the building block for melanin, patients with melanoma are cautioned against it since tyrosine may enhance the progression of this type of cancer. Tyrosine should not be taken with antidepressants called MAO drugs (monoamine oxidase inhibitors) or any other antidepressant unless approved by a physician.

8. Tryptophan, 5-HTP and melatonin

Serotonin is a chemical messenger in the brain that has a calming effect. It also acts to control appetite and reduce carbohydrate cravings. Chronic low levels of serotonin may cause weight gain due to overeating[21] and may also bring on depression in susceptible individuals. In addition, serotonin is the building block for melatonin, which induces sleep.

The manufacture of serotonin in the brain requires tryptophan. Although some people take tryptophan itself, tryptophan has difficulty passing the blood-brain barrier. I prefer to use 5-HTP. It cannot be diverted by the body to make niacin (vitamin

B3), and 5-HTP supplements may therefore be the most effective way to increase levels of brain serotonin. For sleep problems, 50 to 200 mg, taken 30 minutes before bedtime, is usually effective, and an extra 50 mg can be taken if you wake in the middle of the night and cannot get back to sleep. For appetite control or depression, start with 50 mg, increasing to 100 mg three times a day. For weight control, 5-HTP should be taken 20 minutes before eating.

If you want to take higher doses of 5-HTP, work with a knowledgeable practitioner because it is possible for serotonin levels to go too high. This causes a condition called serotonin syndrome, usually due to medications that block the breakdown of serotonin in the brain. There have been suggestions, however, that taking 5-HTP could also increase the risk of this condition,[22] although I have never personally encountered it. Signs of excess serotonin are confusion, fever, shivering, diarrhea and muscle spasms.

Melatonin supplements are popular in Europe as a sleeping aid and for recovery from jet lag; some people find them more effective than 5-HTP. I usually suggest starting with 5-HTP, and if you do not get the result you desire, switch to melatonin. Start with 1 mg at night before bed, and if that is insufficient, increase it up to 3 mg as needed. Like tyrosine, these are natural aids to sleep and should not be taken with sleeping pills. Seek professional advice and approval of your physician before starting them.

9. Citicoline

Citicoline is a natural component of cell membranes. Taken as a supplement, it can help improve deteriorating memory, poor focus and concentration, all of which become more common as we age. It is particularly helpful for supporting and enhancing word recall (verbal memory).[23] Citicoline, also known as CDP-choline, is a well-studied supplement and is very safe; toxic side effects or interactions with medications are uncommon even at high doses.[24] Citicoline may also have antidepressant properties, stimulating the release of dopamine. It has been used successfully to aid recovery of memory after physical injury or stroke.

If you want to reduce or eliminate those senior moments, try adding citicoline to your core regime of daily supplements. Citicoline supplements come as 250 mg capsules, and the dose needs to be individualized. Start with 500 mg twice a day with food. If this is effective, try lowering the dose to 500 mg in the morning and 250 mg in the evening, or even 250 mg twice a day to see if the effect is maintained. If not, go up to the higher dose again. Up to 4000 mg daily has been safely used in clinical studies, but these high doses are rarely needed in otherwise healthy individuals who just want to protect memory and concentration as they age.

10. GABA

Gamma-amino butyric acid or GABA, a naturally occurring amino acid, is made in the brain. It functions as an inhibitory neurotransmitter, blocking nerve transmission. Without GABA, neurons fire too often and too rapidly, and our brain becomes overactive; we feel this as anxiety. That is why GABA, and drugs that mimic the effect of GABA, like Valium, can have a calming effect. It is often claimed that GABA taken as a supplement is ineffective, and that it cannot cross the blood-brain barrier and enter the brain. These statements are rarely supported by any scientific evidence. Although there is not a lot of research to support the usefulness of GABA supplements, one study using healthy volunteers showed that within one hour GABA sup-

plements increased the alpha brainwaves associated with a relaxed state. They have also been shown to decrease anxiety and
boost immunity in volunteers asked to make a high-stress
crossing across an unstable suspension bridge.[25]

In my practice I find low-dose chewable GABA lozenges very
useful for anyone suffering from anxiety or from brain overload.
Chew 100 mg lozenges throughout the day as needed, up to
a maximum of six daily. They can be especially helpful taken
before bed when an overactive brain can interfere with sleep.
If you feel you benefit from low-dose GABA, you may want to
consult a knowledgeable practitioner to find the optimal dose
and dosing schedule that works for you.

If you have not taken supplements before . . .

If you are starting to take supplements for the first time, be prepared for one or two things that you might not have expected.
First, your urine will probably turn bright yellow about one
hour after you take either a multivitamin or a B-complex. This
is because one of the B vitamins—riboflavin, also known as vitamin B2—is a fluorescent-yellow colour. The colour fades over
the course of the day.

Another B vitamin—niacin, or vitamin B3—can sometimes
cause what is known as a niacin flush. Your skin becomes red and
prickly, and you feel slightly overheated, as if you have had too
much sun. A niacin flush usually happens only at doses above
300 mg, but can happen at lower doses in very sensitive people.
If you get a partial flush, which looks blotchy and mottled, you
may think you are having an allergic reaction. Although startling
to look at, both a full or a partial flush are absolutely harmless.
The effect wears off after you take the supplement for a few
days. The upper limit for niacin (35 mg a day) has been set at a

level at which no one will experience this completely harmless reaction. Doses up to 2 grams a day (2000 mg) have been used safely in treating high cholesterol, despite the possibility of a flush.[26]

Some supplements, especially those that contain water-soluble vitamins and minerals, should be taken twice a day, usually with breakfast and dinner. That way you maintain good blood levels both during the day and overnight when nutrients are needed for body repair and maintenance. Fat-soluble vitamins like D and E do not need to be taken more than once daily, but vitamin D should be taken with the largest meal of the day, which for most people is dinner.[27] A few drugs have been shown to interact with nutritional supplements. Calcium, magnesium and iron can interfere with absorption of thyroid medications, and current advice is to allow four hours to elapse between taking these minerals and taking drugs such as l-thyroxine, used to treat thyroid disease. While very few other drugs have been tested for interactions with vitamins or minerals, it is best to get into a routine of taking supplements at a different time of day than you take medication, just in case. Allow at least two hours between taking supplements and taking medications other than those for thyroid.

If for any reason you need to stop supplements, check with a knowledgeable health professional for advice on the best way to do this. Both fish oil (omega-3 fats) and vitamin E supplements should be stopped 10 to 14 days prior to any surgery. If higher doses of vitamin C (500 mg or more) are being regularly consumed, they should not be stopped abruptly, but tapered off over a period of weeks. Over the years, several reports have appeared of scurvy-like symptoms following sudden withdrawal of high doses of vitamin C. Although these reports are anecdotal and there is no strong evidence that this is a common event, I still prefer to err on the side of caution, and suggest that stopping vitamin C supplements should be done gradually. If you want to reduce your intake of vitamin C, come down in 250 mg increments every three to four days, while increasing your intake of vitamin C–rich foods.

How to store supplements

Most supplements are best stored in a cool, dry cupboard, away from light and the heat from stoves or under-cupboard lights. Bottles of flaxseed oil or fish oil are stable at room temperature until opened. Once opened, oils and many probiotic supplements need to be stored in the fridge and used within two to four weeks, depending on manufacturers' instructions. Store gel caps of flaxseed or cod liver oil in the freezer for longer shelf life; they can be taken in their frozen state. This may reduce any tendency for oils to cause burping. Proper storage will help you get the most out of your supplements.

Appendix A

Fruit and Vegetable Diary

▼

This diary should be kept for one week. Repeat from time to time to see how you rate.

Mark each serving of fruits and vegetables you eat by ticking a single box. At the end of the week, total the number of boxes you have ticked, and write your score in the space provided.

FRUIT
(for weight control, limit to 3 servings spread throughout the day)

1 fresh apple or pear	❑❑❑❑❑ ❑❑❑❑❑	½ cup apple sauce (unsweetened)	❑❑❑❑❑ ❑❑❑❑❑
½ cup tinned fruit (no syrup)	❑❑❑❑❑ ❑❑❑❑❑	½ cup berries (fresh or frozen)	❑❑❑❑❑ ❑❑❑❑❑
1 medium banana	❑❑❑❑❑ ❑❑❑❑❑	¼ cup dried fruit (raisins, apricots etc.)	❑❑❑❑❑ ❑❑❑❑❑

1 medium slice of cantaloupe	⬜⬜⬜⬜⬜ ⬜⬜⬜⬜⬜	1 medium orange or large tangerine	⬜⬜⬜⬜⬜ ⬜⬜⬜⬜⬜
1 cup watermelon cubes	⬜⬜⬜⬜⬜ ⬜⬜⬜⬜⬜	½ cup prunes or figs (soaked, no sugar)	⬜⬜⬜⬜⬜ ⬜⬜⬜⬜⬜
½ large grapefruit	⬜⬜⬜⬜⬜ ⬜⬜⬜⬜⬜	1 peach or nectarine	⬜⬜⬜⬜⬜ ⬜⬜⬜⬜⬜
1 apricot (large) or plum (large)	⬜⬜⬜⬜⬜ ⬜⬜⬜⬜⬜	1 cup fresh or tinned pineapple (no sugar)	⬜⬜⬜⬜⬜ ⬜⬜⬜⬜⬜

VEGETABLES
(minimum 3 servings per day; no maximum)

½ glass vegetable juice (tomato, carrot, beet, mixed)	⬜⬜⬜⬜⬜ ⬜⬜⬜⬜⬜	½ cup cooked carrots or cooked mixed vegetables	⬜⬜⬜⬜⬜ ⬜⬜⬜⬜⬜
½ cup fresh or frozen peas or beans (lima, green, etc.)	⬜⬜⬜⬜⬜ ⬜⬜⬜⬜⬜	1 medium potato or medium yam	⬜⬜⬜⬜⬜ ⬜⬜⬜⬜⬜
½ cup broccoli or cauliflower	⬜⬜⬜⬜⬜ ⬜⬜⬜⬜⬜	1 cup shredded lettuce or mixed salad vegetables	⬜⬜⬜⬜⬜ ⬜⬜⬜⬜⬜
1 small onion or 4 spring onions	⬜⬜⬜⬜⬜ ⬜⬜⬜⬜⬜	½ cup cooked spinach or other greens	⬜⬜⬜⬜⬜ ⬜⬜⬜⬜⬜
1 medium tomato, or red or green pepper	⬜⬜⬜⬜⬜ ⬜⬜⬜⬜⬜	1 cup raw spinach (packed)	⬜⬜⬜⬜⬜ ⬜⬜⬜⬜⬜

½ cup tomato sauce (i.e., spaghetti, or pizza)	❑❑❑❑❑ ❑❑❑❑❑	1 stick of celery	❑❑❑❑❑ ❑❑❑❑❑
1 ear of corn (fresh) or ½ cup frozen	❑❑❑❑❑ ❑❑❑❑❑	½ cup bean or alfalfa sprouts	❑❑❑❑❑
½ cup soybeans	❑❑❑❑❑ ❑❑❑❑❑	½ cup beets	❑❑❑❑❑ ❑❑❑❑❑
½ cup eggplant, zucchini, squash or pumpkin	❑❑❑❑❑ ❑❑❑❑❑	3 medium stalks of asparagus	❑❑❑❑❑ ❑❑❑❑❑
½ cup cabbage or coleslaw	❑❑❑❑❑ ❑❑❑❑❑	½ cup lentils (cooked)	❑❑❑❑❑ ❑❑❑❑❑
1 medium raw carrot or 4 large carrot sticks	❑❑❑❑❑ ❑❑❑❑❑	1 cup vegetable, lentil or bean soup	❑❑❑❑❑ ❑❑❑❑❑

Total score for the week ❑

HOW DO YOU RATE?

56–70 Excellent. If you maintain this level of consumption consistently, you should see your efforts repaid in the long term with a stronger immune system, slower aging and a reduced risk of major health problems. Weight control should also be easier. Congratulations.

49–55 Good. Your fruit and vegetable intake is above average, and meets the 7 to 8 now recommended by Health Canada. Try to maintain and improve on this. Choose dark green and orange vegetables, and orange fruits like cantaloupe and mango and purple/red berries and vegetables more often for maximum benefit.

35–48 Fair. Although you may think you are eating enough fruits and vegetables, your intake is lower than the recommended minimum daily servings, and is only adequate for children between the ages of 2 and 6. Plan to have fruit or carrot sticks as a mid-morning or afternoon snack, and on days when it is difficult to get enough fresh produce, drink vegetable juice to supplement your intake.

Under 35 Poor. You are not consuming enough vegetables and fruits. Remember they are no longer considered an optional part of our diet but play a key role in helping us stay healthy and avoid diseases such as diabetes, heart disease and stroke, eye disease, cancer and dementia.

Appendix B

Calcium Diary

▼

Use this diary to calculate your average daily intake of calcium from food on a typical day. You could simply set down what you ate yesterday, or make copies of this page and fill them out for one week to give you a more accurate average. If you do not meet current recommendations (below), you need to increase your intake with supplements.

Recommended dietary intake (mg per day)

Age (years)	Men	Women
19–50	1000 mg	1000 mg
51–70	1000 mg	1200 mg
71 +	1200 mg	1200 mg

Food	Calcium per portion (mg)	Number of servings	Total calcium (mg)
Milk and milk products			
¾ cup 1% yogurt	330 mg	_____	_____
1 cup 1% milk	300 mg	_____	_____
½ cup ricotta	250 mg	_____	_____
1 oz cheddar cheese	200 mg	_____	_____
1 oz feta cheese	140 mg	_____	_____
½ cup cottage cheese	70 mg	_____	_____

Fish and shellfish

1 tin sardines (4 oz)	350 mg	_____	_____
4 oz salmon, canned with bones	200 mg	_____	_____
4 oz rainbow trout	100 mg	_____	_____
4 oz crabmeat	55 mg	_____	_____
4 oz fresh salmon (cooked)	40 mg	_____	_____
4 oz haddock	40 mg	_____	_____

Beans and legumes

4 oz tofu (firm)	225 mg	_____	_____
½ cup hummus	65 mg	_____	_____
½ cup soybeans (edamame)	50 mg	_____	_____
½ cup chick peas	40 mg	_____	_____
½ cup lentils (cooked)	30 mg	_____	_____

Vegetables

½ cup collard greens (cooked)	110 mg	_____	_____
½ cup bok choy (cooked)	80 mg	_____	_____
½ cup kale (cooked)	45 mg	_____	_____
½ cup broccoli (chopped, cooked)	50 mg	_____	_____
1 small sweet potato (baked)	30 mg	_____	_____

Fruit

1 orange (medium)	50 mg	_____	_____
Figs, fresh (2)	35 mg	_____	_____
½ grapefruit (large)	30 mg	_____	_____
1 kiwifruit (large)	30 mg	_____	_____

Nuts and seeds

1 oz almonds (about 24)	75 mg	_____	_____
½ cup sunflower seeds	45 mg	_____	_____
1 tablespoon almond butter	45 mg	_____	_____
1 oz walnuts (about 12)	25 mg	_____	_____

Milk alternatives

1 cup of fortified rice, soy   300 mg   _____   _____
or almond milk. *Check label
as amount of fortification can
vary from product to product.*

Daily Total   _____

Acknowledgments

The authors wish to thank Professor Sampa Bhadra and Professor John Martin for bringing about their collaboration, and their agent, Beverley Slopen, for her perseverance and faith in the project. Many thanks to Dr. Linda Rapson and Dr. Nadine Bukmuz for reading the manuscript, and giving so generously of their time and expert advice. Aileen Burford-Mason is indebted to Professor Ursula Franklin for her friendship and many hours of helpful discussion, and to her two wonderful granddaughters, Hannah and Holly, from whom time was stolen to write this book. For his unflagging encouragement and computer prowess, Judy Stoffman is, as always, grateful to her husband, Daniel.

Endnotes

Introduction

1. Nutrition education in U.S. medical schools: latest update of a national survey. Adams KM et al. *Academic Medicine* 2010;85(9):1537–42.
2. Medical students' perceptions of nutrition education in Canadian universities. Gramlich LM et al. *Applied Physiology, Nutrition and Metabolism* 2010;35(3):336–43.

Chapter 1: Adding Life to Your Years

1. *World Population Data Sheet.* Washington, DC: Population Reference Bureau, 2001.
2. Living longer but doing worse: assessing health status in elderly persons at two points in time in Manitoba, Canada, 1971 and 1983. Roos NP et al. *Social Science and Medicine* 1993;36(3):273–82.
3. High prevalence of coronary atherosclerosis in asymptomatic teenagers and young adults: evidence from intravascular ultrasound. Tuzcu EM et al. *Circulation* 2001;103(22):2705–10.
4. IMS Health Reports Canadian Retail Prescriptions Dispensed Grew 5.5 Percent in 2009, Fueled by Generics. Press release April 2010 (www.imshealth.com).
5. *The Nutritional Cost of Drugs: A Guide to Maintaining Good Nutrition While Using Prescription and Over-the-Counter Drugs.* Pelton R, Lavalle JB. Englewood, CO: Morton Publishing Company, 2004.

6. Metabolic syndrome components worsen lower urinary tract symptoms in women with type 2 diabetes. Tai HC et al. *Journal of Clinical Endocrinology and Metabolism* 2010;95(3):1143–50.

7. The multifaceted and widespread pathology of magnesium deficiency. Johnson S. *Medical Hypotheses* 2001;56(2):163–70.

8. A pilot phase II trial of magnesium supplements to reduce menopausal hot flashes in breast cancer patients. Park H et al. *Supportive Care in Cancer* 2011;19(6):859–63.

9. Apoptosis. Israels LLG, Israels ED. *Stem Cells* 1999;17(5):306–13.

10. Canadian Community Health Survey Cycle 2.2 (2004). Available at Health Canada's website at www.hc-sc.gc.ca/fn-an/surveill/nutrition/commun/index-eng.php.

11. Adaptive dysfunction of selenoproteins from the perspective of the triage theory: why modest selenium deficiency may increase risk of diseases of aging. McCann JC, Ames BN. *Federation of American Societies for Experimental Biology (FASEB) Journal* 2011;25(6):1793–814.

12. Factors impacting human telomere homeostasis and age-related disease. Gilley D et al. *Mechanisms of Ageing and Development* 2008;129: 27–34.

13. The heritability of human longevity: a population-based study of 2872 Danish twin pairs born 1870-1900. Herskind AM et al. *Human Genetics* 1996:97: 319–23.

14. Eat your way to better DNA. *The Scientist* 2006:20(9):50.

Chapter 2: A Short History of Eating

1. The roles and values of wild foods in agricultural systems. Bharucha Z, Pretty J. Philosophical Transactions of the Royal Society of London. Series B *Biological Sciences* 2010;365(1554):2913–26.

2. Paleolithic nutrition: twenty-five years later. Konner M, Eaton SB. *Nutrition in Clinical Practice* 2010;25(6):594–602.

3. *Health and the Rise of Civilization*. Cohen MN. New Haven and London: Yale University Press, 1989.

4. The diabetes and obesity epidemic among the Pima Indians. Krosnick A. *New Jersey Medicine* 2000;97(8):31–37.

5. The effect of Indian or Anglo dietary preference on the incidence of diabetes in Pima Indians. Williams D et al. *Diabetes Care* 2001;24(5):811–16.

6. Changes in USDA food composition data for 43 garden crops, 1950 to 1999. Davis DR et al. *Journal of the American College of Nutrition* 2004;23 (6):669–82.

7. Civilisation and the colon: constipation as the "disease of diseases." Whorton J. *British Medical Journal* 2000;321(7276):1586–89.

Chapter 3: Hidden Hunger: The Discovery of Micronutrients

1. De Morbo puerili Anglorum, quam patrio idiomate indiginae vocant 'The Rickets.' Whistler D. 1645, Leydon.

2. *Essays Medical, Philosophical and Experimental*. Percival T. Vol. 2. 4th Edition. London, 1789.

3. *Biochemical Individuality*. Williams RJ. New Canaan, CO: Keats Publishing, 1998.

4. Body iron excretion by healthy men and women. Hunt JR et al. *American Journal of Clinical Nutrition* 2009;89(6):1792–98.

5. Low micronutrient intake may accelerate the degenerative diseases of aging through allocation of scarce micronutrients by triage. Ames BN. Proceedings of the National Academy of Sciences USA 2006;103(47): 17589–94.

Chapter 4: Fatigue

1. In *The Vitamins in Medicine*. Bicknell F, Prescott F. London: William Heinemann Medical Books, 1942, p. 3.

2. Ipsos Reid. Two-thirds of Canadians Use Natural Products. 1/12/2010.

3. Magnesium content of the food supply in the modern-day world. Marier JR. *Magnesium* 1986;5(1):1–8.

4. Glycemic index of foods: a physiological basis for carbohydrate exchange. Jenkins, DJ et al. *American Journal of Clinical Nutrition* 1981;34 (3): 362–66.

Chapter 5: Hair, Skin and Nails

1. Perceived age as clinically useful biomarker of ageing: cohort study. Christensen K, *British Medical Journal* 2009;339:b5262.

2. Collagen turnover and its regulation in the normal and hypertrophying heart. Bishop JE, Laurent GJ. *European Heart Journal* 1995;16 Suppl C:38–44.

3. Diabetic vascular complications: pathophysiology, biochemical basis and potential therapeutic strategy. Yamagishi S, Imaizumi T. *Current Pharmaceutical Design* 2005;11:2279–99.

4. Scurvy is still present in developed countries. Velandia B et al. *Journal of General Internal Medicine* 2008;23(8):1281–84.

5. Green tea extract suppresses the age-related increase in collagen crosslinking and fluorescent products in C57BL/6 mice. Rutter K et al. *International Journal for Vitamin and Nutrition Research* 2003;73(6):453–60.

6. Trophic implications of altered body composition observed in or near the nails of hemodialysis patients. Kelly MP et al. *Advances in Renal Replacement Therapy* 1998;5(3):241–51.

7. Current status of zinc deficiency in the pathogenesis of neurological, dermatological and musculoskeletal disorders. Sunderman FW Jr. *Annals of Clinical and Laboratory Science* 1975;5(2):132–45.

8. Diffuse hair loss: its triggers and management. Harrison S, Bergfeld W. *Cleveland Clinic Journal of Medicine* 2009;76(6):361–67.

9. Vitamin intake: a possible determinant of plasma homocyst(e)ine among middle-aged adults. Shimakawa T et al. *Annals of Epidemiology* 1997;7(4):285–93.

10. Transposable elements: targets for early nutritional effects on epigenetic gene regulation. Waterland RA, Jirtle RL. *Molecular and Cellular Biology* 2003;23(15):5293–300.

11. Improvement of vitiligo after oral treatment with vitamin B12 and folic acid and the importance of sun exposure. Juhlin L, Olsson MJ. *Acta Dermato-Venereologica* 1997;77(6):460–62.

Chapter 6: Vision and Hearing

1. Association between vision and hearing impairments and their combined effects on quality of life. Chia EM, et al. *Archives of Ophthalmology* 2006;124(10):1465–70.

2. Dietary glycemic load is a predictor of age-related hearing loss in older adults. Gopinath B, et al. *Journal of Nutrition* 2010;140(12):2207–12.

3. Dietary glycemic index and the risk of age-related macular degeneration. Kaushik S et al. *American Journal of Clinical Nutrition* 2008;88(4):1104–10.

4. Nutritional interventions against age-related macular degeneration. Bernstein PS. *Acta Horticulturae* 2009;841:103–12.

Endnotes

5. Risk factors for sudden deafness: a case-control study. Nakashima T et al. *Auris Nasus Larynx* 1997;24(3):265–70.

6. The association of cataract with leukocyte telomere length in older adults: defining a new marker of aging. Sanders JL et al. *Journal of Gerontology Series A. Biological Sciences and Medical Sciences* 2011;66(6):639–45.

7. Aspects of antioxidant foods and supplements in health and disease. Herrera E et al. *Nutrition Reviews* 2009;67 Suppl 1:S140–44.

8. Oxygen Radical Absorbance Capacity (ORAC) of Selected Foods—2007. http://www.ars.usda.gov/nutrientdata.

9. Vitamin E and the risk of prostate cancer: the Selenium and Vitamin E Cancer Prevention Trial (SELECT). Klein EA et al. *Journal of the American Medical Association* 2011;306(14):1549–56.

10. Food and Nutrition Board, Institute of Medicine. Vitamin E. *Dietary reference intakes for vitamin C, vitamin E, selenium, and carotenoids.* Washington D.C.: National Academy Press; 2000:186–283.

11. Anti-inflammatory properties of alpha- and gamma-tocopherol. Reiter E et al. *Molecular Aspects of Medicine* 2007;28(5-6):668–91.

12. High plasma levels of vitamin E forms and reduced Alzheimer's disease risk in advanced age. Mangialasche F et al. *Journal of Alzheimers Disease* 2010;20(4):1029–37.

13. Vitamin E and the risk of prostate cancer: the Selenium and Vitamin E Cancer Prevention Trial (SELECT).

14. Measurement of vitamin E metabolites by high-performance liquid chromatography during high-dose administration of alpha-tocopherol. Morinobu T et al. *European Journal of Clinical Nutrition* 2003;57(3):410–14.

15. Intestinal absorption, serum clearance, and interactions between lutein and beta-carotene when administered to human adults in separate or combined oral doses. Kostic D, et al. *American Journal of Clinical Nutrition* 1995;62:604–610.

16. A 12-wk egg intervention increases serum zeaxanthin and macular pigment optical density in women. Wenzel AJ et al. *Journal of Nutrition* 2006;136(10):2568–73.

17. Consumption of one egg per day increases serum lutein and zeaxanthin concentrations in older adults without altering serum lipid and lipoprotein cholesterol concentrations. Goodrow E et al. *Journal of Nutrition* 2006; 136(10):2519–24.

18. Prevention of age-related macular degeneration. Wong IY et al. *International Ophthalmology* 2011;31(1):73–82.

19. Centrum use and progression of age-related cataract in the Age-Related Eye Disease Study: a propensity score approach. AREDS report No. 21. Milton RC et al. *Ophthalmology* 2006;113(8):1264–70.

20. Vitamin D status and early age-related macular degeneration in post-menopausal women. Millen AE et al. *Archives of Ophthalmology* 2011; 129(4):481–89.

21. The influence of magnesium on visual field and peripheral vasospasm in glaucoma. Gaspar AZ et al. *Ophthalmologica* 1995;209(1):11–13.

22. Pathogenesis of ganglion "cell death" in glaucoma and neuroprotection: focus on ganglion cell axonal mitochondria. Osborne NN. *Progress in Brain Research* 2008;173:339–52.

23. Carotinoid absorption from salad and salsa by humans is enhanced by the addition of avocado or avocado oil. Unlu NZ et al. *Journal of Nutrition* 2005;135(3):431–36.

24. Oral magnesium intake reduces permanent hearing loss induced by noise exposure. Attias J et al. *American Journal of Otolaryngology* 1994;15(1): 26–32.

25. Consumption of omega-3 fatty acids and fish and risk of age-related hearing loss. Gopinath B et al. *American Journal of Clinical Nutrition* 2010;92(2): 416–21.

26. Antioxidant micronutrient impact on hearing disorders: concept, rationale, and evidence. Haase GM et al. *American Journal of Otolaryngology* 2011;32(1):55–61.

27. Exploring the reasons why melatonin can improve tinnitus. Pirodda A et al. *Medical Hypotheses* 2010;75(2):190–91.

Chapter 7: Osteopenia and Osteoporosis

1. Excess mortality following hip fracture: a systematic epidemiological review. Abrahamsen B et al. *Osteoporosis International* 2009;20(10):1633–50.

2. Developmental origins of osteoporosis: the role of maternal nutrition. Cooper C et al. *Advances in Experimental Medicine and Biology* 2009;646: 31–39.

3. Bone remodeling. Hadjidakis DJ, Androulakis II. *Annals of the New York Academy of Sciences* 2006;1092:385–96.

4. Do osteocytes contribute to bone mineral homeostasis? Osteocytic osteolysis revisited. Teti A, Zallone A. *Bone* 2009;44(1):11–16.

Endnotes

5. Drug-induced osteoporosis: mechanisms and clinical implications. Mazz-iotti G et al. *American Journal of Medicine* 2010;123(10):877–84.

6. Bisphosphonate adverse effects, lessons from large databases. Abrahamsen B. *Current Opinion in Rheumatology* 2010;22(4):404–09.

7. A systematic review of the evidence for Canada's Physical Activity Guide-lines for Adults. Warburton DE et al. *International Journal of Behavioral Nutrition and Physical Activity* 2010;7:39.

8. Physical activity in the prevention and amelioration of osteoporosis in women: interaction of mechanical, hormonal and dietary factors. Borer KT. *Sports Medicine* 2005;35(9):779–830.

9. Nutrition Society Medal lecture. The role of the skeleton in acid-base homeostasis. New SA. Proceedings of the Nutrition Society 2002;61(2): 151–64.

10. The DASH diet and sodium reduction improve markers of bone turnover and calcium metabolism in adults. Lin PH et al. *Journal of Nutrition* 2003;133(10):3130–36.

11. Drug-induced osteoporosis: mechanisms and clinical implications.

12. Optimal protein intake in the elderly. Wolfe RR et al. *Clinical Nutrition* 2008;27(5):675–84.

13. Dietary calcium intake and risk of fracture and osteoporosis: prospective longitudinal cohort study. Warensjö E et al. *British Medical Journal* 2011; 342:d1473.

14. Calcium supplements with or without vitamin D and risk of cardiovascular events: reanalysis of the Women's Health Initiative limited access dataset and meta-analysis. Bolland MJ et al. *British Medical Journal* 2011;342: d2040.

15. Institute of Medicine. *Dietary Reference Intakes for Calcium and Vitamin D.* Washington, D.C.: National Academies Press, 2010.

16. Comment on the IOM Vitamin D and Calcium Recommendations. Bischoff-Ferrari H, Willett W. The Nutrition Source. Harvard School of Public Health, May 19, 2011.

17. Vitamin D across the lifecycle: physiology and biomarkers. Prentice A et al. *American Journal of Clinical Nutrition* 2008;88(2):500S–506S.

18. Influence of season and latitude on the cutaneous synthesis of vitamin D3: exposure to winter sunlight in Boston and Edmonton will not promote vit-amin D3 synthesis in human skin. Webb AR, Kline L, Holick MF. *Journal of Clinical Endocrinology and Metabolism* 1988;67:373–78.

19. Sunlight and vitamin D for bone health and prevention of autoimmune diseases, cancers, and cardiovascular disease. Holick M. *American Journal of Clinical Nutrition* 2004;80(6):1678S–1688S.

20. Common genetic variants of the vitamin D binding protein (DBP) predict differences in response of serum 25-hydroxyvitamin D [25(OH)D] to vitamin D supplementation. Fu L et al. *Clinical Biochemistry* 2009;42 (10-11):1174–77.

21. Short-term oral magnesium supplementation suppresses bone turnover in postmenopausal osteoporotic women. Aydin H et al. *Biological Trace Element Research* 2010;133(2):136–43.

22. Optimizing bone health in older adults: the importance of dietary protein. Surdykowski A.K. et al. *Aging Health* 2010;6(3):345–57.

Chapter 8: Sleep Problems

1. Light at night, chronodisruption, melatonin suppression, and cancer risk: a review. Reiter RJ et al. *Critical Reviews in Oncology* 2007;13(4):303–28.

2. The effect of insulin upon the influx of tryptophan into the brain of the rabbit. Daniel PM et al. *Journal of Physiology* 1981;312:551–62.

3. Oral Mg (2+) supplementation reverses age-related neuroendocrine and sleep EEG changes in humans. Held K et al. *Pharmacopsychiatry* 2002; 35(4):135–43.

4. *The Magnesium Factor*. Seelig M, Rosanoff A. New York: Avery Books (A division of Penguin Group USA), 2003, page 5.

5. Torasemide significantly reduces thiazide-induced potassium and magnesium loss despite supra-additive natriuresis. Knauf H et al. *European Journal of Clinical Pharmacology* 2009;65(5):465–72.

6. Statin-associated psychiatric adverse events: a case/non-case evaluation of an Italian database of spontaneous adverse drug reaction reporting. Tuccorri M et al. *Drug Safety* 2008;31(12):1115–23.

7. *The Magnesium Factor*, page 58.

8. Comparison of mechanism and functional effects of magnesium and statin pharmaceuticals. Rosanoff A, Seelig MS. *Journal of the American College of Nutrition* 2004;23 (5): 501S–505S.

9. Genetic renal disorders with hypomagnesemia and hypocalcuria. Knoers NV et al. *Journal of Nephrology* 2003; 16:293–96.

10. Magnesium supplementation and osteoporosis. Sojka JE, Weaver CM. *Nutrition Reviews* 1995;53:71–74.

11. Standing Committee on the Scientific Evaluation of Dietary Reference Intakes, Food and Nutrition Board, Institute of Medicine. *Dietary Reference Intakes. Calcium, Phosphorus, Magnesium, Vitamin D, and Fluoride.* Washington, D.C.: National Academy Press, 1997, page 196.

12. Therapeutic uses of magnesium. Guerrera MP et al. *American Family Physician* 2009;80(2):157–62.

13. Prolonged release melatonin in the treatment of primary insomnia: evaluation of the age cut-off for short- and long-term response. Wade AG et al. *Current Medical Research and Opinion* 2011;27(1):87–98.

14. Magnesium. Burford-Mason A. In *Scientific Evidence for Musculoskeletal, Bariatric, and Sports Nutrition*. Editor: Ingrid Kohlstadt MD. Boca Raton, FL: CRC Press, Taylor & Francis Group, 2006, page 142.

15. The multifaceted and widespread pathology of magnesium deficiency. Johnson S. *Medical Hypotheses* 2001;56(2):163–70.

Chapter 9: Constipation

1. Impact of chronic constipation on health-related quality of life, work productivity, and healthcare resource use: an analysis of the National Health and Wellness Survey. Sun SX et al. *Digestive Diseases and Science* 2011; 56(9):2688–95.

2. Orthomolecular psychiatry: varying the concentrations of substances normally present in the human body may control mental disease. Pauling L. *Science* 1968;160:265–71.

3. Chronic constipation: a survey of the patient perspective. Johanson JF, Kralstein J. *Alimentary Pharmacology and Therapeutics* 2007;25(5):599–608.

4. Impact of functional gastrointestinal disorders on survival in the community. Chang JY et al. *American Journal of Gastroenterology* 2010;105(4): 822–32.

5. Health conditions and mortality in the Japan Collaborative Cohort Study for Evaluation of Cancer (JACC). Suzuki K; Japan Collaborative Cohort Study for Evaluation of Cancer. *Asian Pacific Journal of Cancer Prevention* 2007;8 Suppl:25–34.

6. Constipation and risk of cardiovascular disease among postmenopausal women. Salmoirago-Blotcher E. *American Journal of Medicine* 2011;124(8): 714–23.

7. Effects of dietary fibers on magnesium absorption in animals and humans. Coudray C et al. *Journal of Nutrition* 2003;133(1):1–4.

8. Dietary Reference Intakes. *Calcium, Phosphorus, Magnesium, Vitamin D, and Fluoride*. Washington, D.C.: National Academy of Science, Institute of Medicine, 1997.

9. Dietary calcium and mineral/vitamin supplementation: a controversial problem. Celotti F, Bignamini A. *Journal of International Medical Research* 1999;27(1):1–14.

10. Calcium scores and matrix Gla protein levels: association with vitamin K status. Rennenberg RJ et al. *European Journal of Clinical Investigation* 2010; 40(4):344–49.

11. Vitamin K supplementation and progression of coronary artery calcium in older men and women. Shea MK et al. *American Journal of Clinical Nutrition* 2009;89(6):1799–807.

12. Dietary vitamin K intakes are associated with hip fracture but not with bone mineral density in elderly men and women. Booth SL et al. *American Journal of Clinical Nutrition* 2000;71(5):1201–8.

13. Food and Nutrition Board, Institute of Medicine. Vitamin K. *Dietary Reference Intakes for Vitamin A, Vitamin K, Arsenic, Boron, Chromium, Copper, Iodine, Iron, Manganese, Molybdenum, Nickel, Silicon, Vanadium, and Zinc*. Washington, D.C.: National Academy Press, 2001, pages 162–96.

14. The effect of magnesium supplementation on blood pressure: a meta-analysis of randomized clinical trials. Jee SH et al. *American Journal of Hypertension* 2002;15(8):691–96.

15. Diuretic complications. Greenberg A. *American Journal of Medical Science* 2000;319(1):10–24.

16. Familial clustering of habitual constipation: a prospective study in children from West Virginia. Ostwani W, et al. *Journal of Pediatric Gastroenterology and Nutrition* 2010;50(3):287–89.

17. Magnesium deficiency: a cause of heterogeneous disease in humans. Rude RK. *Journal of Bone Mineral Research* 1998;13:749–58.

18. Magnesium bioavailability from magnesium citrate and magnesium oxide. Lindberg JS et al. *Journal of the American College of Nutrition* 1990;9(1): 48–55.

19. The impact of physical exercise on the gastrointestinal tract. de Oliveira EP, Burini RC. *Current Opinion in Clinical Nutrition and Metabolic Care* 2009;12(5):533–38.

20. Update on the relationship between magnesium and exercise. Nielsen FH, Lukaski HC. *Magnesium Research* 2006;19(3):180–89.

21. Clinical clues to magnesium deficiency. Cohen L, Kitzes R. *Israel Journal of Medical Sciences* 1987;23(12):1238–41.

22. Plasma and dietary magnesium and risk of sudden cardiac death in women. Chiuve SE et al. *American Journal of Clinical Nutrition* 2011;93(2):253–60.

Chapter 10: Depression, Sadness, and Anxiety

1. Omega-3 fatty acids: evidence basis for treatment and future research in psychiatry. Freeman MP, et al. *Journal of Clinical Psychiatry* 2006;67(12): 1954–67.

2. Behavioural effects of nutrients. Wurtman, R.J. *Lancet.* 1983;1(8334): 1145–47.

3. The effects of nutrients on mood. Benton D, Donohoe RT. *Public Health Nutrition* 1999;2:403–09.

4. Meta-analysis of prospective cohort studies evaluating the association of saturated fat with cardiovascular disease. Siri-Tarino PW et al. *American Journal of Clinical Nutrition* 2010;91(3):535–46.

5. The opposing effects of n-3 and n-6 fatty acids. Schmitz G, Ecker J. *Progress in Lipid Research* 2008;47(2):147–55.

6. Evolutionary aspects of diet: the omega-6/omega-3 ratio and the brain. Simopoulos AP. *Molecular Neurobiology* 2011;44(2):203–15.

7. n-6 fatty acid-specific and mixed polyunsaturate dietary interventions have different effects on CHD risk: a meta-analysis of randomised controlled trials. Ramsden CE et al. *British Journal of Nutrition* 2010;104(11): 1586–600.

8. Omega-3 fatty acids: evidence basis for treatment and future research in psychiatry.

9. Polyunsaturated fatty acids and cerebral function: focus on monoaminergic neurotransmission. Chalon S, et al. *Lipids* 2001;36(9):937–44.

10. Docosahexaenoic acid supplementation increases prefrontal cortex activation during sustained attention in healthy boys: a placebo-controlled, dose-ranging, functional magnetic resonance imaging study. McNamara RK et al. *American Journal of Clinical Nutrition* 2010;91(4):1060–67.

11. Evaluation of docosahexaenoic acid deficiency as a preventable risk factor for recurrent affective disorders: current status, future directions, and dietary recommendations. McNamara RK. *Prostaglandins Leukotrienes and Essential Fatty Acids* 2009;81(2-3):223–31.

12. Dietary fat intake and the risk of depression: the SUN Project. Sánchez-Villegas A et al. *PLoS One* 2011; 6(1): e16268.

13. Tolerable upper intake levels for trans fat, saturated fat, and cholesterol. Trumbo PR, Shimakawa T. *Nutrition Review* 2011;69(5):270–78.

14. http.www.hc-sg.gc.ca.

15. Meta-analysis of prospective cohort studies evaluating the association of saturated fat with cardiovascular disease.

16. Effects of normal meals rich in carbohydrates or proteins on plasma tryptophan and tyrosine ratios. Wurtman RJ et al. *American Journal of Clinical Nutrition* 2003; 77(1):128–32.

17. Distribution of the vitamin D receptor and 1 alpha-hydroxylase in human brain. Eyles D et al. *Journal of Chemical Neuroanatomy* 2005;29:21–30.

18. Serum vitamin D concentrations are related to depression in a young adult US population: the Third National Health and Nutrition Examination Survey. Ganji V et al. *International Archives of Medicine* 2010;3:29.

19. Vitamin D deficiency is associated with anxiety and depression in fibromyalgia. Armstrong DJ et al. *Clinical Rheumatology* 2007;26(4):551–54.

20. Schizophrenia and vitamin D related fenes could have been subject to latitude-driven adaptation. Amato R et al. *BMC Evolutionary Biology* 2010;10:351.

21. L-Tyrosine to alleviate the effects of stress? Young SN. *Journal of Psychiatry and Neuroscience* 2007; 32(3): 224.

22. Tyrosine improves cognitive performance and reduces blood pressure in cadets after one week of a combat training course. Deijen JB et al. *Brain Research Bulletin* 1999;48(2):203–09.

23. Health Canada monograph on tyrosine. Available at http.www.hc-sg.gc.ca.

24. Folic acid fortification: why not vitamin B12 also? Selhub J, Paul L. *Biofactors* 2011 Jul;37(4):269–71.

25. Cellular changes in the postmortem hippocampus in major depression. Stockmeier CA et al. *Biological Psychiatry* 2004;56(9):640–50.

26. Vitamin B12 status and rate of brain volume loss in community-dwelling elderly. Vogiatzoglou A. *Neurology* 2008;71(11):826–27.   32.

27. Vitamin C provision improves mood in acutely hospitalized patients. Zhang M et al. *Nutrition* 2011 May;27(5):530–33.

Endnotes

28. Effects of high-dose B vitamin complex with vitamin C and minerals on subjective mood and performance in healthy males. Kennedy DO et al. *Psychopharmacology* (Berl) 2010 Jul;211(1):55–68.

29. Metabolic syndrome predisposes to depressive symptoms: a population-based 7-year follow-up study. Koponen H et al. *Journal of Clinical Psychiatry* 2008;69(2):178–82.

30. Consequences of magnesium deficiency on the enhancement of stress reactions; preventive and therapeutic implications (a review). Seelig M. *Journal of the American College of Nutrition* 1994;13(5):429–46.

31. Depression and magnesium deficiency. Rasmussen HH, Mortensen PB, Jensen IW. *International Journal of Psychiatry and Medicine* 1989;19(1):57–63.

32. Rapid recovery from major depression using magnesium treatment. Eby GA, Eby KL. *Medical Hypotheses* 2006;67:362–70.

Chapter 11: Colds and Flu

1. Role of free radicals and antioxidants in health and disease. Flora SJ. *Cellular and Molecular Biology* (Noisy-le-grand) 2007;53(1):1–2.

2. Cost-benefit analysis of a strategy to vaccinate healthy working adults against influenza. Nichol KL. *Archives of Internal Medicine* 2001;161(5): 749–59.

3. Influenza B in households: virus shedding without symptoms or antibody response. Foy HM et al. *American Journal of Epidemiology* 1987;126(3): 506–15.

4. Viral shedding and clinical illness in naturally acquired influenza virus infections. Lau LL et al. *Journal of Infectious Diseases* 2010;201(10):1509–16.

5. Reactive oxygen species in phagocytic leukocytes. Robinson JM. *Histochemistry and Cell Biology* 2008;130(2):281–97.

6. Reactive oxygen species in immune responses. Grisham MB. *Free Radical and Biological Medicine* 2004;36(12):1479–80.

7. The nutritional regulation of T lymphocyte function. Horrobin DF et al. *Medical Hypotheses* 1979;5(9):969–85.

8. Immune-enhancing role of vitamin C and zinc and effect on clinical conditions. Wintergerst ES et al. *Annals of Nutrition and Metabolism* 2006;50(2): 85–94.

9. Actions of melatonin in the reduction of oxidative stress. A review. Reiter RJ et al. *Journal of Biomedical Science* 2000;7(6):444–58.

10. Increased antioxidant capacity in healthy volunteers taking a mixture of oral antioxidants versus vitamin C or E supplementation. Lara-Padilla E at al. *Advances in Therapy* 2007;24(1):50–59.

11. Flavonoids from almond skins are bioavailable and act synergistically with vitamins C and E to enhance hamster and human LDL resistance to oxidation. Chen C-Y, et al. *Journal of Nutrition* 2005;135(6):1366–73.

12. Cellular antioxidant activity of common vegetables. Song W et al. *Journal of Agriculture and Food Chemistry* 2010;58(11):6621–29.

13. New concepts in the biology and biochemistry of ascorbic acid. Levine M. *New England Journal of Medicine* 1986;314(14):892–902.

14. Nutritional characteristics of wild primate foods: do the diets of our closest living relatives have lessons for us? Milton K. *Nutrition* 1999;15(6):488–98.

15. Vitamin C for preventing and treating the common cold. Douglas R M et al. *Cochrane Database of Systematic Reviews* 2007, Issue 3. Art. No.: CD000980.

16. Work stress and innate immune response. Boscolo P et al. *International Journal of Immunopathology and Pharmacology* 2011;24(1 Suppl):51S–54S.

17. A randomized controlled trial of high dose ascorbic acid for reduction of blood pressure, cortisol, and subjective responses to psychological stress. Brody S et al. *Psychopharmacology* (Berlin) 2002;159(3):319–24.

18. Vitamin D controls T cell antigen receptor signaling and activation of human T cells. von Essen MR et al. *Nature Immunology* 2010;11(4):344–49.

19. Randomized trial of vitamin D supplementation to prevent seasonal influenza A in schoolchildren. Urashima M et al. *American Journal of Clinical Nutrition* 2010;91(5):1255–60.

20. Vitamin D status has a linear association with seasonal infections and lung function in British adults. Berry DJ et al. *British Journal of Nutrition* 2011;106(9):1433–40.

21. Serum 25-hydroxy D and the incidence of acute viral respiratory tract infections in adults. Sabetta R et al. PLoS Ont. 2010;5(6):e11088.

22. Reduction in duration of common colds by zinc gluconate lozenges in a double-blind study. Eby GA et al. *Antimicrobial Agents and Chemotherapy* 1984;25(1):20–24.

23. Zinc lozenges may shorten the duration of colds: a systematic review. Hemilä H. *The Open Respiratory Medicine Journal* 2011:5:51–58.

24. Zinc and inflammatory/immune response in aging. Vasto S et al. *Annals of the New York Academy of Science* 2007;1100:111–22.

25. The effect of age on plasma zinc uptake and taste acuity. Bales CW et al. *American Journal of Clinical Nutrition* 1986;44(5):664–69.

26. Reduced thymus activity and infection prematurely age the immune system. Gress RE, Deeks SG. *Journal of Clinical Investigation* 2009;119(10): 2884–87.

27. Hypogeusia and zinc depletion in chronic dialysis patients. Atkin-Thor E et al. *American Journal of Clinical Nutrition* 1978;31(10):1948–51.

28. Antimicrobial effect of garlic (Allium sativum). Goncagul G, Ayaz E. *Recent Patents on Anti-Effective Drug Discovery* 2010;5(1):91–93.

Chapter 12: Weight Gain and Obesity

1. Canadian consumer trends in obesity and food consumption. Government of Alberta. http://www1.agric.gov.ab.ca/$department/deptdocs.nsf/all/sis8438.

2. Canadian Health Measures Survey 2007-2009. http://www.statcan.gc.ca.

3. Obesity. Haslam DW, James WP. *The Lancet* 2005;366(9492):1197–209.

4. Cardiovascular disease under the influence of excess visceral fat. Després JP. *Critical Pathways in Cardiology* 2007;6(2):51–59.

5. Overweight, obesity, diabetes, and risk of breast cancer: interlocking pieces of the puzzle. La Vecchia C et al. *Oncologist* 2011;16(6):726–29.

6. Central obesity in the elderly is related to late-onset Alzheimer Disease. Luchsinger JA et al. *Alzheimer Disease and Associated Disorders* 2011 Jun 9. [Epub ahead of print]

7. Dietary predictors of 5-year changes in waist circumference. Halkjaer J et al. *Journal of the American Dietetic Association* 2009;109(8):1356–66.

8. Quantification of the effect of energy imbalance on bodyweight. Hall KD et al. *Lancet* 2011;378:826–37.

9. Circulating glucose levels modulate neural control of desire for high-calorie foods in humans. Page K et al. *Journal of Clinical Investigation* 2011;121(10):4161–69.

10. Comparison of abdominal adiposity and overall obesity in predicting risk of type 2 diabetes among men. Wang Y et al. *American Journal of Clinical Nutrition* 2005;81: 555–63.

11. Prevalence of metabolic syndrome in the Canadian adult population. Riediger ND, Clara I. *Canadian Medical Association Journal* 2011;183(15): E1127–34.

12. Soft drink consumption and risk of developing cardiometabolic risk factors and the metabolic syndrome in middle-aged adults in the community. Dhingra R et al. *Circulation* 2007;116(5):480–88.

13. High-intensity sweeteners and energy balance. Swithers SE et al. *Physiology and Behavior* 2010;100(1):55–62.

14. Effect of long term intake of aspartame on antioxidant defense status in liver. Abhilash M et al. *Food and Chemical Toxicology* 2011;49(6):1203–07.

15. Stevioside and related compounds: therapeutic benefits beyond sweetness. Chatsudthipong V, Muanprasat C. *Pharmacology and Therapeutics* 2009; 121(1):41–54.

16. Ibid.

17. Quantification of sleep behavior and of its impact on the cross-talk between the brain and peripheral metabolism. Hanlon EC, Van Cauter E. *Proceedings of the National Academy of Sciences* 2011; 108(3):15609–15616.

18. Symposium overview: do we all eat breakfast and is it important? Giovannini M et al. *Critical Reviews in Food Science and Nutrition* 2010;50(2):97–99.

19. The addition of a protein-rich breakfast and its effects on acute appetite control and food intake in 'breakfast-skipping' adolescents. Leidy HJ, Racki EM. *International Journal of Obesity* (London) 2010l;34(7):1125–33.

20. Eating meals irregularly: a novel environmental risk factor for the metabolic syndrome. Sierra-Johnson J et al. *Obesity* (Silver Spring) 2008;16(6):1302–27.

21. Increasing the volume of a food by incorporating air affects satiety in men. Rolls BJ et al. *American Journal of Clinical Nutrition* 2000;72(2):361–68.

22. Epidemiology of gallstones. Stinton LM et al. *Gastroenterology Clinics of North America* 2010;39(2):157–69.

23. Inverse associations between long-term weight change and serum concentrations of persistent organic pollutants. Li JS et al. *International Journal of Obesity* 2011;35:744–47.

24. Apiaceous vegetable constituents inhibit human cytochrome P-450 1A2 (hCYP1A2) activity and hCYP1A2-mediated mutagenicity of aflatoxin B1. Peterson S et al. *Food Chemistry and Toxicology* 2006;44(9):1474–84.

25. Edward Stanley, Earl of Derby and British statesman. The Conduct of Life, address to Liverpool College, Dec. 20, 1873.

26. Exercise is required for visceral fat loss in postmenopausal women with Type 2 diabetes. Giannopoulou I et al. *Journal of Clinical Endocrinology and Metabolism* 2005; 90:1511–18.

27. Phytochemicals in the control of human appetite and body weight. Tucci SA. *Pharmaceuticals* 2010; 3(3):748–63.

28. The nutritional characteristics of a contemporary diet based upon Paleolithic food groups. Cordain L. *Journal of the American Neutraceutical Association* 2002;5:15–24.

29. Long term effects of a Mediterranean-style diet and calorie restriction on biomarkers of longevity and oxidative stress in overweight men. Esposito K et al. *Cardiology Research and Practice* 2011;29316.

30. Dairy calcium intake, serum vitamin D, and successful weight loss. Shahar DR et al. *American Journal of Clinical Nutrition* 2010;92(5):1017–22.

31. Low vitamin D linked to the metabolic syndrome in elderly people. The Endocrine Society (2010, July 6). ScienceDaily. Retrieved September 26, 2011, from http://www.sciencedaily.com/releases/2010/07/1007010726 58.htm.

Chapter 13: Cholesterol and Hypertension

1. Brain cholesterol: long secret life behind a barrier. Björkhem I, Meaney S. *Arteriosclerosis, Thrombosis, and Vascular Biology* 2004;24: 806–15.

2. http://www.statcan.gc.ca/pub/2010001/article/11136-eng.htm.

3. The effect of including C-reactive protein in cardiovascular risk prediction models for women. Cook NR et al. *Annals of Internal Medicine* 2006;145(1): 21–29.

4. Canadian Cardiovascular Society position statement—Recommendations for the diagnosis and treatment of dyslipidemia and prevention of cardiovascular disease. McPherson R et al. *Canadian Journal of Cardiology* 2006; 22(11):913–27.

5. Vitamin C treatment reduces elevated C-reactive protein. Block G et al. *Free Radical Biology and Medicine* 2009;46(1):70–77.

6. Strawberry intake, lipids, C-reactive protein, and the risk of cardiovascular disease in women. Sesso HD et al. *Journal of the American College of Nutrition* 2007;26(4):303–10.

7. Serial arteriography in atherosclerosis. Willis GC et al. *Canadian Medical Association Journal* 1954;71(6):562–68.

8. The effect of chronic hypovitaminosis C on the metabolism of cholesterol and atherogenesis in guinea pigs. Ginter E et al. *Journal of Atherosclerosis Research* 1969 Nov-Dec;10(3):341–52.

9. The reversibility of atherosclerosis. Willis GC. *Canadian Medical Association Journal* 1957;77(2):106–08.

10. Persistent dyslipidemia in Austrian patients treated with statins for primary and secondary prevention of atherosclerotic events—Results of the DYSlipidemia international study (DYSIS). Drexel H et al. *Wiener Klinische Wochenschrift* 2011 Oct;123(19-20):611–17.

11. Simvastatin causes changes in affective processes in elderly volunteers. Morales K et al. *Journal of the American Geriatric Society* 2006;54(1):70–76.

12. Association between statin-associated myopathy and skeletal muscle damage. Mohaupt MG et al. *Canadian Medical Association Journal* 2009;181(1-2):E11–E18.

13. Lovastatin decreases coenzyme Q levels in humans. Folkers K et al. *Proceeding of the National Academy of Sciences USA 1990*;87(22):8931–34.

14. Reducing exercise-induced muscular injury in kendo athletes with supplementation of coenzyme Q10. Kon M et al. *British Journal of Nutrition* 2008;100(4):903–09.

15. Magnesium: forgotten mineral in cardiovascular biology and atherogenesis. Altura BM, Altura BT. In: Nishizawa N, Morii H, Durlach J, editors. *New Perspectives in Magnesium Research* 2007. Springer pp. 239–60.

16. Effects of long-term dietary intake of magnesium on oxidative stress, apoptosis and ageing in rat liver. Martin H et al. *Magnesium Research* 2008;21(2):124–30.

17. Comparison of mechanism and functional effects of magnesium and statin pharmaceuticals. Rosanoff A, Seelig MS. *Journal of the American College of Nutrition* 2004;23(5):501S–505S.

18. The importance of lost minerals in heart failure. Newman KP et al. *Cardiovascular and Hematological Agents in Medicinal Chemistry* 2007;5(4):295–99.

19. Magnesium: nature's physiological calcium channel blocker. Iseri LT, French JH. *American Heart Journal* 1984;108:188–93.

20. Niacin inhibits surface expression of ATP synthase beta chain in HepG2 cells: implications for raising HDL. Zhang LH et al. *Journal of Lipid Research* 2008;49(6):1195–201.

21. Niacin: a critical component to the management of atherosclerosis: contemporary management of dyslipidemia to prevent, reduce, or reverse atherosclerotic cardiovascular disease. Mason CM, Doneen AL. *Journal of Cardiovascular Nursing* 2011 Jul 29. [Epub ahead of print]

22. The use of diet and dietary components in the study of factors controlling affect in humans: a review. Young SN. *Journal of Psychiatry and Neuroscience* 1993;18(5):235–44.

Endnotes

23. Meta-analysis of prospective cohort studies evaluating the association of saturated fat with cardiovascular disease. Siri-Tarino PW et al. *American Journal of Clinical Nutrition* 2010;91(3):535–46.

24. A low carbohydrate Mediterranean diet improves cardiovascular risk factors and diabetes control among overweight patients with type 2 diabetes mellitus: a 1-year prospective randomized intervention study. Elhayany A et al. *Diabetes, Obesity and Metabolism* 2010;12(3):204–09.

25. Lycopene and cardiovascular diseases: an update. Mordente A et al. *Current Medicinal Chemistry* 2011;18(8):1146–63.

26. Vitamin D status is associated with arterial stiffness and vascular dysfunction in healthy humans. Al Mheid I et al. *Journal of the American College of Cardiology* 2011;58(2):186–92.

27. Diverse associations of 25-hydroxyvitamin D and 1,25-dihydroxy-vitamin D with dyslipidaemias. Karhapää P et al. *Journal of Internal Medicine* 2010;268(6):604–10.

28. Dietary fatty acids and cardiovascular health—an ongoing controversy. Mensink RP. *Annals of Nutrition and Metabolism* 2011;58(1):66–67.

29. Trans fatty acids: current contents in Canadian foods and estimated intake levels for the Canadian population. Ratnayake WM et al. *Journal of Association of Official Analytical Chemists International* 2009;92(5):1258–76.

30. Omega-3 polyunsaturated fatty acids and cardiovascular diseases. Lavie CJ et al. *Journal of the American College of Cardiology* 2009;54(7):585–94.

31. Why and how to implement sodium, potassium, calcium, and magnesium changes in food items and diets? Karppanen H et al. *Journal of Human Hypertension* 2005;Suppl3:S10–S19.

32. Paleolithic nutrition. A consideration of its nature and current implications. Eaton SB, Konner M. *New England Journal of Medicine* 1985;312: 283–89.

33. Reduction in blood pressure with a low sodium, high potassium, high magnesium salt in older subjects with mild to moderate hypertension. Geleijnse JM et al. *British Medical Journal* 1994 August 13; 309(6952): 436–40.

34. Anti-atherogenic effects of resveratrol. Ramprasath VR, Jones PJ. *European Journal of Clinical Nutrition* 2010;64(7):660–68.

35. Polyphenolics in grape seeds—biochemistry and functionality. Shi J et al. *Journal of Medicinal Food* 2003;6(4):291–99.

36. Oenology: red wine procyanidins and vascular health. Corder R et al. *Nature* 2006;444(7119):566.

Chapter 14: Memory Problems

1. Neuronal basis of age-related working memory decline. Wang M et al. *Nature* 2011;476(7359):210–13.

2. Single neurons in the monkey hippocampus and learning of new associations. Wirth S et al. *Science* 2003;300(5625):1578–81.

3. Growth hormone, insulin-like growth factor I and cognitive function in adults. Van Dam PS et al. *Growth Hormone and IGF Research* 2000;10 Suppl B: S69-S73.

4. Arterial stiffness as an independent predictor of longitudinal changes in cognitive function in the older individual. Scuteri A et al. *Journal of Hypertension* 2007;25(5):1035–40.

5. Current serum lipoprotein levels and FMRI response to working memory in midlife. Gonzales MM et al. *Dementia and Geriatric Cognitive Disorders* 2011;31(4):259–67.

6. Haemorheological predictors of cognitive decline: the Edinburgh Artery Study. Rafnsson S et al. *Age and Ageing* 2010;39(2):217–22.

7. Proneness to psychological distress and risk for Alzheimer's disease in a biracial community. Wilson RS et al. *Neurology* 2005;64(2):380–82.

8. A cognitive training program based on principles of brain plasticity: results from the Improvement in Memory with Plasticity-based Adaptive Cognitive Training (IMPACT) study. Smith GE et al. *Journal of the American Geriatric Society* 2009;57(4):594–603.

9. Navigation-related structural change in the hippocampi of taxi drivers. Maguire EA et al. *Proceedings of the National Academy of Sciences* 2000; 97(8): 4398–403.

10. Exercise training increases size of hippocampus and improves memory. Erickson KI et al. *Proceedings of the National Academy of Sciences* 2011; 108(7):3017–22.

11. Exercise-induced cognitive plasticity, implications for mild cognitive impairment and Alzheimer's disease. Foster PP et al. *Frontiers in Neurology* 2011;2:28.

12. The behavioural effects of nutrients. Wurtman R. *The Lancet* 1983;321 (8334):1145–47.

13. Reduced ventrolateral fMRI response during observation of emotional gestures related to the degree of dopaminergic impairment in Parkinson disease. Lotze M et al. *Journal of Cognitive Neuroscience* 2009;21(7): 1321–31.

14. Behavioural effects of acute phenylalanine and tyrosine depletion in healthy male volunteers. Grevet EH et al. *Journal of Psychopharmacology* 2002;16(1):51–55.

15. Role of serotonin in memory impairment. Buhot MC et al. *Annals of Medicine* 2000;32(3):210–221.

16. Choline: needed for normal development of memory. Zeisel SH. *Journal of the American College of Nutrition* 2000;19(5 Suppl):528S–531S.

17. The supply of choline is important for fetal progenitor cells. Zeisel SH. *Seminars in Cell Development and Biology* 2011 Aug;22(6):624–28.

18. Citicoline: update on a promising and widely available agent for neuroprotection and neurorepair. Saver JL. *Reviews in Neurological Diseases* 2008; 5(4):167–77.

19. The supply of choline is important for fetal progenitor cells.

20. Glutamate: its role in learning, memory, and the aging brain. McEntee WJ, Crook TH. *Psychopharmacology* 1993;111(4):391–401.

21. Vitamin D and cognitive impairment in the elderly U.S. population. Llewellyn DJ et al. *Journal of Gerontology* Series A, Biological Sciences and Medical Sciences. 2011;66(1):59–65.

22. Reduced risk of Alzheimer disease in users of antioxidant vitamin supplements: the Cache County Study. Zandi PP et al. *Archives of Neurology* 2004; 61(1):82–88.

23. Cognitive and cardiovascular benefits of docosahexaenoic acid in aging and cognitive decline. Yurko-Mauro K. *Current Alzheimer Research* 2010; 7(3):190–6.

24. Homocysteine, B-vitamins and CVD. McNulty H et al. *Proceedings of the Nutrition Society* 2008;67(2):232–37.

25. Hyperhomocysteinemia and low pyridoxal phosphate. Common and independent reversible risk factors for coronary artery disease. Robinson K et al. *Circulation* 1995;92:2825–30.

26. Vitamin B12 deficiency. Oh RC, Brown DL. *American Family Physician* 2003;67(5):979–86.

27. Dementia associated with vitamin B(12) deficiency: presentation of two cases and review of the literature. Goebels N, Soyka M. *Journal of Neuropsychiatry and Clinical Neurosciences* 2000;12(3):389–94.

28. Vitamin B12, cognition, and brain MRI measures: a cross-sectional examination. Tangney CC et al. *Neurology* 2011;77:1276–82.

29. Understanding the serum B12 level and its implications for treating neuropsychiatric conditions: an orthomolecular perspective. Prousky J. *Journal of Orthomolecular Medicine* 2010;25(2):77–88.

30. Effects of acute psychological stress on glucose metabolism and subclinical inflammation in patients with post-traumatic stress disorder. Nowotny B et al. *Hormone and Metabolic Research* 2010;42(10):746–53.

31. Fruit and vegetable intake and cognitive decline in middle-aged men and women: the Doetinchem Cohort Study. Nooyens AC et al. *British Journal of Nutrition* 2011;106(5):752–61.

32. Neurodegenerative memory disorders: a potential role of environmental toxins. Caban-Holt A et al. *Neurology Clinics* 2005;23(2):485–521.

Chapter 15: Food for Health

1. Beneficial metabolic effects of regular meal frequency on dietary thermogenesis, insulin sensitivity, and fasting lipid profiles in healthy obese women. Farshchi HR et al. *American Journal of Clinical Nutrition* 2005; 81(1):16–24.

2. Whey protein but not soy protein supplementation alters body weight and composition in free-living overweight and obese adults. Baer DJ et al. *Journal of Nutrition* 2011;141(8):1489–94.

3. A solid high-protein meal evokes stronger hunger suppression than a liquefied high-protein meal. Martens MJ et al. *Obesity* (Silver Spring) 2011; 19(3):522–27.

4. Nutrition, brain aging, and neurodegeneration. Joseph J et al. *Journal of Neuroscience* 2009; 14;29(41):12795–801.

5. Vegetarian diet improves insulin resistance and oxidative stress markers more than conventional diet in subjects with Type 2 diabetes. Kahleova H et al. *Diabetic Medicine* 2011;28(5):549–59.

6. Attention-deficit/hyperactivity disorder and urinary metabolites of organophosphate pesticides. Bouchard MF et al. *Pediatrics* 2010;125(6):e1270–77.

7. Dietary intake and its contribution to longitudinal organophosphorus pesticide exposure in urban/suburban children. Lu C et al. *Environmental Health Perspectives* 2008;116(4):537–42.

8. www.ewg.org.

9. Antioxidant effectiveness of organically and non-organically grown red oranges in cell culture systems. Tarozzi A et al. *European Journal of Nutrition* 2006;45(3):152–58.

10. Phytochemical phenolics in organically grown vegetables. Young J E et al. *Molecular Nutrition and Food Research* 2005;49(12):1136–42.

11. Association of alcohol consumption with selected cardiovascular disease outcomes: a systematic review and meta-analysis. Ronksley PE et al. *British Medical Journal* 2011;342:d671.

12. Moderate wine consumption is associated with better cognitive test results: a 7 year follow up of 5033 subjects in the Tromsø Study. Arntzen KA et al. *Acta Neurologica Scandanavica* 2010;(190):23–29.

13. Relationship between physical activity level, telomere length, and telomerase activity. Ludlow AT et al. *Medicine and Science in Sports and Exercise* 2008;40(10):1764–71.

14. Aerobic fitness reduces brain tissue loss in aging humans. Colcombe SJ et al. *Journals of Gerontology* Series A: Biological and Medical Sciences 2003; 58(2):176–80.

15. The fittest person in the morgue? Sheppard MN. *Histopathology* 2012; 60(3):381–96.

16. Monocyte and t-cell responses to exercise training in elderly subjects. Shimizu K et al. *Journal of Strength and Conditioning Research* 2011;25(9): 2565–72.

17. Stretching exercise program improves gait in the elderly. Cristopoliski F et al. *Gerontology* 2009;55(6):614–20.

Chapter 16: Building a Core Supplement Regime

1. Effect of dietary intervention on human micronucleus frequency in lymphocytes and buccal cells. Thomas P et al. *Mutagenesis* 2011;26(1): 69–76.

2. www.hc-sc.gc/fn-an/nutrition/reference/dri-ques-ques_anref-eng.php.

3. Long-latency deficiency disease: insights from calcium and vitamin D. Heaney RP. *American Journal of Clinical Nutrition* 2003;78(5):912–19.

4. Investigation of gastroduodenal mucosal injuries caused by low-dose aspirin therapy in patients with cerebral infarction. Nema H, Kato M. *Journal of Gastroenterology and Hepatology* 2010;25 Suppl 1:S119–21.

5. Acute water intoxication during military urine drug screening. Tilley MA, Cotant CL. *Military Medicine* 2011;176(4):451–53.

6. Folate and vitamin B6 from diet and supplements in relation to risk of coronary heart disease among women. Rimm EB et al. *Journal of the American Medical Association* 1998;279(5):359–64.

7. http://www.osteoporosis.ca.

8. Vitamin D and muscle function. Pfeifer M et al. *Osteoporosis International* 2002;13(3):187–94.

9. Vitamin D. How much is Enough? Many Americans are deficient, studies show. *Harvard Public Health Review*. Spring/Summer 2007.

10. Glycemic changes after vitamin D supplementation in patients with type 1 diabetes mellitus and vitamin D deficiency. Aljabri KS et al. *Annals of Saudi Medicine* 2010; 30(6):454–58.

11. Vitamin D2 is much less effective than vitamin D3 in humans. Armas LA et al. *Journal of Clinical Endocrinology and Metabolism* 2004;89(11):5387–91.

12. Why the IOM recommendations for vitamin D are deficient. Heaney RP, Holick MF. *Journal of Bone and Mineral Research* 2011;26(3):455–57.

13. Unique features of the enzyme kinetics for the vitamin D system and the implications for cancer prevention and therapeutics. Vieth R. In: *Vitamin D and Cancer*, Editors: Trump DL, Johnson CS. Published Springer New York 2011.

14. The importance of the ratio of omega-6/omega-3 essential fatty acids. Simopoulos AP. *Biomedicine and Pharmacotherapy* 2002;56(8):365–79.

15. Omega-3 supplementation lowers inflammation and anxiety in medical students: A randomized controlled trial. Kiecolt-Glaser JK et al. *Brain, Behaviour and Immunity* 2011 Nov;25(8):1725–34.

16. Tocotrienols, the vitamin E of the 21st century: its potential against cancer and other chronic diseases. Aggarwal BB et al. *Biochemical Pharmacology* 2010;80(11):1613–31.

17. Mood, performance and pain sensitivity: Changes induced by food constituents. Lieberman HR et al. *Journal of Psychiatric Research* 1983;17:135–45.

18. Tyrosine for depression. Gelenberg AJ et al. *Journal of Psychiatric Research* 1983;17:175–80.

19. Neurochemical and behavioral consequences of acute, uncontrollable stress: Effects of dietary tyrosine. Lehnert H et al. *Brain Research* 1984;303:215–23.

20. L-tyrosine ameliorates some effects of lower body negative pressure stress. Dollins AB et al. *Physiology and Behavior* 1995;57:223–30.

21. Brain serotonin, carbohydrate-craving, obesity, and depression. Wurtman RJ, Wurtman JJ. *Advances in Experimental Medicine and Biology* 1996; 398:35–41.

22. Serotonin Syndrome. Martin TG. *Annals of Emergency Medicine* 1996;28(5):520–26.

23. Citicoline improves verbal memory in aging. Spiers PA et al. *Archives of Neurology* 1996;(10):441–48.

24. Efficacy and safety of oral citicoline in acute ischemic stroke: drug surveillance study in 4,191 cases. Cho HJ, Kim YJ. *Methods and Findings in Experimental and Clinical Pharmacology* 2009;31(3):171–76.

25. Relaxation and immunity enhancement effects of gamma-aminobutyric acid (GABA) administration in humans. Abdou AM et al. *Biofactors* 2006;26(3):201–8.

26. A "hot" topic in dyslipidemia management—"how to beat a flush": optimizing niacin tolerability to promote long-term treatment adherence and coronary disease prevention. Jacobson TA. *Mayo Clinic Proceedings* 2010;85(4):365–79.

27. Taking vitamin D with the largest meal improves absorption and results in higher serum levels of 25-hydroxyvitamin D. Mulligan GB, Licata A. *Journal of Bone and Mineral Research* 2010;25(4):928–30.

Index

Index

vitamin B3. *See* niacin.

vitamin B12, 9, 64, 153, 155,
233–34

vitamin C, 21, 35, 55, 56, 59, 60, 72,
98, 129, 152, 154, 167, 204, 231,
257

atherosclerosis and, 204–205

cataracts and, 76–77

colds and, 168–71

deficiency, 10, 29, 39, 45, 60, 61,
231

RDA, 169, 270

stopping supplementation, 277–78

vitamin D, xix, xx, xxi, 11, 36, 40, 46,
57, 60, 76, 100, 154, 211, 263–66,
277

blood levels of, 16, 93–94, 97, 147,
172, 265

brain function and, 147, 231

calcium and, 93–94

cholesterol and, 211

deficiency, 57, 61, 95, 97, 147, 196,
264

immune system and, 171–72

RDA, 40, 46

supplementation amounts, 96–97,
264–66

weight and, 196

vitamin E, xx, 36, 58, 72–73, 80, 167,
214, 257, 261, 270, 277

vitamin K, 98, 128–29, 174, 262, 271

vitamins, fat soluble vs. water soluble,
36

Vitamins in Medicine, The (Bicknell
and Prescott), 44–45

vitiligo, 64

vision. *See* eyes.

Walsh, Mary, 73

water, 126, 191

Watson, Lyall, 219

weight loss:

diets, 183–85

rapid, 191–92

whole grains, 246

Willett, Walter, 94

Williams, Roger, 38–39

Willis, G. C., 204–05

World Health Organization (WHO),
4, 5

xenobiotics, 191–92

zeaxanthin, 73

zinc, 59–60, 62, 172–73, 175

Zeisel, Steven, 226